GOVERNMENT AND ADMINISTRATION IN WESTERN EUROPE

Edited by

F.F.Ridley

St. Martin's Press . New York

ISBN 0-312-34113-X

Library of Congress Cataloging in Publication Data
Main entry under title:
Government and administration in Western Europe.
  Bibliography: p.
  Includes index.
   1. Europe--Politics and government--Addresses,
essays, lectures. 2. Comparative government--Addresses,
essays, lectures. I. Ridley, Frederick F.
JN94.A5G68 1979   354'.4   79-13518
ISBN 0-312-34113-X

Phototypeset by Pioneer Associates Ltd. Flimwell, East Sussex
Printed and bound by Richard Clay (The Chaucer Press) Ltd.,
Bungay, Suffolk.

Contents

David Hine is grateful to the Research Committee of the University of Newcastle upon Tyne for financial assistance enabling him to visit Italy during research for Chapter 5.

CHAPTER ONE

Introduction

The fact that governments change but administrations remain may be a cliché, but it is true for all that. While electoral fortunes remove one government and bring another to power, Conservatives replacing Labour in Britain and Labour Conservatives, the permanent civil service works on, adjusting itself to new masters without upheaval. In countries which have not enjoyed the constitutional stability of Britain, it is not just governments but regimes that pass while the administration remains. Germany and Italy adopted their present constitutions just thirty years ago, France twenty; but their administrative structures were established well before and their bureaucracies are even older. Of the Third and Fourth French Republics it used to be said that the republican order had merely been imposed on the imperial: the political institutions of democracy the visible, but relatively unimportant, eighth of the iceberg above the surface, the Napoleonic administration the effective seven-eighths below. The Fourth Republic, not so long ago, was characterised by toppling cabinets, but few citizens noticed it except as a news' item: the police remained on duty, taxes were collected, public services ran and the multifarious regulations of the state were enforced. In Italy, where there still seem to be times when no cabinet is in charge at all, government continues in its set patterns, its anarchic administrative features part of its own routine. Politics is not always the froth on the governmental system, sometimes political forces play a decisive role, sometimes even parliaments, but administration accounts for the larger part of government quantitatively and, in many views, tends to be the dominant partner qualitatively also.

That we live in an era of big government is another undeniable truism. It is not just that government shapes all aspects of our collective life, but that we are subject to it daily as individuals. Its rules set the framework of what we may and may not do; we utilise its services continuously — schools, hospitals, roads — the list is endless; we depend on it for licences, permits, allowances, subsidies and other advantages it can grant or withhold — its benefits, indeed, can be claimed by others in our name at cradle and grave; and we pay for all this through a variety of burdensome taxes all the time. Politics may be studied as an academic subject, but citizens need to understand the ways of government as an applied rather than a pure science. There is much talk these days of political education which would teach the citizen of the future about political issues, their ideological and material aspects, as well as about the conflicting forces that determine the policy of our rulers. To participate in the policy-making process requires, among other skills, some understanding of how the political system works. For most people, however, most of the time, policies resemble acts of God, accepted as inevitable like good weather or bad. They want to get their rights within the rules. We may try to change the rules for the future, transform society even, but here and now it is the administration of policies that is likely to cause the individual concern. We are increasingly administered, subject to ever more difficult regulations applied by an ever more bewildering complex of offices. Unless we can identify the structures of the system, the physical layout of its offices, we will be lost in the governmental maze before we start, never able to confront the mysterious 'them' with our demands; unless we know the formal rules they apply in making decisions, we shall be left stammering ineffectually when we do track them down. It will help us, then, if we also have some idea of the informal structures of the system, channels of influence for example, as well as the informal attitudes we are likely to meet. Administrative literacy, in other words, may pay more immediate dividends than political literacy. While this book is primarily for the student of government rather than the administered citizen and describes administrative systems at a higher level than would be required for a plain man's guide to practice, this point is worth making as an additional reason for the focus on government rather than politics.

This focus implies no clear demarcation. Concentration on the administrative side of government does not mean exclusion of the political. In democracies that is impossible because administrations react to the political environment of parties, pressure groups and public opinion; in Western Europe doubly so because government departments are headed by politicians answerable to parliament. The fact that the executive consists of ministers and civil servants makes it impossible to separate the two spheres even notionally, while the openness of government to external influences makes it impossible to draw a practical line between them. Government administration is unavoidably a subsystem of the political system, not just related to it through inputs and outputs but dependent upon it for its basic structures and influenced by it in its values. If administrative systems cannot be understood except by reference to their political environment, the point here for the political scientist, returning to the opening explanation of our focus, is that political systems cannot be understood without study of the administration. The administration not only forms the largest part of government, it lies at the centre of the policy-making process.

The factor of bigness — space occupied, people employed, business transacted, money spent — is sometimes forgotten by those who see government in terms of politics — party programmes, the outcome of elections, votes in parliament, pressure of interests, cabinet leaks, ministerial statements and similar newsworthy items. We need not trace the development of state functions or catalogue its range of activities to illustrate the size of government. Other indicators are the growth of public expenditure and the proportion of the active population that work for the state. Both are bedevilled by problems of definition, but however defined central government, local authorities and public corporations between them dominate spending and employment. Politics apart, they merit attention as vast organisations in our organisational society. While the administration plays an important role in policy, moreover, the bulk of its work is implementation, either by the provision of services itself or by the regulation of others. Political scientists have tended to concentrate on the more exciting aspects of the political system — voters, parties and pressure groups, even on relatively impotent parliamentarians. Measured by the work of its personnel, however, government is overwhelmingly about administration. A good deal may seem trivial except to those directly concerned, many decisions apparently unpolitical when looked at in isolation — but taken together, that is what government is about just as much as grander decisions of policy. Whether entitled 'Politics in Britain' or 'British

Government', books which have but a chapter on the executive, and then devote that to the Cabinet and relations between ministers and their senior officials, offer the reader a totally misleading picture of reality.

With the expansion of state activities the machinery of government has become increasingly complex. In France as in Britain ministries have been reshuffled at regular intervals; functions have been diversified and new units established within the sphere of central government, the Central Policy Review Staff, for example; new levels of decentralized central administration have been added, such as the French regions. Local government has been reformed throughout Europe. A host of new agencies have appeared, quasi-governmental and quasi-nongovernmental, often, like the Manpower Services Commission, hard to define in constitutional status. The map of public bodies gets ever more confusing, another reason why citizen and student alike require adequate guidelines. An encyclopaedia rather than a book would be needed to do justice to all this. For practical reasons, and because of its political centrality, the focus here is on the machinery of central government. Because they partake of the functions of central government elsewhere, the provincial governments of Germany and Italy are also covered. Local authorities and public corporations are referred to, nevertheless, to explain the distribution of state functions, the character of the public service and similar matters.

What interests the political scientist is that the administration is central to the policy-making process as well as being responsible for its execution. In Britain, more decisions are made in Whitehall than in Westminster or the Cabinet Room. Even those made by Cabinet and ministers are heavily influenced by senior officials expressing their own views or acting as channels of communication for interested bodies outside. Power has shifted from legislatures to executives throughout the democratic world for reasons that have been well rehearsed, as have the reasons for the shift from politicians to bureaucracy within the executive. Civil servants are permanent, their posting unaffected by government change in Britain, while even in those countries of Europe where senior posts are at the government's disposal those who fill them are generally career officials in a way that few politicians are career ministers. While ministers are generally professionals only in politics, with the Fifth Republic as something of an exception, officials are experts, some by training, all by experience. For these and other reasons they are bound to influence ministerial decisions, while the sheer volume of governmental work makes it inevitable that many important decisions are delegated entirely to them. It is impossible for the outsider to distinguish between advice, influence and decision. As advice on new policies arises out of the officials' experience of implementation in the past, moreover, and as the manner of implementation itself gives shape to policy, becoming part of it in the eyes of the recipient, it is almost as hard to distinguish between policy-making and execution.

If politics, as popularly used, is concerned with inputs into the decision-making system, attempts by citizens individually or through their organisations to influence the outputs of government, then the administration is at the centre of the conversion process. In so far as that process is directed by the politicians within government, responding to demands from the political system, it is the administration which turns their broad objectives into practical guidelines for action. It is not policies but rules which are implemented, and while parliamentary committees in some countries have an influence on legislation, laws are drafted and regulations made within the administration. In any case many of the demands on government, most perhaps, are direct inputs to the administration and do not pass through political institutions. European parliaments undoubtedly have lobbyists but nowhere is their role akin to that of their American counterparts: interests prefer the corridors of Whitehall to the lobby of Westminster where possible.

While a systems approach is not used in this book, the role of the administration can nevertheless be expressed in system terms. Seen thus, it does more than convert inputs into outputs. The conversion process is influenced by the character of the administration, as are those policy initiatives that arise within the administration itself. Together, these factors have been described as 'withinputs'. This means, first, the formal structure: institutional arrangements and regularised procedures. It means, second, the attitudes of the bureaucrats who inhabit the institutions and operate the procedures. Because no organisation works entirely according to its organisation chart, it means, third, informal aspects of the administrative system, relationships of authority and influence, work methods and lines of communication. Such matters are generally reserved for books on public administration. Books which claim to describe the government and politics of a country are often distorted as a result. The administration is not only what government is about in everyday experience, it is just as important to the big decisions which shape the way society goes.

Why study foreign governments and administration? Travel broadens the mind seems a good first answer, but there are many purposes, some utilitarian, others scientific, overlapping no doubt, and none exclusive. Study of a foreign country and its politics can also be a self-contained pursuit. Students of history have no difficulty in this: some history books, biography above all, can be enjoyed as stories, not read as contributions to something else. Politics can occasionally be approached in the same way. One thinks of Laurence Wylie on French village life, a contribution to political culture, just as one thinks of Richard Cobb's essays on French history. Among political scientists this justification of their subject is much underrated these days, which may explain why so little makes armchair reading. Public administration, in any case, does not have this potential appeal and it would be foolish to sell a study of the machinery of government, even superbly written, as leisure reading, though there must be some devotees of the subject (as there are of all subjects) who disprove this generalisation. Let us therefore turn to other purposes as a further prospectus for this book.

The first need involve no element of comparison. We live in an ever more interdependent world (the reader will see how hard it is to avoid clichés if one needs to state the obvious) and the governmental decisions of foreign countries are likely to affect us in many ways. Study of foreign governments enables us to understand how these decisions are made and to guess rather better than otherwise what decisions the immediate future may bring. A rapid glance at the daily press unfortunately reminds us how many actors there are on the international scene, many of whose policies may affect us, Japan as an exporter, for example, or Iran as an oil producer. It would need an encyclopaedia once more, rather than a textbook, to understand the ways of the world around us. But

Europe is a special case. Proximity apart (and those without a Channel are more conscious than we that common frontiers bring problems), member states of the European Community increasingly pursue common policies and citizens are gradually being subjected to its rules in their everyday affairs: how we may describe the food we eat and what it may contain, for example, or the weight of lorries driven through our streets. The study of British politics therefore needs to be reinforced by the study of EEC politics and that, in turn, requires an understanding of the member states.

Such knowledge, of course, is more relevant to those whose profession (or prospective careers) involves them in dealing with foreign countries, whether in government or some other capacity. This book has such people in mind. True, the man at the Foreign Office desk may not receive as much help from the conflicting interpretations of academic Kremlinologists as the latter would like to believe, but Europe, once more, is different. Its governmental institutions are more transparent and less arbitrary. The following chapters describe the machinery of government in the major countries of Western Europe, placing this in the context of national politics and administrative culture. In this way the reader should obtain a broad outline of the formal structures — useful as a map of administrations with which one may have to deal — as well as some notions of the administrative process, how policies are made, clues therefore to the behaviour of those involved. To cover all the branches of administration and all the rules of administrative procedure that a negotiator might conceivably meet would require separate volumes for each country. The chapters therefore emphasise general characteristics, the necessary background to make sense of more detailed information particular specialists will acquire at work.

To follow another tack. Travel books are among the oldest form of literature. Explorers described the curious ways of the people they met. Writers on politics used these reports for their own purposes: sometimes they asked why other societies were so differently organised from their own — early comparative politics; more often their real interest lay in critique nearer home. The study of foreign governments still throws some light on one's own. Country by country accounts serve as a guided tour of foreign lands, showing the various ways in which societies can be governed: the student may thus acquire perspectives which allow him to consider more critically the assumptions which underlie the system he knows from personal experience. Once more, there is a case for concentrating on Western Europe. We have here countries comparable in size, socio-economic structures, basic political values and governmental functions. On closer inspection, however, they turn out quite different, not just in their institutional arrangements but in the principles upon which these rest and the behavioural norms which guide their operation. There are more obvious lessons to be learnt from countries which are similar but different than from cultures totally strange.

Some reference to ways of managing things in such countries serves in two ways to broaden the student's critical appreciation of his own system. First, it underlines the simple fact that democratic government as we understand it can be organised in many ways. It may be that we no longer need books to argue that the grass is greener over the water — and the reader will soon find that the following chapters make no such claims: a critical eye, indeed, is cast on each country in turn. Despite the 'what's wrong with Britain?' literature, however, one still meets a disconcerting tendency to assume that certain arrangements are the natural order, an unawareness that the principles underlying them may not be shared in other democracies or that similar principles may be translated into practice in other ways. You cannot see what is commonplace and what is strange in your own ways, what works as well as might be expected and what might be done better, until you have looked elsewhere.

That brings one, second, to the study of foreign systems as an aid to discussion of domestic reform. Warnings about the difficulty of transplanting institutions are hardly needed. An institution obviously depends upon its environment, both formal and behavioural; it is unavoidably a piece in a complex jigsaw. The way it works depends on innumerable factors. It is usually hard to be sure why a particular arrangement works well (or badly) at home; it is certainly harder to predict how it will function if transferred elsewhere. But too much is made of these difficulties by political scientists immersed in methodology on the one hand, by practitioners socialised into the values of their own system on the other. One can look at foreign experience simply for ideas. Would we have come up with the idea of a Parliamentary Commissioner of the Administration if we had not heard of the Ombudsman? One can go further. Despite all the differences between European systems of government, they face similar administrative problems, thus similar questions of administrative reform as the following chapters brings out. Although some reforms are clearly constrained by their institutional and cultural setting, similar problems sometimes get different solutions less because of environmental constraints than because reformers have reasoned differently. While administrative science is unlikely to produce many laws, foreign studies should add to our stock of knowledge — insights and reasonable expectations — as effectively as other forms of inquiry and should be more suggestive than some. Comparison as a practical activity has only limited relevance for the student reading Politics as a humanities subject, though it should be different for those with a vocational intent. There is always the temptation to lecture on the reform of government as if this could have practical results. Few teachers have future influentials in their class, however, and by the time those few reach positions of influence their studies will probably have been forgotten even if the problems have not changed. This book deliberately avoids prescriptions, therefore. The hope remains that travel through the governmental systems of neighbouring countries will broaden the mind and thereby contribute to reformist thinking in the longer run.

Changing tack again, the study of political institutions can illuminate political theory. We may ask: are the various forms taken by government in Western democracies simply different ways of doing the same thing, each appropriate to its own nation, or are they trying to produce fundamentally different results? The original question of political science, after all, is 'what is the good society and what the best form of government to obtain it?' This can be studied through political thinkers of the past or contemporary political ideologies, but it can just as well be discussed by reference to existing forms, moving from description of governmental systems to the principles that underlie them, and working from there to a more general consideration of political ideas. We tend to assume that parliamentary democracies are based on a set of common principles, drawing these, on the whole, from our own experience. A survey of Europe quickly dispels that notion. Contrast the British doctrine of the sovereignty of Parliament with the French doctrine that democracy means a national assembly expressing the will of the people; and contrast both with German constitutionalism which limits the sovereignty of all institutions in the name of human rights. Contrast the centralised Republic One and Indivisible that the French have deduced from the twin principles of national will and the equality of citizens with British pluralism that in principle (if not practice) regards local diversity as a good thing. Contrast the connection Germans make between democracy and the rule of law (Rechtsstaat), administrative procedures fettered by rules and the citizen protected through courts, with British emphasis on responsible government, broad discretion checked by answerability to a political institution, the House of Commons. Concepts of the state differ and with it ideas about the relationship between politicians and bureaucracy, administration and law, government and interests, central and local authorities: in many such fundamental respects one finds quite different assumptions underlying the machinery of government. At a time when we ourselves are discussing basic principles — federalism, a Bill of Rights, further protection of the citizen against the state — a comparative view may help to clarify some of the values at stake as well as the administrative implications that follow.

Here, perhaps, we come closer to the study of comparative government proper. Many textbooks claim to use a framework by virtue of which their country by country chapters actually contribute to the development of a body of generalisations about political and administrative systems. In practice, this is rarely achieved. It is difficult to combine the coherent description of several national systems with the thematic approach usually required for genuine comparison. Even for the student of comparative politics, however, more interested in cross-national generalisations than particular nations, some straightforward single country accounts are necessary. Without some feeling how systems as a whole really operate, thematic generalisations are likely to remain abstract; without it, students cannot test such generalisations, apparently logical, for their practical likelihood. That, certainly, is the view of this book.

It remains true, however, that for the development of political science one must search administrative structures and administrative behaviour for recurring patterns, attempting causal explanation by relating these to other variables. This exercise may be undertaken because the political scientist takes a scholarly delight in pursuing the elusive laws of politics for their own sake; some may seek only to increase their understanding of politics, others to underpin reforms thereby. Whether disinterested or utilitarian, we hope that the student of comparative government will find some stimuli for theorising in the following chapters as well as facts to underpin such theories.

WHY EUROPE?

A European, we have suggested, has practical reasons for studying the government of his neighbours. While the states of Western Europe are no longer great powers in the world, they influence each other's politics through membership of the European Community. The student of politics, for his part, does well to look at governmental systems nearby before surveying entirely different political cultures around the globe or even that other exemplar of Western democracy, the United States, with its rather different constitutional order and political traditions. There should at least be some familiarity which will help make sense of the differences. But no assumption need be made that the Briton has some instinctive understanding of France, the German of Italy, nor, indeed, that the reader is a European at all. The fact remains that Western Europe forms a convenient area for comparative politics, like the communist bloc, Latin America or the Arab world. As democracies and in other ways the states of Western Europe have sufficient in common for comparison to go beyond the juxtaposition of systems. Similarities are matched by dissimilarities of political values, institutional arrangements, bureaucratic structures and administrative style. This should make the exercise more fruitful than a run around Britain, United States and Soviet Union, the standard three of introductory texts.

Limits of space enforce some restriction. Britain, France, Germany and Italy pick themselves for their size. Indeed, after the USA they are the four largest democracies in the world (give or take Japan). No offence to the smaller democracies is intended by the fact that they are represented by Belgium and the Netherlands alone. The others also have distinguishing features which it would have been useful to describe. Sweden for example, has a unique system of small policy-making ministries and autonomous administrative agencies headed by boards (precursors of the hived-off

Manpower Services Commission in Britain) and is the home of the Ombudsman institution, adapted not only in Britain but elsewhere. Ireland would have been interesting as a support to Britain, here outnumbered five to one by countries in the continental tradition on matters such as ministerial responsibility and administrative law. The range could only have been extended, however, by compressing each chapter to superficiality. Further chapters would have been doubly superficial because of the absence of other textbooks in English: for Britain, France and Germany, to a lesser extent Italy, textbooks on government and politics are available. We assume some readers of the present volume to be students of comparative administration, and for them such books are useful background reading; others may be studying the politics of one or several of the countries covered here, and for them this book should cover aspects of government not well covered in the other texts.

The common features of Western European states are obvious enough. They have advanced (complex and industrialised) economies with considerable mixed-economy elements; urbanised societies with relatively high living standards, extensive social services and educated populations; liberal-democratic political values, parliamentary institutions, free elections and competitive parties, interest group participation in policy-making; complex administrative systems, diversified functionally and geographically, subject to the rule of law and a variety of controls; large professional bureaucracies, highly competent, linked by hierarchical structures of authority to a political summit; extensive public services operated by the state and extensive state intervention in economic and social affairs, matched by public expectations that the state will promote material prosperity and social justice. They face similar social and economic problems which overloaded governments find it increasingly hard to solve and, as we shall see, a range of not dissimilar machinery of government problems also.

There are nevertheless many points of contrast, some fundamental, others technical. While the four largest states are fairly close in size, there are interesting differences in socio-economic development as regards Italy, for example, which affect the operations of government. Their historical experiences have been different, even in such simple matters as the acquisition of statehood and the establishment of democracy. Germany is still sufficiently worried about whether democracy is secure to investigate all who want to join the public service for their positive support of the constitutional order. National unity is under challenge in Belgium and on the periphery of Britain, with implications for the machinery of government. Though all are liberal democracies, their constitutional arrangements do not coincide. France is a unitary state, as is Britain (so far); Germany has a unique federal system (which really needs contrasting with the American model); the regionalism of Italy is halfway between, as, in a different way, is Belgium's experiment with separate ministers for the two linguistic communities in a centralised administration. All except France have cabinets that emerge from parliament and are answerable to it; it is France in this case which has a unique system halfway between parliamentary and presidential government. We move from Germany, where the rights of the citizen are guaranteed in the constitution and enforced by a constitutional court, through Italy with a lesser court, to Britain and the doctrine of parliamentary sovereignty. Relations between central and local government differ, as does the distribution of state functions between them: the fact that teachers appear in opposite columns is apparent as soon as one compares the size of the French and British civil services. While all have professional bureaucracies, they differ quite remarkably in character, with generalists (or 'amateurs') in Britain, economists and engineers (or 'technocrats') in France and jurists in Germany. They are organised differently, too: a unified service in Britain (but with specialists set apart), centrally managed; a unified service decentrally managed in Germany; a corps system in France. Control of the administration is primarily through ministerial responsibility to Parliament in Britain, while administrative courts play a major role elsewhere. Britain has its Ombudsmen for central and local government, Germany only for the armed forces, France a somewhat different 'mediator'. The arrangement of central government institutions shows a wide range of possibilities, for example in the allocation of functions between ministries (Finance and Economic Affairs but one of the interesting points of comparison), the hierarchical structures within them (single permanent head or numerous directors), and the extent of their field services (the prefectoral system of France, with its weaker copy in Italy, has no counterpart in Britain). The special position of the Chancellor deserves note in Germany, as does in France the juxtaposition of the President's and the Prime Minister's offices. Underlying all are different administrative cultures, perceptions of the role of the state and its servants for example, and different administrative styles, as in the balance between discretion and rules in individual decisions.

These and similar features allow comparisons at many levels, between systems as a whole, explaining each in terms of environmental factors, between bureaucracies or between institutions. The student can read each chapter to further his understanding of that country's government; he can pick from all to develop his own comparisons or fill in the framework of more theoretical works on comparative administration.

It often seems that more has been written about the methodology of comparative administration than on its substance. Works of substance have often focused on the bureaucracy, perhaps because Max Weber started a tradition, perhaps because its behavioural aspects lend themselves to survey and quantification. It is much harder to reduce the machinery of government to comparable units for analytic comparison across states, harder yet to describe an entire machine in a way that remains meaningful but is simple enough to allow the comparison of national systems as such. While methodology is not our concern here, the question of 'approach' remains, meaning by that no more than the way in which material is presented. We are all familiar with books which open with a theoretical section, followed by a case study in the author's framework which substantiates his generalisations but fails to give us a rounded picture of the system in question. Such authors typically close with the hope that others will produce parallel studies to test the framework further. Agreement on hypotheses may be a prerequisite for the move from description to science: political scientists being what they are, however, this rarely happens. More to the point, lecturers, in Britain at least, rarely teach to someone else's order. Books introducing political science or public administration, the government and politics of Britain, France or Germany, rarely serve as more than background reading to lectures. A textbook, therefore, does well to cover standard topics in as neutral a framework as possible. Our purpose here is to provide a volume that will describe the administrative systems of the major countries of Western Europe in a manner that allows the chapters to be used by students being taught in quite different ways.

That does not solve the problem of framework, of course. Material has to be presented in some order that makes sense unless one is writing a reference work, in which case topics can be treated under separate headings without too much worry. If theory is excluded, it is focus that will probably determine the way information is organised. Many foci are possible: institutions, behaviour patterns, systems, policies and so on. The debate between institutional and behavioural approaches is no longer as acute as it seemed a while ago, when the behavioural new broom tried to sweep out all the institutional accounts as misleadingly formal. While behavioural studies are a good way of understanding how particular organisations work, it is hard to describe the machinery of government as a whole through behavioural eyes. Systems analysis is now the fashion, but it has similar problems, as do studies which centre on the policy-making process. Administration can be seen as patterns of policy making and policy implementation. An obvious difficulty is the absence of a flow chart along which inputs and withinputs move until they reach the output stage. Too many institutions are involved in too many ways, interrelating in different ways from case to case, for a conveyor belt account of the machinery of government. Policy studies may be written in this way, not a geography of the administration. Systems thinking is valuable, nevertheless, because it reminds one of the need to relate the administration to its environment, not just in terms of demand-inputs but of the broader cultural forces that influence its behaviour.

The focus of this book is on the machinery of government. That does not mean institutional in the legalistic sense. The attempt is made to put institutions in their historical and political frame, to explain why they came to be as they are and why they work as they do: relations in the French executive between President and Prime Minister, for example, depend on political forces quite as much as on constitutional provisions. Formal arrangements, organisation charts and procedural rules are the framework in which administrators operate. In public administration behaviour is probably more constrained in this way than in the private sector: in administrative law countries, for example, the implementation of laws is regarded as a quasi-judicial process, while in Britain, as in the rest of Europe, those who manage the bureaucracy do not have the discretion of personnel managers in business. There are dangers in too legalistic an approach, however, though this is more likely to be found among students of continental Europe who combine the study of public administration with law than among political scientists here. Within their constraints, sometimes breaking them, indeed, actors have their own behaviour patterns, shaped by the values they hold, and these depend on all sorts of factors. There is an administrative culture just as there is a political culture. Organisation charts show the formal structures of government, its units and their functions, the relationships of officials within units and the relationships between offices. These are generally the truth in constitutional democracies, though sometimes broken, but they are not the whole truth. Formal structures are necessarily complemented — and may be distorted — by informal relationships, patterns of influence and channels of communication. To understand how governments operate, one needs to look at the institutional bricks and mortar, the bureaucratic inhabitants and the processes that operate within the system: stage, actors and play. The following chapters attempt within the limits of space to cover all these.

The modern state is a complex machine made up of numerous parts, relating to one another in a variety of ways. Even if the broad outlines are the same in all the states of Western Europe, it would not be easy to decide on the most logical order in which to describe it. It is hard to break into the system in one place and string out the parts in a line, as coherent treatment on consecutive pages really needs. In its simplest form, the problem is illustrated by standard textbooks on British government and politics which permute Public-Parliament-Cabinet-Administration in every possible way. The more features are introduced — civil service, internal and external controls, courts, regionalism, local government — the harder it gets. The difficulty is compounded when one remembers that the governmental systems studied here contain different building blocks, the states of German federalism and the French Council of State, for example. An attempt has nevertheless been made to order each chapter in broadly similar ways: historical and constitutional background and other political factors which influence the character of the system; the political side of the executive and the institutions of central government; decentralisation in its various forms;

structure and character of the civil service; control and consultation; problems of the system.

Within that framework, a good deal of latitude must necessarily be allowed to each contributor, not just because of the formal differences already mentioned but to bring out the different characteristics and to stress the issues that seem important in each case. What the chapters show is the diversity of systems and the diversity of principles on which they are based. Illuminating, nevertheless, is the recurrence of themes: the conflict between continuity and change, trends towards decentralisation, modernisation of the civil service, problems of politicisation within the bureaucracy, difficulties of external control, for example. In single chapters the student should find an introduction to the geography of that country's administration as well as material necessary for understanding its politics which he may miss in more politically orientated textbooks. Reading the book as a whole, similarities and dissimilarities of administrative style should provide stimuli for the study of comparative administration proper; common problems with different solutions should offer useful clues to the more practical study of governmental reform.

CHAPTER TWO

Britain

The character of contemporary public administration in Britain
has been strongly influenced by the fact that the system of
government has developed gradually with only a few sharp breaks
in its evolution. Many of the important institutions and processes
have their origins in the nineteenth century and earlier. As the role
of government has changed, so they have been adapted to perform
new tasks in a different environment.

Two examples of such institutional adaptation make this point
clearly. First, there is the convention that ministers are responsible
to Parliament for all the actions of their departments, a doctrine
which is of crucial importance in determining the relationship of
the executive to the legislature and that between ministers and
their civil servants. It was originally formulated in the mid-
nineteenth century before the development of a disciplined party
system and before the growth in the scale of government which has
occurred in the last seventy years. This has led to some modification
in the convention, for instance ministers are no longer expected to
resign for every departmental mistake that is uncovered, but it has
by no means been superseded. Indeed in 1978 the traditional
doctrine was re-asserted by the government.

Another example is provided by the civil service itself. Many of
its principal features were established in the nineteenth century
when the scale of government was small and its functions mainly
regulatory. The work of contemporary civil servants has altered
dramatically. Governments now intervene in many economic
matters that formerly were the preserve of private individuals and
organisations; in the social field they are also responsible for the
provision of a vast number of benefits and services. As a result
there has been a dramatic increase in the size of the civil service and

18

many new kinds of staff with appropriate expertise for the new tasks have been recruited. But the most senior posts in the civil service are still occupied by men who are recruited and deployed along lines very similar to those adopted in the 1850s and their relationship with their political masters is still based on ground rules that were elaborated more than one hundred years ago.

Too much, however, must not be made of the continuity of evolution of British administration. The civil service has been diversified through the recruitment of large numbers of staff with specialist qualifications. New institutions and procedures have also been developed to supplement the traditional ones. Two such developments are of particular importance. First, during the twentieth century there has been a dramatic growth in field administration such that in the 1970s 70 per cent of non-industrial civil servants worked outside headquarters offices. Most departments now have a network of regional and local offices which handle a high proportion of their work and are the main points of contact for the citizen with the administration. Second, there has been a large and steady increase in the number of public bodies which are neither parts of ministerial departments nor of local authorities. Thus special bodies have been created to manage the nationalised industries and to take responsibility for many of the new areas of state intervention. Combined with the rapid growth of local government during this century, this development has altered the pattern of public administration dramatically. For instance, the civil service now only employs one-tenth of the public workforce, compared with about one-quarter in 1914.

Thus the evolutionary development of the administrative system must not be allowed to overshadow the major changes that have occurred. Nevertheless it is important in any understanding of the distinctive character of British administration which differs in so many respects from that of its European neighbours. This is not to say, however, that the system has not been challenged. Indeed in the last twenty years there has been an almost constant flow of criticism directed against most of the institutions of British government, some of it in the traditional evolutionary mould but much of it seeking radical constitutional change.

In the 1950s any discussion of the administrative system would have been based upon two premises: first, the high degree of integration in Britain, both socially and geographically and, second, the extent to which the executive dominated the governmental process. Both these generalisations still hold in 1979 but they need to be advanced rather cautiously. Britain remains highly integrated by the standards of most countries and this is still reflected in the informal nature of many of its constitutional rules and in its unitary system of government. However, during the 1970s there have been various signs of strain. Political debate has generally been more bitter and the differences between the Conservative and Labour parties have become more marked. There has also been an increase in protest with powerful groups adopting extra-parliamentary tactics to oppose the decisions of government. It would be an exaggeration to talk of a collapse of the stable consensus that has characterised British politics since 1945 but at times it has looked rather frayed and there has certainly been a decline in public confidence in the institutions of government. One aspect of this change has been the growth of nationalist movements in Scotland and Wales demanding independence for their countries. Partly in response to their electoral success, plans have been approved for setting up assemblies in Scotland and Wales which, if confirmed in referenda to be held in March 1979, will radically alter the character of British government.

The administrative system is also still founded in the principle of executive domination. The fusion of executive and legislative functions means that the government owes it position to the fact that it commands a majority in the House of Commons. The initiative in decision making therefore lies with the Cabinet which generally has experienced few problems in gaining the assent of the House of Commons. Indeed, in the 1960s a number of writers were talking of the demise of parliamentary government. Nor has the power of the executive traditionally been challenged by the judiciary. The role of the courts accords with the sovereignty of Parliament and is therefore confined to ensuring that the executive operates within the law.

However, in recent years the domination of the system by the executive, although still intact, has looked less secure. Whereas in 1951 the Conservative and Labour parties won almost 97 per cent of the popular vote, in October 1974 they achieved only 75 per cent. This has meant that the number of minor parties represented in the House of Commons has increased, and for seven months in 1974 and again since 1977 the Labour Party has been in office without a parliamentary majority. One consequence has been a revival of parliamentary influence which many consider irrevocable even if one of the parties obtains an overall majority at the next general election. There have also been signs of growing assertiveness on the part of the courts. Neither of these developments has yet given rise to basic alterations in the administrative system but they have placed it under strain and, if they are not reversed, they may well lead to significant changes.

In any case, the emphasis that has in the past been placed upon executive domination has perhaps been exaggerated through too much attention being given to the formal structure of government at the expense of political realities. The freedom of action of any government is now severely constrained by its international commitments and by domestic pressures. The significance of the former has been stressed in the debate about British membership of the European Economic Community and was highlighted during the economic crisis of 1976-77 when British economic policy was largely determined by the necessity of obtaining substantial international financial assistance. Domestically, the 1970s have provided many illustrations of the need for the government to win the consent of affected interests if its decisions are to be implemented successfully. In 1974 a Conservative government was forced into a premature general election as a result of its failure to persuade a powerful trade union to abide by its pay policy. Its successor experienced fewer difficulties in this area, at least initially, but has generally failed to persuade industry to undertake the investment needed for British economic recovery. Thus, although there are few formal obstacles confronting the Cabinet, its ability to act in most fields depends very much upon its success in persuading and cajoling others to cooperate with it.

There are, therefore, two points that need to be borne in mind in any discussion of the administrative system in Britain. First, its evolutionary character has contributed to what one observer called its 'labyrinthine complexity'. Only in 1918 was a comprehensive official examination of the entire system undertaken and few of its recommendations were implemented. In general, existing institutions have been adapted to perform new tasks and new organisations have been added piecemeal, often with little consideration being given to how well they fitted in with what was already in existence. Second, many aspects of the system have in recent years been the subject of critical scrutiny. This has led to a number of reforms but the fundamental character of the administrative process has not been changed. Whether this trend will continue and what its overall effect will be in ten years' time can only be a matter of speculation: it does, however, induce caution in predicting the future development of the system.

THE INSTITUTIONAL FRAMEWORK

The focus of this section is upon central administration. However, to understand its structure and processes fully some attention must be paid to the pattern of public administration generally. Public organisations in the United Kingdom can be divided into three broad categories: first, central departments which are headed by ministers (often known as Secretaries of State) who are members of one of the houses of Parliament, and staffed by civil servants; second, local authorities whose powers and duties are confined to a particular locality and whose members are elected by the voters of that area; third, a vast number of special-purpose authorities with their own powers and responsibilities, which here will be called non-departmental organisations.

Employees in the Public Service, 1978

Civil Service	750,000
National Health Service	1,000,000
Local Authorities	3,000,000
Non-departmental Organisations	2,000,000
	6,750,000

As the table indicates, the civil service accounts for only 11 per cent of the public workforce (excluding the armed forces) in the United Kingdom. Local authorities employ more than 40 per cent and non-departmental organisations (including the nationalised industries) a further 30 per cent. The remaining 15 per cent work in the National Health Service which, although formally under ministerial control, is in practice managed by regional and area health authorities whose staff are not classified as civil servants. This pattern of employment reflects the fact that central departments do not themselves provide many public services, most of these — education, welfare, housing, police and fire services — being the responsibility of local authorities.

The Government

At the apex of the government is the Cabinet. It is composed of the senior members of the party that commands a majority in the House of Commons. It is chaired by the Prime Minister who also selects it members, most of whom are the heads of government departments (and usually have the title of Secretary of State). The others are either non-departmental ministers (many of whom hold historic offices such as Paymaster-General and Lord Privy Seal) or second-tier ministers in departments that have politically important responsibilities. Outside the Cabinet, there are two ministerial levels, both appointed by the Prime Minister. First, there are those of 'ministerial rank outside the Cabinet'. In recent years they have mainly been second-tier ministers in departments headed by Cabinet ministers (most with the title of Minister of State) but in the past it was common for smaller departments to be headed by ministers who did not sit in the Cabinet. Secondly, there are junior ministers (usually called Parliamentary Under Secretaries) who assist their senior colleagues in their departmental work. Together, all these ministers, and the whips who manage the government's business in Parliament, constitute 'the government', which in 1978 numbered 110.

The Government in 1978	
Cabinet Ministers	24
Ministers outside the Cabinet	30
Junior Ministers	34
Government Whips	22
	110

The Cabinet has two main functions: first, it takes the lead in initiating most legislative and administrative action; and second, it is the ultimate forum for the coordination of all the activities of government. These functions have a major effect upon the Prime Minister's freedom of choice in choosing the Cabinet: the first normally requires him to select the most senior members of his party, many of whom may be rivals as well as colleagues; the second makes it desirable that all the major departments are represented. However, the Prime Minister retains a considerable amount of discretion both in deciding who to include and in allocating portfolios and this gives him considerable influence over the Cabinet.

The powers of executive action in Britain are legally vested not in the Cabinet or in the government as collective bodies but in ministers individually. However, politically it is accepted that ministers share responsibility for decisions and are subject to the authority of the Cabinet. Whether or not he is a member of the Cabinet, the only alternatives for a minister who disagrees with a decision are to remain silent or to resign. There have been a few occasions when this convention of collective responsibility has been relaxed, most recently during the referendum on Britain's continuing membership of the European Community in 1975. Frequently, ministers also bend the rules by leaking their views to the media but there are fairly strict limits on the extent to which this will be tolerated by the Prime Minister and this convention is the major 'cause' of ministerial resignations.

Because ministers are individually responsible to Parliament for the affairs of their departments they must all be members of either the Commons or the Lords. They are the spokesmen of their departments in Parliament and can be held to account for departmental, as well as personal, mistakes. In the past this doctrine was thought to entail resignation when serious mistakes occurred but now it is generally accepted that the scale of most departments makes it impractical to hold ministers responsible in this way. The doctrine, however, remains very important in other respects. First, it determines the relationship between ministers and their civil servants. All official action is taken in the name of the minister; civil servants therefore remain largely anonymous. Within departments generally, great care is taken to ensure that the minister is not exposed to parliamentary criticism and this possibility has a major impact upon the way in which decisions are taken. Second, the doctrine affects the relationship between ministers. As constitutionally no minister can issue directions to another, disagreements have to be resolved by striking compromises between the parties to a dispute. Politically, of course, their strengths vary and ultimately the Cabinet adjudicates in disputes. But below the

Cabinet there is an elaborate machinery of inter-departmental committees which is founded on the principle of securing agreement among all the interested parties, regardless of their size.

Later in this section, the adequacy of ministerial responsibility as a means of controlling executive action will be examined. At this point we are interested only in its effect upon the functioning of the executive. Two questions have attracted a considerable amount of attention in recent years: first, the power of the Prime Minister and, second, the disintegration of the Cabinet into smaller committees. In the first case, it is clear that a number of factors, not least the development of television, have increased the prominence of the Prime Minister. But this is not to say that the Prime Minister has taken over the functions of the Cabinet. In certain circumstances the Prime Minister may appear to wield almost presidential powers but his role is dependent upon his ability to carry his colleagues and particularly those who have significant support of their own both in the party and in the country. Similarly, although the workload of the Cabinet has necessitated the use of committees and has led to experiments with various types of small inner cabinets, generally such procedures are successful only when they are accepted by all the members of the Cabinet, who in the last resort can require issues to be discussed in the Cabinet itself. Thus, although it is difficult to generalise about the styles of different governments, as they vary according to the personalities of their members and political circumstances, the system remains essentially a collegiate one in which responsibility is shared by a group of ministers bound by party ties.

Central Departments

The department of state is the traditional and still the most important form of central administrative organisation. In 1978 there were eighteen ministerial departments and a number of others which were under the ultimate control of a minister in charge of a major department but which enjoyed some degree of autonomy.

Main Departments and Staff Numbers in January 1978

Defence[1]	253,400
Health and Social Security	96,900
Treasury[2]	77,600
Environment	54,600
Home Office	32,950
Employment	24,100
Agriculture, Fisheries and Food	14,800
Transport	14,600
Foreign and Commonwealth Office[3]	12,100
Scottish Office	10,250
Lord Chancellor's Office	10,100
Industry	9,550
Trade	7,400
Civil Service Department	4,900
Education and Science	2,800
Welsh Office	1,500
Energy	1,300
Prices and Consumer Protection	340

1 Excluding military personnel
2 Of whom 76,500 work for the Inland Revenue, Customs and Excise, and National Savings Departments
3 Including Ministry of Overseas Development

As the table indicates, departments vary widely in size, reflecting differences in the nature of their responsibilities. Most of the smaller ones are primarily concerned with the formulation of policy and the regulation of the activities of both private individuals and organisations and other public bodies, such as local authorities and the nationalised industries. For instance, the small size of the Department of Education and Science reflects the fact that it is not directly responsible for running any schools or colleges and does not therefore employ any teaching staff. Other departments, however, are themselves responsible for administering policy and conducting executive operations. In many such cases, although the minister at the head of the department retains ultimate responsibility, executive work is actually carried out by sub-departments or agencies enjoying considerable degrees of day-to-day autonomy. Thus in the Treasury over 98 per cent of its staff work in the three sub-departments concerned with the collection of taxes and the operation of the national savings system. Similarly, in the Department of the Environment those staff concerned with the construction and maintenance of government buildings work for the Property Services Agency which enjoys some independence within the department on financial and staffing matters.

These variations in the size and the tasks of departments make it difficult to generalise about their structure or their methods of operation. It is possible, however, to identify a number of factors which generally affect both the distribution of functions between departments and their internal organisation.

Departments are artificial creations in the sense that there is no one way in which the tasks of government can be grouped together. The aim of grouping is of course to achieve the benefits of specialisation by linking activities that are related. But there are various ways in which this can be done. In Britain, as elsewhere, two bases of organisation predominate. Most important is specialisation according to the task to be done or the objective to be attained. Thus, as can be gauged from their titles, the pattern of most departments reflects the main functions of government — defence, transport, energy, and so on. There are also some departments, such as the Scottish and Welsh Offices, that are organised on the basis of the area that is served: within these, however, the functional approach emerges at lower levels. Thus the Scottish Office is divided into functional parts dealing with education, development, etc.

On taking office, each government inherits a set of departments which it usually modifies to meet its own political and administrative needs. This is normally done in piecemeal fashion but on a very few occasions, the most recent being in 1970, comprehensive reviews of the machinery of government have been undertaken. Some of the changes made may be largely symbolic: the creation of a new department is often an effective way of indicating the government's determination to tackle a problem. Others may reflect little more than the personal preferences of the Prime Minister and his senior colleagues. But most usually changes reflect a shift in the government's political priorities. For instance, in 1970 concern about uniformity of treatment of public and private industry led to a unification of most of the government's powers in relation to industry in a single department, the Department of Trade and Industry. By 1973, however, this aim had been overshadowed by the problem of energy supplies following the increase in the price of oil. Thus a separate Department of Energy was created and this process of disintegration was taken further in 1974 by a different government whose priorities were the provision of assistance to particular sectors of industry and action to protect consumers against price increases.

Decisions about the machinery of government are generally taken by the Prime Minister. Never far from his mind is the problem of Cabinet size. On the one hand the Prime Minister is concerned to restrict the size of the Cabinet if it is to provide effective political direction and leadership; on the other hand, if it is to perform its coordinating function successfully, all the major areas of activity need to be represented. Various attempts have been made to resolve this dilemma. Most recently there has been a trend towards the amalgamation of departments. Earlier, as the government had assumed new responsibilities there had been a gradual increase in the number of departments. Thus it grew from eighteen in 1914, to twenty-six in 1956. Between 1966 and 1972, however, the number fell to seventeen with the emergence of so-called 'giant departments', e.g. Department of Health and Social Security and Department of Trade and Industry. A smaller Cabinet was not the only advantage seen in amalgamation. It also allowed conflicts (such as that between transport and environmental protection) to be resolved within a single department rather than through interdepartmental compromise, and it made possible economies of scale in management and analytic resources.

As departments have increased in size, so their ministerial teams have become larger: in 1978, twelve departments had teams of four or more. They have also become more complex. In most departments there are now three ministerial ranks and in some there are four. Increasingly, also, junior ministers are publicly charged with responsibility for particular areas of a department's work and this is often reflected in their titles, e.g. Minister of State for Sport and Recreation, Parliamentary Under Secretary (Disablement). Indeed, for a Prime Minister this may be an attractive alternative to setting up a separate department. But as long as a function remains within a department, the ultimate responsibility to Parliament rests with the Secretary of State and his ability to cope with this burden therefore places a limit on the size of departments. It is difficult to generalise as to the maximum size that is tolerable in this sense. The available evidence suggests that it depends upon such factors as the political implications and the degree of integration of a department's work, and upon the ability of particular ministers — something which varies widely for ability in this sense is only one of a number of qualifications for ministerial office — both to master departmental business and to work together in a team.

Departments do not only vary in their size. There are also differences in the way in which they are organised internally. In many respects they share common features which result from their political accountability to Parliament and from standard rules relating to financial and staff management. Thus the levels in each department reflect grades in the civil service; and a hierarchical structure follows from the minister's liability to be called to account for any action of the department and from the senior administrative official's responsibility as accounting officer.

Administrative Hierarchy and Staff Numbers, 1978

Permanent Secretary	42
Deputy Secretary	180
Under Secretary	560
Assistant Secretary	1,200
Principal	4,400
Senior Executive Officer	7,900
Higher Executive Officer	22,300
Administration Trainee	600
Executive Officer	47,200
Clerical Officer	89,700
Clerical Assistant	76,600

However, increasingly the organisation of departments has been modified to take account of the needs of particular kinds of work. For instance, those which employ specialist staff, such as economists or engineers, have modified their structure to give such staff a major role in decision making.

Attempts have also been made to delegate responsibility away from the minister and from top official staff. This has been done partly through the transfer of functions outside the departmental

framework. But within departments there are now a growing
number of 'agencies' which, although under the direction of a
minister and staffed by civil servants, are distinguished from the
conventional pattern of departmental organisation by having their
own executive heads and accounting officers and by a larger degree
of freedom in staff management. The two most important such
agencies are the Procurement Executive in the Ministry of Defence
and the Property Services Agency in the Department of the
Environment.

Functional Decentralisation

The growth in the workload of government which led to changes in
the departmental framework has also been one of the factors behind
moves to transfer responsibility for certain activities away from
ministers and to vest them in other public bodies. This process of
decentralisation is advocated on many other grounds as well. For
instance, the management of certain tasks, such as the operation of
commercial activities in the public sector, is generally thought to
require greater financial and organisational flexibility than can be
provided in a department that is subject to ministerial and
parliamentary supervision. Similarly, decentralisation may make
it easier to adapt services to local conditions and to the wishes of
particular communities.

Analytically it is helpful to distinguish two dimensions to
decentralisation, although in practice they are closely intertwined.
The first is functional decentralisation, a process — often known as
hiving-off — in which a special body is set up to assume responsibility for a particular function or group of functions, usually but
not necessarily on a national basis. Second is decentralisation which
is primarily areal in focus, a process in which responsibility for
decision making in particular areas is vested in either bureau-
cratically-controlled 'outstations' of central departments or in
democratically-elected local authorities.

Non-departmental organisations have been part of the structure
of public administration in Britain since the nineteenth century
and some can even be found in earlier periods. Their importance,
however, has grown dramatically since the end of the First World
War, particularly in connection with many of the new tasks
undertaken by government. An important step in their develop-

ment was the decision of the Labour Party between the wars that the management of any industrial or commercial activities brought into public ownership needed greater autonomy than existed in either ministerial departments or local authorities and should therefore be entrusted to agencies specially created for the purpose. After 1945 this decision was implemented not only for the nationalised industries but also in other new areas of government social and economic intervention. Moreover, responsibility for certain tasks has been transferred from departments to non-departmental organisations. Thus in 1968 the postal services ceased to be run by a minister and became the responsibility of a corporate body, the Post Office Corporation; during 1973 and 1974 the size and character of the Department of Employment were transformed by the transfer of its job-finding, training, health and safety, and conciliation and arbitration services to three independent agencies: the Manpower Services Commission, the Health and Safety Commission and the Advisory Conciliation and Arbitration Service.

The number of non-departmental organisations now in existence and their variety almost defies classification. Some idea of their scope can be gained by dividing them into three very broad groups. First, there are those which perform commercial or quasi-commercial functions. Within this category are the nationalised industries proper, e.g. the British Railways Board and the British Gas Corporation, and an increasing number of publicly-owned companies, e.g. Rolls-Royce Ltd and British Leyland, which remain subject to private company law. Second, there is a group of bodies, e.g. the Monopolies and Mergers Commission, the Commission for Racial Equality and the Price Commission, which relieve ministers of responsibility for investigating the affairs of other individuals and bodies and which take decisions of a quasi-judicial kind. Third, there are bodies in which decision making is entrusted either to relevant experts or to the representatives of affected interests, both to insulate the field from the political arena and to increase the likelihood of decisions being accepted once they have been taken — falling into this category are the University Grants Committee, the Arts Council and the Advisory Conciliation and Arbitration Service.

There is also great variety in their constitutions. The characteristics of a non-departmental organisation have not been prescribed legally and no standard model has been followed each time a body of this kind has been set up. Nevertheless, they all have formal constitutions, set out either in legislation or a royal charter, which confer corporate status and independent legal personality. But, beyond this, it is almost impossible to make generalisations. In most cases their staff are not civil servants but there are exceptions, e.g. the Manpower Services Commission. They all also enjoy some degree of independence from direct political control by ministers and Parliament. The extent of their autonomy, however, varies widely according to such factors as the way in which they are financed, the membership and security of tenure of their controlling boards, the powers of control given to ministers and the basis on which they are staffed. Thus a body which owns revenue-bearing assets and is financially self-supporting is freed from the close control exercised by the Treasury over expenditure that is financed out of parliamentary appropriations. Similarly, board members who do not owe their positions entirely to ministerial patronage and who are not liable to summary dismissal will feel more able to stand up to ministerial pressure. Staff who are not civil servants are also less subject to central control and will approach their work differently than if they were members of a career service with a likelihood of later being transferred to other departments.

Although the aim of setting up a non-departmental organisation is to confer independence, some control over activities that remain in the public sector must be maintained. The duties of each body, and the powers which enable it to carry them out, are laid down formally, usually by statute, and in the last resort it is thus subject to regulation by the courts. In practice, however, judicial control has been of little importance in this field; regulation has been achieved through ministerial powers of direction and influence, and through the retention of limited parliamentary oversight. Ministers are normally able to guide the activities of non-departmental organisations by means of their powers of direction and approval of certain key decisions. Parliament's role has largely been confined to the questioning of ministers on the exercise or non-exercise of their powers of intervention but some direct contact between MPs and non-departmental organisations is achieved by means of select committee enquiries into their activities.

The general aim of this framework is to strike a balance between independence and control. In practice, however, it has proved very difficult to sustain under the pressure of events. Neither ministers nor MPs have been content not to interfere in the day-to-day decisions of many non-departmental organisations. The problem is that it is frequently these decisions which have political repercussions and are the subject of political pressure. Similarly, governments have been concerned to use the public sector as a tool of economic management and have therefore sought to intervene in many individual decisions. For instance, for most of the post-war period the pricing decisions, investment plans and wage settlements of the nationalised industries — all matters which semi-autonomous status was intended to protect from political interference — have been subject to extensive formal or informal ministerial control.

Geographical Decentralisation

The unitary• nature of British government has given rise to a popular view that it is highly centralised. In one sense this is of course true. The writ of Parliament does extend throughout the country and all other public bodies are subordinate to it. But it is very misleading to imagine that the United Kingdom is governed from London. Even as far as central government is concerned, 75 per cent of civil servants work outside Greater London; and local authorities provide the majority of important public services.

Most central departments and other national organisations have systems of regional and local offices. While formal responsibility for decisions taken in such offices remains with the minister, decisions are actually taken by officials who operate within the framework of centrally drawn-up rules and procedures but who enjoy extensive discretion. The system of decentralised administration in Britain does not always receive sufficient attention, partly because such officials do not enjoy the prestige or the publicity of, for instance, their counterparts at prefectoral level in France. It is important, however, not only because of the volume of work that is performed at local and regional levels but because it is at these levels that most citizens have their principal contact with government.

A complex system of local government emerged towards the end of the nineteenth century. Throughout the country there is now a multi-tier system but the pattern varies in different parts of the country. Even in England, there are three systems. In each case, county councils are responsible for police (except in London) and fire services, structure planning and major roads, and district councils for housing, local planning and environmental health. Responsibility for education and social services, however, varies: in non-metropolitan areas it is at county level, in metropolitan areas and Greater London it is at district level.

Local Government Structure in England

	Non-metropolitan areas	Metropolitan areas[1]	Greater London
First tier	County Councils (39)	County Councils (6)	Greater London Council (1)
Second tier	District Councils (296)	District Councils (36)	London Borough Councils (32)
Third tier	Parish Councils[2]		

1   e.g. West Midlands, Greater Manchester, Merseyside
2   These are found in many rural areas: their main function is to represent the views of their residents to the principal authorities

Although local authorities are the principal operational level of government, their powers are laid down by Parliament and central government retains control over many aspects of their work. Certain decisions require ministerial approval and in general the independence of local authorities is limited by their dependence upon central government for over 50 per cent of their current expenditure. Recently, also, there have been a number of attempts to increase central control over issues that previously were left to local discretion. Nevertheless they retain a significant degree of autonomy both in setting priorities and in deciding how services should be provided, and this is reflected in wide variations in standards and practices in different parts of the country.

Britain lacks an elected regional tier of government. From 1921 until 1972 Northern Ireland had its own parliament and Cabinet which, although remaining constitutionally subordinate to the UK

Parliament, wielded extensive powers on most domestic issues. These arrangements were, however, suspended in 1972 following the breakdown of law and order in the province and a system of 'direct rule' from Westminster was introduced. The province is now governed by the Secretary of State for Northern Ireland, a member of the UK Cabinet, on a basis which has many similarities with that found in Scotland and Wales. Scotland has never been fully integrated into the UK and has retained its own distinctive legal and educational system and its own established church. Since 1895 it has had a separate Secretary of State in the UK Cabinet in charge of the Scottish Office which now contains four departments and is responsible for most government functions in Scotland. On many issues separate Scottish legislation is enacted by Parliament and significant differences exist between Scottish practice and elsewhere. A similar system applies in Wales but it is of more recent origin and does not cover as wide a range of activities. This is reflected in the fact that there is less divergence in Wales from English practice. In England the only form of regional government is a system of advisory economic planning councils, appointed by ministers from among people qualified by expert knowledge or as representatives of regional interest groups.

The degree of centralisation in the UK will be radically altered if plans to devolve extensive powers to assemblies in Scotland and Wales are implemented. Restoration of regional self-government in Northern Ireland is also likely if security conditions permit and agreement can be secured among the different communities of the province. There has been discussion of introducing stronger regional government in England but there is little public demand for such a change and major reform is unlikely.

Coordination

An important issue in the debate on devolution to Scotland and Wales has been the question of striking a balance between local autonomy and the need for central control. This has arisen not just because of concern about the variations in levels of service provision that would probably result. It is also the result of worries, strongly expressed by the Treasury, as to the effects of devolution on the management of the economy. The Treasury is reluctant to permit significant variations in tax levels and insists that central control of the level of public expenditure, if not its distribution, is essential. Its arguments have been underpinned by Britain's economic difficulties which have persisted throughout the post-war period. These problems have generally enhanced the importance of coordination in government of a positive kind — the setting of priorities and the careful planning of public spending — which has been added to traditional coordination, concerned with the resolution of disputes between different branches of government and the smooth running of the machine.

One of the main functions of the Cabinet is coordination and it is supported in this by the Cabinet Secretariat. Traditionally the Secretariat has been responsible for the servicing of the Cabinet and its committees, taking minutes and recording decisions which are transmitted as impulses for action throughout Whitehall. Since the 1960s, however, it has begun to assume a more positive role. It has provided the base for a number of senior government advisers, and special units for important areas of decision making, e.g. European policy and devolution, have been located there. Most important, however, has been the creation of the Central Policy Review Staff (CPRS) in 1971 which 'physically and constitutionally' is part of the Cabinet Office.

The main task of the CPRS is 'to offer advice to ministers collectively which will help them relate their policies and decisions to the government's strategy as a whole'. It attempts to do this by taking stock at fairly regular intervals of the problems facing the government and of its progress in achieving its commitments, by undertaking a number of in-depth studies, by assisting in departmental policy reviews and by preparing briefs on matters coming before the Cabinet and its committees. Such briefs supplement departmental papers and are designed to bring out the main issues involved and to point out implications which departments may have overlooked. The CPRS has about sixteen to nineteen members, half of whom are career civil servants on secondment from their departments and the rest recruited from outside — from universities, industry, financial institutions and international organisations.

On financial matters coordination is provided by the Treasury, which is responsible both for economic and financial policy and for the control of public expenditure. Since the mid-nineteenth century an elaborate system has been developed for controlling depart-mental spending that is linked closely to the requirements of the annual parliamentary appropriations procedures. Originally the main aims of this system were to check the legality of public spending and to restrict its growth, but over the years the Treasury has increasingly become concerned with securing value for money. Modifications have also been introduced to give departments greater delegated authority to incur expenditure without the specific approval of the Treasury. However, in the years after the Second World War increasing doubts were expressed about the adequacy of the control of public spending. Much expenditure could not properly be regulated on an annual basis. Nor did the form in which financial information was presented permit debate about the cost of different programmes, so that spending could be linked to the government's overall priorities. Following an official report in 1961, a new system of public expenditure planning — known as the Public Expenditure Survey System (or PESC after one stage of the process) — has been developed. An annual survey of public expenditure looks at spending plans in terms of a number of broad functional programmes (such as defence, housing, or roads and transport) over the next five years, with the current financial year as year one. Since 1969 the end-product has been an annual White Paper setting out the government's plans and relating them to the prospects for the economy. PESC is primarily a planning device but since 1974 it has been modified so that it also has a role to play, alongside the traditional system, in controlling spending. Its importance cannot be overstated. Although it came under great strain in the serious economic crisis in Britain in the mid-1970s, it provides the forum for an annual debate both within the government and outside on spending priorities and is seen by ministers and officials as being of crucial importance.

The Civil Service

In January 1977 the size of the civil service was 746,000 — of whom 572,000 were non-industrial officials. The remaining quarter of the service were industrial workers, most of whom worked for the Ministry of Defence in the ordnance factories and naval dockyards. This section is concerned only with non-industrial civil servants.

Their numbers have grown about three-and-a-half times since 1939 and have more than doubled since 1960. It is this trend which has given rise to the popular image of a vast army of bureaucrats inhabiting comfortable Whitehall offices far-removed from the people they are supposed to be serving. In fact this picture is misleading. 75 per cent of non-industrial civil servants work outside Greater London and 40 per cent work in local offices which have direct contact with the public. Although its numbers have recently begun to fall, the Ministry of Defence is still the largest employer, followed by the Department of Health and Social Security and the Inland Revenue. Together these three departments employ more than half the total.

Within the non-industrial civil service there is a great variety of personnel, ranging from the most senior officials to messengers and cleaners. Until the 1970s the service was divided into classes, both horizontally (between higher and lower in the same broad area of work) and vertically (between different skills, professions or work areas), 47 of which covered the whole service while the rest (numbering about 1,400) related only to particular departments. A civil servant was recruited to a particular class and this determined his prospects and the range of jobs on which he could be employed.

This system was strongly criticised in 1968 by the Fulton Committee on the Civil Service which considered that it impeded the efficiency of the service by imposing barriers in the way of an able civil servant being promoted as far as his talents justified and by making it difficult to transfer staff between posts which, often for historical reasons, were the preserve of different classes. It therefore recommended that the class system should be replaced by a unified grading structure covering the entire service. This proposal was accepted in principle by the government but, following further investigation, it has only been partially implemented. A unified structure, known as the Open Structure, has been established at the very top of the service. Below this level, however, all that has happened is that there have been mergers of related classes to form occupational groups for the purposes of pay, recruitment and personnel management.

From the table listing the largest groups it can be seen that 44 per cent of the civil service belong to the Administration Group: this was formed in 1971 by the merger of the three general service classes — Administrative, Executive and Clerical — to which most non-specialist civil servants had belonged since the end of the First World War. If those who are engaged in local and regional casework in connection with tax collection and social security, and secretarial staff are added, almost 75 per cent of the civil service may be said to be engaged in general administrative work. The rest are members of a wide range of professional, technical and specialised occupations, including engineers, architects, doctors, economists, scientists and their supporting staffs.

Non-Industrial Civil Service: Principal Staff Groups in 1977

Administration	251,400
Inland Revenue	52,400
Social Security	43,800
Professional and Technology	43,500
Secretarial	29,000
Science	18,100
Others[1]	133,800

1   More than 30 groups ranging in size from 30 to 12,000 members

Administrators

The Administration Group includes staff ranging from the grade of Clerical Assistant to that of Assistant Secretary. There are three principal points of entry, each with its own level of educational attainment. Applicants for clerical posts must normally have passed General Certificate of Education (GCE) Ordinary level examinations (usually taken at age 16). Recruits at Executive Officer level must have at least five GCE passes, including two at Advanced level (usually taken at age 18) but in practice many of them — amounting to as many as 45 per cent in 1977 — are graduates. Originally, however, it was intended that the normal graduate point of entry would be the Administration Trainee (AT) grade. Graduate applicants at this level compete with internal candidates, who were originally appointed at lower levels, for entry into the Administration Trainee scheme. Most ATs are promoted to the grade of Higher Executive Officer (A) and thence to Principal without having to serve in the intermediate grade of Senior

Executive Officer. The remainder become Principals more slowly, first passing through the grades of Higher and Senior Executive Officer.

The Open Structure at the top of the service covers about 800 staff at the level of Under Secretary and above. Posts at this level are filled by the most suitable people without regard to their academic background or previous employment in the civil service. All posts are related to a unified grading structure although a wide variety of titles is still used.

The principles of recruitment in the civil service were laid down in the second half of the nineteenth century. For administrative posts, recruitment is on the basis of open competition and is the responsibility of a body of independent Civil Service Commissioners, first appointed in 1855 to counter patronage and corruption. Since 1968 the Commission has been part of the Civil Service Department which is headed by the Prime Minister but enjoys complete independence in individual selection decisions. Traditionally these decisions were based upon written examinations set by the Commission in academic subjects but, since the Second World War, these have gradually been abandoned in favour of procedures based on interviews and a variety of tests, both written and oral, designed specifically to test general ability and aptitude for particular types of work. Nevertheless, participation in these procedures still depends on achieving a certain level of academic attainment.

The recruitment of Executive Officers is based primarily upon interviews but since 1973 the number of applicants at this level has necessitated the introduction of a written qualifying examination consisting of objective tests and job-related problems to be solved. Administration Trainees are recruited by a procedure which is in three parts: first, written qualifying tests which include a passage to precis and various statistical and verbal exercises; second, a series of tests, exercises and interviews at the Civil Service Selection Board which last for two days and are designed to test candidates' aptitude for administrative work; and third, a conventional interview before the Final Selection Board composed of senior civil servants and outsiders.

When the AT scheme was established it was intended that about 250 or 300 should be recruited each year, of whom no more than 175 would be external candidates. In practice the number recruited has

varied between 170 and 240, depending upon departmental requirements and overall manpower restrictions, and since 1973 all
vacancies have been filled. However, the proportion of in-service
appointees, which has varied between 11 and 31 per cent, has fallen
far short of original intentions. In this respect the scheme has not
met one of the aims which lay behind its creation, that of ensuring
that a higher proportion of those in charge of policy and management have had experience of working at lower levels. That this has
not happened in part points to the success of the new scheme in
attracting large numbers of well-qualified external applicants but,
in the view of the staff associations representing middle management, it is also a result of paying too much attention in selection to
academic ability rather than practical experience. They have
therefore pressed for the abolition of the scheme and for all graduate
recruitment to take place at the level of Executive Officer.

By increasing the size of the graduate entry, it was also hoped to
widen its social and educational composition. This aspect of the
senior civil service has frequently been criticised, especially in the
last twenty years. A survey of the Administrative Class in 1967
revealed that 67 per cent had fathers in the managerial and
professional classes, that 56 per cent had been educated at either
private or semi-private schools and that 64 per cent were Oxford
and Cambridge graduates. Moreover, although there had been a
steady post-war increase in the proportion of recruits educated at
state schools, their social background had not altered significantly
and the proportion from Oxford and Cambridge had also remained
static, despite the declining share of these two universities in the
annual output of graduates. Such narrow recruitment was considered to be harmful because it meant that most senior officials
were very much out of touch with the community. It was also
considered to be unfair in that the statistics suggested that there was
a bias towards candidates with certain kinds of background.

This latter question was examined in the late 1960s by an official
committee. It concluded that there was no bias in the selection
procedures and that the pattern of recruitment can largely be
explained in other terms. For instance, the standards of entry into
Oxford and Cambridge are generally higher than those at other
universities. Thus, if the civil service is seeking to recruit the most
able people, it is hardly surprising that these two universities
supply a high proportion. Equally, graduate recruitment is in-

evitably middle-class because the university population is heavily biased in this direction. However, such factors cannot account entirely for the nature of recruitment to the civil service; for instance, the proportion of recruits from private schools is more difficult to explain. It is also clear that these statistical biases are more pronounced in successful candidates than in the overall pool of applicants. Moreover, it is striking that the increase in the size of the graduate entry at this level since 1971 has not had the effect that was expected. In 1975 the proportion of entrants from managerial and professional backgrounds had actually risen to 78 per cent and the figures from private education and Oxford and Cambridge had only fallen to 50 per cent and 60 per cent respectively. The question of bias is difficult to prove or disprove but concern about this led the government in 1978 to propose that the membership of the Civil Service Commission and its selection boards should be widened.

But, regardless of its origins, the unrepresentative nature of the civil service at this level is said to raise more fundamental issues. It is widely considered that greater representativeness is desirable as an objective in itself because it would set an example of equality of opportunity in employment, and that it would facilitate the work of government by reducing the distance between those in senior positions and both their subordinates and the community. On the other hand, although such sentiments gain wide approval, it is not clear how far the aim of representativeness should be pursued, for instance by the imposition of quotas for women and certain 'minority' groups, to the possible detriment of the technical efficiency of government. Moreover, it may be that other factors, such as the nature of civil service work and the system of socialisation after entry, are equally important influences upon civil servants' attitudes.

Another aspect of graduate recruitment which has been controversial in recent years has been the question of the relevance of candidates' academic studies to government work. Since the mid-nineteenth century the policy of the civil service has been to recruit the most able men available, regardless of the relevance of their academic qualifications for the conduct of official business. Thus in 1967 70 per cent of the graduate members of the Administrative class had degrees in arts and humanities, mainly in history and classics. This situation concerned a majority of the members of the

Fulton Committee who recommended that the selection procedures should be modified to give preference to those whose academic studies were in very general terms relevant to government work. The other members of the Committee however disagreed, believing that it would deprive the service of some of the most able recruits and that it would increase the already strong pressure on school-leavers to choose between university courses at a time when they were not fully aware of the implications of their decisions. The government, for its part, rejected the majority proposal. Since 1970 the proportion of entrants with 'relevant' backgrounds has increased but this reflects changes in the pattern of university study and in graduate employment opportunities rather than any official change in recruitment policy.

Training and Management

Recruitment policy has major implications for civil service training. If candidates are selected on the basis of their general ability, any skills or knowledge which they need to perform their duties must be provided post-entry. Traditionally the civil service has laid great emphasis on informal training by means of practical experience of working under the supervision and guidance of senior staff. This remains very important, but since 1945 there has been a marked expansion of formal training. Most of this is 'job-related' in that it provides trainees with skills needed for the particular jobs they will undertake on completion of the course, and is organised by departments which either run their own courses or send staff to outside institutions such as technical and further education colleges. Only since about 1960 has much attention been paid to the provision of 'developmental' training for senior officials, the aim of which is to prepare a civil servant for the rest of his career generally.

In 1963 a Centre for Administrative Studies was opened to provide central training, mainly in economics, for graduate entrants to the Administrative Class in their first and third years of service. This development was endorsed by the Fulton Committee in 1968 which called for a general increase in the central training effort and proposed the establishment of a Civil Service College. Such a college was opened in 1970 and given three main functions: first, it runs courses which provide general managerial training for staff at the level of Higher Executive Officer and above; second, it provides a wide variety of job-related specialised courses, attended largely by more junior staff, in fields such as management services and automatic data processing; and third, it conducts research into problems of administration and the machinery of government. The College, which now operates at two centres in southern England, is part of the Civil Service Department which has overall responsibility for civil service training, 90 per cent of which still takes place within departments.

The largest single component of the College's work is the Administration Trainee programme, which accounts for one-quarter of its effort. ATs attend the College for two ten-week periods, at the end of their first and second years of service. The first period comprises courses in statistics, economics, law and public administration; in the second they all take courses on staff management, policy studies and financial management, including the control of public expenditure, and choose between a further course on government and industry and one on social policy and administration. When they are not at the College, ATs work in a variety of posts carefully selected to enable them to gain some idea of the range of official duties. Between their second and fifth years of service, a streaming decision is made. About 80 per cent are 'fast-streamed' and are appointed to the grade of HEO(A) and thence directly to Principal after a further two to five years. Originally, HEO(A)s attended the College for a further period of training but this course was one of the victims of a cutback in training in 1977.

The Civil Service College has been widely criticised ever since its inception in 1970. Much of the trouble has arisen because of a failure by the government to define its objectives clearly and because of the very wide spread of its activities. However, underlying much of the criticism are basic disagreements as to the relative importance of practical experience and formal study in the training of administrators, and about the timing and content of the various components in the programme. There are still many senior officials who doubt the value of formal training, believing that administration is more of an art than a science, and this is reflected in difficult relations between the College and departments. Their doubts are shared by many ATs themselves who have disliked having to leave their departments in order to take courses which they see as being excessively academic. Others, however, have criticised the AT programme for its superficiality, believing that a course of only ten weeks duration in economics or public administration is insufficient and that theory ought to play a larger part. In this respect the College has been compared unfavourably with its French counterpart, the Ecole Nationale d'Administration (ENA), where the training for the equivalents of ATs is very much longer and the contrast is all the more striking when it is realised that entry to ENA is dependent upon passing academic examinations in many of the subjects it teaches. However, this comparison is somewhat unfair to the College. ENA is an elitist institution dedicated to the preparation of non-specialist administrators whereas the AT/HEO(A) programme is only one part of the College's work. Indeed, the College was deliberately not established in ENA's 'image' but was intended to meet the training needs of a wide variety of staff.

Official attitudes towards formal training for administrators in Britain thus remain rather ambivalent. It is still widely believed that those who will in future occupy senior positions are best prepared for such duties by wide experience of working in different posts. This sort of preparation is facilitated by the system of career management. The first point to be stressed is the fact that most civil servants are appointed when they are young and remain in the service until retirement age: in 1971, 72 per cent of the higher civil service had spent their entire working lives in the service. Only a few officials are appointed other than to one of the main recruitment grades; nor do many leave early either through resignation or dismissal.

During a career in the service, an official is assured of several more or less automatic promotions, according to principles agreed with the staff associations. Since Fulton, greater flexibility in promotion has been introduced but seniority remains important. Most officials spend their entire working-lives in a particular department but they move fairly frequently between posts. Thus, in 1977 the average tenure of a post at Under Secretary or Assistant Secretary level in the Department of the Environment was 2½ years and in the Treasury it was only 1¼ years and 1¾ years respectively. At the very top of the service, staff are also exchanged between departments. The Civil Service Department is involved in appointments to posts at Under Secretary level and above and attempts to ensure that most staff at this level have experience of more than one department and that many of them have worked at some stage in one of the 'central departments' (Treasury, Civil Service Department and Cabinet Office).

Recruitment, training and career management are therefore designed to produce a type of administrator to which the label of 'generalist' is usually applied. Selection is based upon general ability and personal qualities; in training practical experience is generally regarded as more important than attendance at formal courses; and career management is designed to develop general knowledge and experience of different types of government work. The reasons for this distinctive pattern of staffing will be examined below, after a brief discussion of the employment of specialist officials in the civil service.

Specialists

About 25 per cent of the non-industrial civil service are professional, scientific or technical staff, who are generally known as 'specialists'. The range of officials included within this term is extremely wide. Some, such as doctors, architects and lawyers, are members of established professions which have their own regulatory bodies which control entry to the profession and enforce certain standards of conduct. Others, such as economists and statisticians, have high-level qualifications but do not enjoy formal professional status. The seniority of many specialist staff is reflected in the fact that they constitute 60 per cent of those working at the salary level of Principal and above, and that 40 per cent of the posts in the Open Structure at the top of the service are held by staff with a specialist background. But there are also large numbers of staff with only technical qualifications, working for instance in scientific establishments and in drawing offices.

Specialist staff are organised separately from administrators. Almost half of them are members of two occupational groups: the Professional and Technology Group which comprises over 40,000 officials such as engineers, architects, surveyors and their supporting technical staff; and the Science Group with 18,000 scientific staff. The largest employer is the Ministry of Defence which has 60 per cent of both these groups. The other major employer is the

Department of the Environment where 50 per cent of the non-industrial staff are specialists, most of whom work for the Property Services Agency as architects, engineers, surveyors, etc.

The recruitment, training and career management of specialists raises fewer questions that are special to public administration. Recruitment is the responsibility of the Civil Service Commission and is based upon open competition; however, candidates are also generally required to possess the qualifications needed for the post for which they are applying. Consequently, there is less need for post-entry training, although junior staff do of course obtain additional qualifications through attending courses run both departmentally and by outside institutions. There is also less movement between jobs. Specialist staff are recruited to a specific range of posts for which their qualifications are appropriate and, as long as they remain in the service, they expect to remain in this field. While this is what most of them want to do, it does not mean that specialists are satisfied with their position in the service or with their career prospects.

Traditionally, specialist civil servants have worked outside the main stream of administration. The task of advising ministers on policy has mainly been undertaken by generalists, who have also been exclusively responsible for financial control, stemming from the fact that the senior administrative official in each department, the Permanent Secretary, is designated the accounting officer. As a result, specialists have generally been employed in separate hierarchies outside the line of management in the department. They have also had little prospect of being promoted to the most senior positions in the service.

This pattern — in which specialists are 'on tap but not on top' — has come under great pressure in recent years. Growing recognition of the importance of specialist contributions to policy has led to significant increases in the numbers recruited. For instance, the number of professional economists working in Whitehall grew from 19 in 1963 to nearly 400 in 1977. In addition, attempts have been made to enhance their position in the service through structural changes and improvements in their career prospects. A number of integrated hierarchies have been introduced in which specialists and administrators work alongside each other under the direction of an official, selected because of the appropriateness of his qualifications and experience rather than because he was a member of a particular occupational group. At the top of the service the creation of the Open Structure has provided better opportunities for those with specialist backgrounds and, to ensure that specialists are able to compete effectively for these posts, a special training scheme in management has been instituted.

However, despite considerable pressure from the staff association representing specialist staff, the pre-eminence of the generalist in the civil service has not been altered fundamentally. It is important not to exaggerate the subordination of the specialist — in certain fields specialist staff have always been very influential and individually a number of them are very close to ministers — but it is nonetheless apparent that these changes have not had a major effect. Although 40 per cent of those in the Open Structure were previously employed as specialists, most of them are working in posts which are natural extensions of their earlier careers. Nor has much encouragement been given to departments to make alterations in their structure and the number of experiments with integrated hierarchies has been small.

This pattern of staffing is unusual in comparison with other countries and with other areas of public administration in Britain. In many countries, there is no real equivalent of the generalist; for instance, in France the ENA graduate is really a trained specialist in administration and many senior posts are in any case filled by those with professional qualifications. In British local government specialist staff occupy the highest posts, with generalist support staff only occupying fairly junior positions in most departments. It is necessary therefore to consider why the generalist performs the role that he does in the civil service.

Two factors seem to be most important. First, it is widely considered in Britain that specialists are unsuitable for administrative work. Administration is seen as a process of arbitrating between special interests as represented by experts within departments and by pressure groups outside. The successful administrator therefore needs to be detached from any particular field and through his training and experience he needs to be able to find a balance between different interests. In doing this he is assisting the political head of his department and it is the minister's needs which provide the second argument in favour of the generalist. As few ministers are experts in the fields to which they are appointed, it is argued that they need the advice and assistance of officials who are able to translate the ideas of experts into terms which ministers can understand and who are themselves experts in operating the government machine and in implementing ministerial wishes. Similarly, it is argued that the breadth of experience of the generalist facilitates the overall coordination of government according to the general priorities established by the Cabinet. In contrast, specialists are generally considered unable to view problems in the same way as the minister or to take a broad view of the needs of the government as a whole; moreover, they could only obtain expertise in operating the machine by ceasing to become experts in their own fields.

Those who advocate an enhanced role for specialists argue that the complexity of modern government is such that generalists can no longer cope and that an excessive amount of experts' time is spent in converting issues into terms which they can understand. They also question the traditional view of the nature of the administrative process in Britain, believing that too much importance is placed upon the smooth running of the machine at the expense of purposive and committed management. Thus, in the last resort the roles of generalists and specialists depend upon one's view of the administrative process. What is clear, however, is that it is the system of political accountability and of collegiate government which in large part account for the present pattern of staffing.

Conditions of Service

Unlike most countries where the rights of state employees form an important branch of administrative law, the civil service in Britain is regulated by arrangements that are basically non-legal in character. Formally, civil servants are 'servants of the Crown' and they therefore hold office 'at the pleasure of the Crown' and are liable to dismissal at any time; equally, they have no contractual rights that are enforceable through the courts. In practice, however, their position is very different. They enjoy great security of tenure and invariably their conditions of service are negotiated through elaborate procedures involving representatives of their staff associations. Nor do they lack legal rights entirely. They have always enjoyed the right to strike and, particularly in recent years, they have been covered by legislation conferring rights upon employees against unfair dismissal or discrimination on grounds of colour or sex.

In Britain the powers of executive action are conferred upon ministers personally rather than upon departments as corporate bodies or upon civil servants. The overriding duty of a civil servant is thus to serve his minister who alone is answerable to Parliament. As a result, the civil service is characterised by its political neutrality and its anonymity. To be able to serve ministers of any political persuasion impartially it is necessary, first, that senior civil servants eschew most open political activity and second, that their relationship with their political masters is largely a confidential one.

About 200,000 civil servants, including not only senior administrative and professional grades but also many executive and clerical staff, are debarred from taking part in national politics and may only participate in local politics with departmental permission. They can, of course, vote in all elections and, after resigning from the service, may stand as candidates. It has recently been proposed, however, that such severe restrictions should be retained only for about 23,000 officials who deal directly with ministers or who work in sensitive areas, including those in contact with members of the public.

The ethic of confidentiality and anonymity is deeply engrained in the civil service. In part it flows from the need for trust in any relationship between an employer and his personal assistants. But in the civil service it is reinforced by the Official Secrets Act and by the convention that the minister is the sole spokesman of the department in Parliament and elsewhere. The former makes it an offence for civil servants to communicate information obtained in the course of their official duties unless authorised to do so. Its scope is therefore extremely wide and while the law is frequently ignored in practice, it remains a significant barrier to more open government. In principle it has been accepted that new legislation should be introduced narrowing the area in which unauthorised disclosure would be a criminal offence but this had not been done at the end of 1978.

More important is the convention that civil servants are reticent in public so as not to reveal their own personal views on issues of policy, which might well differ from those of ministers. The extent of this reticence varies according to circumstances. Many civil servants spend a considerable amount of time in consultation with outside bodies and some, particularly senior professional officers, express views on policy matters in published reports and speeches. However, on matters of political controversy they are expected to be discreet. In recent years this has become rather more difficult as civil servants have increasingly been called to give evidence to parliamentary committees that have been examining current issues, many of them of major political importance. The role played by particular officials in decision making has also become known as a result of the investigations of the Parliamentary Commissioner for Administration. Both these developments will be examined further in the next section; here it is only necessary to state that they have had an effect on the traditional anonymity of the civil service.

The traditional position of officials has also been placed under strain by other recent trends in British government. Of these, the most important is the increase in its workload. Only a very small proportion of departmental business is actually seen by ministers and as a result civil servants have frequently to act without explicit ministerial instructions. In the past, most departments were relatively small with a single minister at the head, supported by perhaps one or two junior ministers, and a close relationship existed between him and his senior officials. The latter were therefore able to get to know the minister's mind and it was fairly easy for them to take decisions which reflected his own views and priorities. Now, however, most departments have ministerial teams of four or five and the number of senior civil servants is often very large. As a result, it is very much more difficult for a close relationship to be established between ministers and their officials, a situation which has given rise to concern on both sides.

Ministers have been worried that their wishes are not being fully implemented in their departments. These doubts are not new. Rather, they are endemic in a system in which an incoming minister relies almost exclusively upon the assistance of staff who hours previously were advising his predecessor who may well have been a member of the opposing political party. There have therefore been frequent allegations from politicians that officials have conspired to conceal information and to frustrate ministerial instructions. Such charges are difficult to prove or disprove, not least because the relationship between ministers and civil servants is largely confidential, but they point to the complexity of this relationship. In any case, it is partly fears of this kind which have led ministers in recent years to bring into their departments personal advisers whose appointments end when the minister himself leaves office. This practice has grown steadily since 1964 and in 1977 there were twenty-eight such advisers, generally known as special advisers, working in departments. Some of them have been experts in the fields to which they have been appointed; others have been younger and less experienced, providing general staff assistance to their political master. The number of special advisers is, however, too small for the basic relationship between ministers and their permanent officials to be altered. The minister still depends upon the civil service for political advice and expects complete loyalty from them.

In recent years civil servants have also sought clarification as to the extent of this loyalty. There have always been certain qualifications to the rule that the paramount duty of an official is to carry out the instructions of his minister. Thus, in his capacity as accounting officer, a Permanent Secretary can state his objection in writing to expenditure he considers to be improper and need only incur the expenditure on written instruction from the minister overruling his objection. This is a rare occurrence but it does happen. For instance, in 1975 the Permanent Secretary in the Department of Industry questioned the expenditure of money for the support of various workers' cooperatives. But, even in these circumstances, which are very exceptional, the civil servant still carries out the instructions of the minister. The only well-established exception concerns the minister's extra-parliamentary activities. Thus, although it is not always easy in practice to distinguish between a minister's official and party duties, civil servants will refuse to issue speeches that are to be delivered to party meetings or to assist the minister in his constituency affairs.

More controversial has been the question of the extent to which civil servants should assist ministers in their parliamentary duties, especially in so far as this involves forestalling the Opposition, and a recent attempt to provide guidance on this matter failed to allay the worries of many senior civil servants, who have also found themselves more exposed in recent years to criticism when mistakes have occurred. Their increasing vulnerability in this respect will be examined in more detail in the next section. What is clear, however, is that all these trends have combined to make civil servants less certain as to their loyalties. Unlike most other countries, Britain has no written code of conduct for civil servants to follow. Certain rules have been laid down but they are very general and in practice the behaviour of civil servants has been determined by 'a network of understandings and practices', most of which are unwritten.

It may well be that the kind of developments that have been outlined here point to a need to define and articulate the existing unwritten principles of professional conduct. Some would also advocate the formulation of new principles giving civil servants a wider duty than that of undivided loyalty to ministers, for instance by including a duty to protect the 'public interest'. At present, however, there is little evidence of a willingness on the part of the government to take up this issue. Thus, in 1978 the government merely re-asserted the traditional position that officials are the loyal and confidential assistants of ministers, as if nothing had changed. Nonetheless it is clear that things have changed and that this issue will not disappear.

In other respects, too, the conduct of the civil service has become more controversial in recent years. A number of cases of corruption, mainly involving local government officers but also affecting civil servants, have highlighted the problem of conflict between public and private interests and have led to the introduction of new rules. More generally, the doctrine of undivided loyalty to ministers has been brought into question by increasing militancy on the part of civil servants. In 1973 the civil service had its first experience of industrial action on a national scale and since then there have been a number of disputes involving staff at many different levels.

A major cause of this unrest has been dissatisfaction over pay. In 1955 it was accepted that civil service pay should be determined by fair comparison with earnings in comparable work outside the service. Formal pay agreements were therefore drawn up embodying this principle and establishing pay research procedures to establish the factual basis for such comparisons. Since the early 1960s, however, government incomes policies have on a number of occasions disrupted the implementation of increases assessed in this way. Indeed the procedures were suspended completely in 1975 on the introduction of the first stage of the Labour government's pay policy. Not only have civil servants lost money as a result, they also feel that they have been treated more harshly than other workers. This is not the place to assess the validity of these claims — to do so would necessitate examination of other benefits, such as pensions where civil servants do very well. What is clear is that dissatisfaction has manifested itself in growing militancy, to be seen not only in strikes but also in the success of left-wing candidates in recent staff association elections and in the decision of all the major associations to affiliate to the Trades Union Congress. Nor is it just pay that has caused dissatisfaction. In departments such as the Inland Revenue or Health and Social Security, staff have on a number of occasions taken action to obtain additional payment for implementing ministerial decisions which they considered placed additional demands upon them. There has also been widespread unrest about government plans for the dispersal of jobs from the London area to other parts of the country.

The general effect of all this has been to complicate the work of ministers. It has always been necessary for them to take the reactions of the staff associations into account and to discuss decisions with them — indeed the civil service has a reputation for successful staff consultation and negotiation — but the cooperation of staff is now rather more difficult to obtain. This applies much less, of course, to the senior officials in closest contact with ministers but generally it has altered the climate in which ministers work.

THE CONTROL OF ADMINISTRATION

Britain has a complex system for controlling the activities of public organisations. At the heart of the system is Parliament. It is the forum in which the representatives of the electorate attempt to influence the activities of the executive and in which they can raise their constituents' grievances. Its ability to do these things stems from the fact that it lays down the functions of all public bodies and provides them with the means of carrying them out. Parliament is not only important in itself: it also influences all the other institutions and procedures of redress. Thus the courts exist not to challenge Parliament but to enforce its will. Similarly, although there are now other important channels, such as ombudsmen and administrative tribunals, they have all been fitted into what is still essentially a parliamentary system. In this section the system of public accountability will be outlined and particular attention will be paid to its effects upon central administration. The emphasis will be upon formal institutions and procedures but it is important not to overlook the role played by informal channels, such as the press and pressure groups, both of which conduct campaigns to influence decision making and to reverse decisions that have given rise to grievances.

Pressure groups have long been important in British politics. Their efforts have been directed primarily at the executive rather than the legislature because of the former's control over the latter. Many groups enjoy very close relationships with particular departments and are invariably consulted before decisions are taken, either informally or through the elaborate machinery of advisory bodies that has been created for this purpose. In recent years their involvement in government has been taken a stage further. First, the peak organisations representing business and labour, the Confederation of British Industry and the Trades Union Congress, are now consulted on almost every aspect of economic policy either bilaterally or in the National Economic Development Council which was set up in 1962 to provide a tripartite forum for such discussions. Second, representatives of various interests have been appointed to serve on a number of non-departmental organisations, e.g. the Manpower Services Commission and the Health and Safety Commission. It is too soon to talk, as some have done in the 1970s, of the emergence of a corporate state in Britain but these trends do clearly have an effect upon the role of Parliament and upon the way in which decisions are taken.

Ministerial Responsibility

Parliamentary oversight of the executive hinges upon the doctrine of ministerial responsibility. Ministers are accountable to Parliament both for their own actions and for those of their departments. They can therefore be called to explain and justify what has been done in their name and they are liable to be held responsible, and ultimately may be censured by Parliament.

In practice, however, the operation of this doctrine has been modified by the scale of contemporary government. It is generally accepted that it is no longer possible to hold a minister personally culpable for every departmental decision, most of which he will not have taken and some of which may even have been contrary to his instructions. In any case it is most unlikely that a vote of censure would be passed on an individual minister. Assuming that his party had an overall majority in the House of Commons, this could only happen through loss of support among his own supporters which would be unlikely to occur as it would affect adversely the standing of the party as a whole. Nor, for the same reasons, do ministers often resign as a result of departmental mistakes. The only such resignation since the Second World War occurred in 1954 and in that case there were a number of special circumstances. All other 'enforced' resignations have been the result of disagreement between a minister and the rest of the government or of personal failings unrelated to the work of the department.

However, although it has been modified, the doctrine of ministerial responsibility remains important in determining the relationship between ministers and Parliament and between ministers and their civil servants. This is not to say that it is adequate as a means of controlling executive action. This is a separate question which can only be answered once the system of public accountability has been outlined as a whole. At present it is important only to note the continuing influence of this constitutional doctrine.

This is to be seen very clearly in the institution of Parliamentary Questions which enables MPs to table questions to particular ministers on any matter which falls within their sphere of responsibility. If they merely want to obtain information they may seek a written reply which is printed in the official record of proceedings. But if they want to raise an issue publicly and to be able to ask a supplementary question to the minister's reply, the question is tabled for oral answer. Question Time, which comes at the beginning of business each day, is a great parliamentary occasion and one in which ministerial reputations are often made and lost. As a means of controlling the executive, however, it is not very effective. The number of questions is so great that each minister only comes up for questioning about once a month and time is too short for individual issues to be pursued satisfactorily. Nor does an able minister, with the backing of his civil servants, have much difficulty in parrying most of the hostile questions that are directed at him. Nevertheless, the system of questions has a major impact upon departments. First, it places a considerable administrative burden upon officials. In an average week in 1976, 77 questions received an oral answer and 787 a written reply. Answers had to be prepared both for these and for possible supplementaries. The chance that a question might be asked about any aspect of departmental business also has a wider effect in ensuring that all officials remain sensitive to the possibility of public scrutiny and the risk of political embarrassment for ministers. They are therefore cautious in straying far from ministerial instructions and take care to treat individuals fairly and with consideration.

If an MP is not satisfied with the answer he receives to his question, he can take the matter further by writing to the minister concerned or by raising it in an adjournment debate in the House of Commons. Both of these tactics are frequently used but neither is entirely satisfactory. As a result, Parliament has increasingly looked to committees to undertake the work of scrutinising executive action and other institutions have also come to play an important part in the resolution of individual grievances.

Select Committees

A select committee is a committee, usually consisting of about fifteen or twenty MPs chosen to reflect the party balance in the House of Commons, that is appointed to investigate and report to the House of Commons on particular issues. To enable them to do this, committees are empowered 'to send for persons, papers and records'. Their importance has grown in the last fifteen years and the present system of committees was established in 1971, following an experiment into the desirability of extending this kind of review.

Two committees, the Public Accounts Committee and the Expenditure Committee, deal with expenditure. The former was established in 1861 and is the traditional watchdog of government expenditure. It considers the reports of the Comptroller and Auditor General, who audits the accounts of each department, and summons officials to explain any items which are drawn to its attention as being unusual or irregular. It therefore reviews spending after it has been incurred but increasingly in recent years it has been interested not just in the regularity of expenditure but in its efficiency and it has made recommendations that are designed to lead to improvements in the future. The Expenditure Committee, established in 1971, takes as its starting point the government's forward projections of public expenditure which are set out in an annual White Paper. It has wide terms of reference which allow it to look both at the policies involved and at the machinery of government itself, and operates through six sub-committees, each one covering an area of government activity.

Four committees specialise in particular subjects: Nationalised Industries, Overseas Development, Race Relations and Immigration, and Science and Technology. The Select Committee on Nationalised Industries, established in 1956 to improve the relationship between Parliament and the industries, conducts regular enquiries into individual industries and occasionally examines issues which affect them all. The other committees are more recent in origin. Each deals with a subject that is considered appropriate for scrutiny by a bipartisan group of MPs in that it is relatively self-contained and generally does not raise issues of inter-party controversy.

The Select Committee on Statutory Instruments, which now works for much of the time with the corresponding committee in the House of Lords, scrutinises delegated legislation, drawing MPs' attention to abuses of this system or any unusual features contained in particular regulations. The Select Committee on European Secondary Legislation, first appointed in 1974, attempts to digest the mountain of proposals emanating from the agencies of the EEC and to select those which merit debate by the House as a whole. Finally, there is the Select Committee on the Parliamentary Commissioner for Administration which will be examined later.

It is not appropriate to attempt a full assessment of the work of these committees; in this context the concern is only with their impact upon government. At one level, they have a similar effect to that of Parliamentary Questions. A substantial amount of work is involved in preparing papers for committees and in briefing those who appear as witnesses, while the possibility that any part of a department may be subjected to parliamentary scrutiny also has general repercussions for the way in which work is performed.

Unlike Question Time, which is handled exclusively by ministers, the burden of giving evidence to committees is borne largely by civil servants. Between 1970 and 1974, for instance, over three hundred civil servants appeared before the Expenditure Committee and the four other subject specialist committees, whereas only fourteen ministers gave evidence during the same period. This has major implications for the relationship between ministers and their officials. Under skilful cross-examination by MPs, sometimes now advised by experts appointed to assist them in assimilating evidence and framing questions, it is difficult for civil servants to avoid expressing personal views on questions which may not accord fully with those of the minister.

In general, and this may be accentuated by the broadcasting of Parliament which started in April 1978, the effect of committees has been to open up the decision-making processes of Whitehall to public scrutiny. They have also led to more informed discussion of issues both in Parliament and outside. Their impact upon actual decisions is more difficult to gauge: it is difficult to find many instances when the work of committees can be said to have been decisive. This is not altogether surprising as the role of committees is basically determined by the relationship between the executive and the legislature. Thus, they operate within limits which effectively are laid down by the government as a result of its control of the House of Commons and they also depend upon the government for most of the information on which to base their enquiries. Only very rarely has the government actually withheld information or prevented committees from hearing particular witnesses but its willingness to confide fully in committees is likely to be affected by the degree to which it feels the enquiry is worthwhile and likely to produce useful results. Thus, if a committee wants its report to be adopted, it will generally avoid issues that are likely to cause serious embarrassment to the government. However this inevitably limits their contribution to the formulation of policy on major issues.

Parliamentary Commissioner for Administration

Parliamentary channels are not adequate for the redress of individual grievances. The volume of complaints is now so great that there is insufficient time for them all to be raised in the House of Commons and many of them neither require nor are really suitable for resolution in what is primarily a political arena. On the other hand, many MPs attach great importance to this aspect of their work and redress of grievances lies at the heart of the traditions of Parliament. Both these factors have influenced the nature of the office of the British ombudsman, known officially as the Parliamentary Commissioner for Administration (PCA), which was created in 1967. The PCA is an officer of Parliament appointed by the government but secure from dismissal except by parliamentary motion. So that he does not undermine the relationship between an MP and his constituents, he may only investigate complaints that are referred to him by MPs and he reports his conclusions to the MP, not directly to the complainant. In other respects, too, close links were established with Parliament: thus a select committee was appointed to oversee his work and to follow up his reports.

The PCA's role is to investigate cases of alleged maladministration. No statutory definition was provided of this term but generally it covers defects in the conduct of officials or in administrative procedures which do not amount to breaches of law, e.g. arbitrariness, bias, unjustifiable delay or failure to take proper considerations into account. He is not permitted to question policy or to question the merits of discretionary decisions, provided they were taken legally and in accordance with an appropriate administrative procedure. Originally a very restrictive approach was adopted by the PCA but, with experience the scope of his review has widened such that he sometimes comes close to considering the merits of individual decisions or the informal rules applied by a department in making a particular class of decisions.

The PCA's jurisdiction is restricted so as to ensure that he does not infringe upon the responsibility of ministers by substituting his decisions for theirs. For the same reason, his recommendations are not binding. Generally they have been implemented but in some cases this has only happened after the matter has been pursued by the Select Committee. The PCA is also limited in that he can only investigate complaints against government departments and a small number of other public bodies; he is precluded from investigating complaints which relate to personnel matters in the civil service and the armed forces. Originally this constituted a major limitation in the scope of the ombudsman concept in Britain but his office has subsequently been complemented by the creation of separate ombudsmen for local government, the National Health Service and the police. The most controversial area still excluded is personnel questions but the government has refused to lift this restriction on the grounds that to do so would interfere with established procedures for dealing with staff disputes.

The effect of all these restrictions has meant that the role of the PCA as the citizen's defender is much more limited than that of many of his overseas counterparts. It has also given rise to widespread public misunderstanding and disappointment. Most complainants do not understand the precise nature of the office and are more concerned with the outcome of the decision-making process than the propriety of the manner in which it was made. This is reflected in the high proportion of complaints which the PCA has to reject as lying outside his jurisdiction.

Between 1967 and 1976 a total of about 2,500 complaints have been fully investigated by the PCA and he has found an element of maladministration in about 500. As many of these cases were only referred to the PCA after other channels of redress had been exhausted, this amounts to a significant achievement. On the other hand, his office, which has only ninety staff, is so small that in itself it cannot have had a major impact upon departments. However, the fact that he has access to all departmental papers, other than those submitted to the Cabinet, adds to the tendency of officials to be cautious and to stick closely to the rules. It is also likely to impair delegation within departments, forcing all decisions up to a higher level. On the other hand, the existence of the PCA has not had the adverse consequences upon 'the prompt and efficient despatch of public business' which was predicted in the early 1960s and it may well have had a tonic effect upon decision making generally. The PCA may also increase the control exercised by ministers over their departments: in assembling details of decisions for the PCA, ministers and senior officials become acquainted with work of which they would otherwise know little and his investigations may reveal irregularities and weaknesses which might not otherwise have come to their attention.

Judicial Review of Administrative Action

It is often claimed that the courts play little part in controlling the executive in Britain. This is true in the sense that they are unable to invalidate statutes or to protect certain 'reserved' rights. Nor is there a formal system of administrative law with special courts to adjudicate disputes between different public institutions and between government and the citizen. Britain is also unusual in the small number of civil servants that are legally qualified and in the low importance given to law in the training of administrators.

However, it would be seriously misleading to conclude from these observations either that the rule of law is unimportant or that the courts do not have important powers of intervention. Although there are no limits to the powers that Parliament may confer upon the executive, there are limits to the powers which Parliament has already conferred. The fundamental principle of judicial review in Britain is *ultra vires* and the courts are able to prevent the executive from exceeding its powers or from failing to exercise its powers in accordance with any procedures or conditions that may be laid down by statute. Not only can they restrain the executive on these grounds, they can also require it to undertake duties that have been prescribed by Parliament.

In this way judicial review fits in with the doctrine of the sovereignty of Parliament. The courts do not challenge the authority of Parliament; rather, they exist to ensure that the will of Parliament is respected by the executive. Traditionally the courts have also been reluctant to interfere with a minister's responsibility to Parliament. Partly for this reason they have mainly been involved with disputes concerning lower levels of administration, notably local authorities whose powers are fairly tightly defined by statute. However, in recent years, there have been signs of a significant extension of judicial review. Many statutes give ministers discretion in deciding whether they should act in particular cases. While in the past it was thought that the courts would not question the exercise of such discretionary powers, in a number of recent cases the courts have begun to look into the motives behind decisions. For instance, in 1976 the courts quashed the action of the Secretary of State for Education and Science in ordering a local authority not to unpick the school re-organisation scheme that had been drawn up by its predecessor. The Secretary of State had acted under a statutory provision which empowered him to intervene if a local education authority behaved 'unreasonably'. In reaching their decision the courts indicated that they were prepared to examine the quality of the evidence said to support the exercise of the minister's discretion. Similarly, in other cases, the courts have penetrated beyond the outward semblance of legality to examine the motives that lie behind decisions, for instance to see whether a particular decision furthers the general aims of the statute under which it was taken.

In this and other ways the courts have also thrown off a largely self-imposed restriction that they would only intervene in areas in which the executive was under a duty to act judicially or quasi-judicially. This view was based upon a ruling in 1914 by the Court of Appeal that judicial standards did not apply to administrative decisions, but it now appears to have been over-turned. Nevertheless the courts remain cautious about intervening in 'political' matters for fear of provoking conflict between the judiciary and the other branches of government.

Although few administrators in the civil service are legally qualified, they have the advice of legal colleagues — many of them highly specialised — in the drafting of legislation and in ensuring that particular decisions fall within the powers that Parliament has granted. Moreover, although the cost of taking a case to the courts is prohibitive for most individuals, the possibility of legal action against the executive has been increased by the formation of a number of organisations whose purpose is to protect individual rights, both against the encroachment of the state and in the field of welfare rights.

Tribunals and Enquiries

The growth of government intervention has increased the likelihood of conflict arising between citizens and the administration, both on questions of individual treatment and where private interests are threatened by public policy. An aggrieved citizen does of course have the right of access to his MP and this does ensure that a decision, which may have been taken by a fairly junior official, will be reviewed at higher levels. But in many cases, for instance concerning entitlement to a welfare benefit, a political form of redress would be inappropriate. The citizen also has recourse to the courts but this is expensive, lengthy and generally intimidating and the courts have traditionally been reluctant to intervene in many areas of decision making. Increasingly, therefore, special bodies have been set up to adjudicate on disputes between individuals and the administration. They are of two types. First, tribunals which carry out an impartial review of a case and make a decision that is legally binding upon both parties: these are most common in fields such as social security and taxation. Second, in a number of areas, notably planning, there is provision for the holding of a public enquiry before a final decision is taken. They are held by a representative of the minister who follows a quasi-judicial procedure before making his recommendation to the minister, but the latter is then free to accept or reject it.

The distinctive feature of tribunals and enquiries is that they are less formal and cheaper than the courts and are able to reach decisions more quickly. They also permit a higher degree of specialisation than is possible within the present judicial system. On the other hand these very qualities give rise to doubts as to their fairness and impartiality. In the 1950s, following an official report that criticised many aspects of their procedure, a Council on Tribunals was established to keep their constitutions and working under continuous review but it is only advisory and has no executive or appellate powers. Increasingly, also, individuals have chosen to be legally represented at hearings. While this has led to greater regularity in procedure, it has also led to greater formality and expense and there are dangers that the case for the establishment of such quasi-judicial bodies in the first place will gradually be eroded as they begin to take on many of the features of the ordinary courts.

CONCLUSION

In this survey, a recurring theme has been the importance of historical and political factors in determining the character of British central administration. Thus the consensual nature of British society and the gradual evolution of its institutions have led to greater reliance on informal rules and procedures than in most other countries. Many important elements in the administrative system, such as the relationship between ministers and officials, have never been formally codified. Similarly, the style of administration tends to be informal. This is not to suggest that there are not important areas in which formal procedures have not been promulgated or that care is not taken to ensure that administrative action falls within the boundaries of existing legislation. But many statutes confer extensive discretionary powers upon ministers and, although the courts have been more assertive in recent years, such decisions are generally subject to political rather than legal challenge. Equally, the relations between public bodies tend to be conducted informally and without recourse to the courts. This administrative style is reflected in the low importance attached to law in the recruitment and training of civil servants.

The most important single factor determining the nature of administrative institutions and processes in Britain is probably the system of political accountability. Great importance is attached to maintaining the traditional doctrine that officials are subordinate to elected politicians. Changes in the scale of government since this doctrine was first established have necessitated some modifications in its application but formally it is still the case that ministers are answerable to Parliament for all the actions of their departments. This accounts for the emphasis given to equity in the treatment of particular cases and is one of the factors behind the elaborate arrangements that exist for consulting affected interests before decisions are taken. The fact that even minor decisions may be the subject of parliamentary enquiry also accounts for the hierarchical structure of departments and imposes strict limits on the extent to which responsibility can be delegated within the departmental framework. A further consequence is the reticence of the civil service. Again, there have been a number of recent developments that have increased the visibility of officials but they remain extremely cautious about expressing opinions on matters of policy, both to avoid embarrassing their political masters and to preserve the 'myth' that it is ministers alone who are responsible for taking decisions.

It is not only individual ministerial responsibility that is important in determining the character of British central administration. Collective responsibility also has major consequences. It is the cause of the elaborate system of interdepartmental committees in Whitehall and leads to a disposition to seek agreement and to narrow areas of dispute between departments. This is not to deny that officials fight hard to defend their departmental interests but ultimately they know that disagreements that are unresolved will be referred for collective decision to the Cabinet. The principle of reciprocity in their relations with colleagues is underlined by the fact that they are members of a unified service, the most senior members of which are liable to be transferred between departments.

The administrative process thus reflects the social and political environment in which it operates. And it is changes in this environment which have recently given rise to doubts about many of its traditional features. The complexity of contemporary government and the specialised decision-making techniques now available have led to demands for change in the pattern of recruitment of both politicians and officials. The increasing importance attached to egalitarianism in society has made it difficult for the civil service to continue to recruit and nurture an administrative elite; similarly, pressure for worker-participation has affected authority relations in the civil service, with the staff associations seeking a larger role in decision making. The apparent decline in political consensus will, if confirmed, affect the ability of civil servants to serve ministers regardless of party and may make it necessary to formalise their relationship with their political masters. In 1979 it appears that the civil service has been remarkably resilient during a period of social and political uncertainty. At present few fundamental changes have occurred in either the political or administrative systems. There can be no doubt, however, that permanent changes in the former will lead to equivalent changes in administrative organisation.

CHAPTER THREE

France

THE BACKGROUND

Since 1789 the French political system has often appeared weak and unstable. Revolutions and coups have been attempted with alarming frequency, written constitutions have known brief and unhappy lives, and strong executive-dominated regimes have alternated with periods of feeble parliamentary government. The most recent parliamentary regimes, the Third and Fourth Republics (1870 to 1940 and 1946 to 1958), were both characterised by excessive governmental instability: in the twelve years of the Fourth Republic France had no fewer than twenty-five governments and fifteen Prime Ministers. Even the present Fifth Republic (1958 to the present), normally dominated by a stable presidential executive, has faced challenges from army revolts in Algeria, OAS and nationalist terrorists, and revolting students and striking workers in May 1968. In short, the development of the modern administrative system in France has taken place in the context of a political system marked by profound changes of objectives, organisation and personnel.

In comparison to this troubled process of political modernisation, the evolution of the French administrative system appears to have been a slow, stable process. Although there were great changes during the Revolutionary and Napoleonic periods (1789-99 and 1799-1815), since then the administrative organisation has had remarkable continuity. There are even Napoleonic institutions (the Council of State, Court of Accounts and prefectoral system are good examples) which still exist today. As during most of the last two centuries, the administration today is both praised and attacked for its size, competence and power, its centralisation, its legalism and red-tape, but also for its internal Byzantine politics.

This comparison of political discontinuity and weakness with administrative continuity and strength is, however, misleading in many respects. First, successive regimes and governments have not hesitated to purge the top personnel or to reform basic structures to meet their political goals: governments of the Fifth Republic have made many changes of both kinds. Second, the elements of administrative continuity which do exist are themselves reflections of an underlying political consensus about the ways in which France should be ruled. Whilst the political disputes over rival dynastic claims, Church-state relations, electoral systems and parliamentary prerogatives have been long and bitter, some features of the French state have faced only rare and unsuccessful challenges and could be considered as forming a kind of unwritten constitution. We shall now examine three of these features.

State Intervention

Throughout Western Europe the role of the state has expanded vastly during the twentieth century. In France, however, this growth has caused neither the surprise nor the antagonism it has engendered elsewhere, and in part this reflects the tradition of the French state playing a large, dynamic role in society. Even before 1789, the absolutist monarchy had claimed virtually unlimited powers and successive kings, aided by able ministers (e.g. Richelieu, Mazarin and Colbert), had gradually built up the powers of the central government, particularly in the spheres of law-making, taxation, military organisation, justice, religion and economics. They also consolidated its possessions of land, forests and factories. At the same time, they sought to confine to relatively minor roles all rivals to royal authority — feudal barons, guilds, corporations, independent cities and charter towns, provincial assemblies and even the Church. If in practice these policies met considerable, and often effective, opposition, the absolutist ambitions of the kings were never reduced: as agents of God, they claimed the right to intervene in any sphere of the activities of their subjects.

While the successors of the *ancien régime*, the Jacobins and Napoleon, were no more limited in the extent of their power claims, they traced their all-embracing authority not to God, but to the people. Thus, the 'general will' and 'popular sovereignty' replaced 'divine will' and 'absolutism' but the idea that the scope of the state action should be completely unlimited retained all its force. The attack on traditional loyalties and rival power claimants continued with such measures as the abolition of all feudal privileges (1789); the replacement of the provinces, duchies and counties by uniform *départements* (1790); the Le Chapelier law (1791) which prohibited all voluntary 'intermediary bodies' between the citizens and the state; and the Concordat (1802) by which Napoleon gained effective control of the French Church. Furthermore, through the codification of criminal and civil law and the sweeping reforms of the systems of taxation, education, local administration and justice, and of the army, they attempted to extend the influence of the state and to make its intervention more effective.

During the four regimes which followed the fall of the Empire — the Restoration (1815-30), the July Monarchy (1830-48), the Second Republic (1848-52) and the Second Empire (1852-70) — the administration not only continued to grow in size and scope but also became deeply involved in politics. In each of these regimes, the government was appointed by the head of state but needed a majority in parliament and hence had to win general elections. Increasingly, the administrative machine was used to bribe and cajole electors into voting for the government's candidates and to keep the loyalty of the deputies elected. Jobs and favours were awarded to political friends, whilst the political activities of opponents were rigorously repressed. The introduction of universal male suffrage in 1848 made this political role much more difficult, whilst the subsequent 'great fear' of an electoral victory (or a revolution) by the radicals made it much more essential. Hence during 1849 and the 1850s the administration was involved in the creation of an embryonic 'police state'. Those critical of the government were dismissed from state jobs, whilst those who remained were expected to take part in political spying, repression, propaganda and election campaigning. In practice, the efficiency of the electioneering was very questionable, whilst the repressive activities reinforced the hostility of republicans and radicals to Napoleon III and made them profoundly suspicious of civil servants. Administrative political repression declined after 1870 (although it reappeared during the Vichy regime of 1940 to 1944), whilst administrative electioneering was greatly reduced after the victory of the republicans in 1877. Nonetheless, there remains a tradition of distrust by politicians, especially those on the Left, of governmental misuse of administrative jobs and contracts for electoral ends — and of the willingness of senior civil servants to cooperate in this.

Although the purely administrative tasks of the state grew steadily during the nineteenth century, it was in the first half of the twentieth century that the 'great leap forward' in state intervention took place. The need for total control of the economy during and immediately after three major wars (1870-71, 1914-18 and 1939-45) was one cause. A second was the increased demand for full employment, economic growth and welfare services. The achievements of the Third Republic included the education and postal systems, the first pension schemes and the nationalisation of the Bank of France. The Provisional Government (1944 to 1946) nationalised many key sectors of the French economy, established national health and social security systems, created structures for medium-term economic planning and controlled prices and credit for day-to-day economic management. This massive expansion of the economic role of the state received support not only from the Communists and Socialists but also from the Christian Democrats and General de Gaulle himself. There were few who openly challenged the underlying assumption that constant large-scale state intervention was the only way of achieving continued reconstruction and growth. In short, the rulers of the Fifth Republic inherited not only a huge administrative machine, an enormous public sector and a vast armoury of powers for economic control, but also a tradition that the state should play a positive and all-pervasive role in society.

Centralisation

Through centuries of central control by the state the many distinct and disparate elements of France have gradually been welded into a single political society. The French state had to create the French nation. Centralisation was a natural instinct for all kings of France; their kingdom had been created by military conquest and dynastic marriage out of the independent feudal territories around the Ile-de-France and there existed vast differences of cultures and customs, laws and languages to prevent effective royal control. With provinces as different as Burgundy and Brittany, Alsace and the

Auvergne, Provence and the Basque countries, France had only a very fragile national fabric. The kings attempted to compensate for this by the creation of a strong centralised state: to this end they strove to reduce the powers of the feudal nobility and provincial representative assemblies (the *Parlements* and *Etats*) and to concentrate effective control of all local administrative and financial questions in the hands of royal officials (the *Intendants*) who resided in the provinces they administered.

Whilst there was considerable resentment of the growing powers of the Intendants, the Revolution did not lead to the establishment of a more decentralised system, as might have been expected. On the contrary, the Jacobins (and later Napoleon) believed even more strongly in the merits of centralisation than their predecessors in government. Their faith that popular sovereignty was indivisible − that the general will could only be articulated through one central national representative agency − led to a concentration of all political powers in Paris, first in the Assembly but subsequently in the person of the Emperor. Thus the advent of the 'one and indivisible Republic' meant a renewed effort to replace local self-government by local administration. Moreover, this belief in centralisation was also reinforced by the Jacobin preoccupation with equality: if all were to be equal before the state, there must be no local divergences from national norms and hence all political decisions must be made in Paris and executed uniformly in the provinces. There was, then, from the time of the Revolution an egalitarian, democratic, republican belief in politico-administrative centralisation − a belief which contrasts greatly with the Anglo-saxon liberal ideal of the pluralist democratic value of local government.

After the Revolution the Jacobins redrafted the administrative map of France: the 38,000 parishes, renamed as *communes*, were retained as the lower tier local units, whilst the feudal counties and provinces were replaced by eighty-nine départements, all roughly equal in size. Napoleon retained these 'republican' territorial units but appointed central government officials to direct all administrative activities within them. The implementation of the government's policies in the département was made the responsibility of the Prefect, the sole representative of the whole government. Within the département he gave orders and instructions through his subordinates, the subprefects, to the mayors of the communes.

Local councils were downgraded to advisory roles and all local services were reorganised under prefectoral supervision. Like his superior, the Minister of the Interior in Paris, the Prefect in his département was directly responsible for every kind of state intervention except those concerning justice, taxation and the army. In short, the Napoleonic prefectoral system reflected the basic beliefs that all political issues were national and to be decided by the government in Paris and, therefore, that in provincial France there should be no local government but only local administration.

The development of the local administrative system during the next 150 years demonstrated the strength of these basic beliefs: specialisation and democratisation made the structures more complex but it required the massive urbanisation of the Fourth and Fifth Republics to bring about a major reorganisation. Hence, until recently it was normally the case that new ministries were created when the scope of state intervention in a particular area outgrew the capacity of the relevant bureau in the Ministry of the Interior (the Ministries of Education and Agriculture are good examples of this). In general, a new ministry would either continue to use officers in the prefectures as its local representatives or create separate field services in the départements under prefectoral supervision (or do both), but it would very rarely delegate functions to mayors or local councils. Thus, in the administrative 'capitals' of the départements the prefectures and the increasingly numerous field services became the main agents of local administration. In short, all policy decisions emanated from the central government and were implemented by civil servants in the provinces.

The reforms of 1871 and 1884 gave theoretically wide powers to the elected councils (*Conseils généraux* in the départements and *Conseils municipaux* in the communes) and provided for the communal councils to choose their own mayors. Relatively few mandatory functions were delegated, however, and smallness, fragmentation and lack of resources meant that only the few large urban communes developed local government functions and services of any importance. But if most local councils remained theoretically weak, there were important links between local and central politics through the accumulation of offices: it was neither illegal nor rare for senior Parisian civil servants to hold office as mayors or local councillors and it was the normal practice for ministers, deputies and senators to do so. Despite the impact of urbanisation, this pattern of centralisation through the central control of all local admninistrative actions and the local roots of central government politicians has remained largely unchanged.

Conflict of Legitimacies

Traditional studies of public administration have stressed the unity and coherence of administrative action in France in contrast to the visibly divided administrative systems in Britain or the USA. Indeed, the French concept of the state (a concept little used in British analyses) implies a unified, integrated structure of government, a single entity over and above the sectional interests which divide society, serving only the general interest of the whole people. It was a state of this kind which both the Jacobins and Napoleon sought to create and which subsequent generations of 'state idealists' have wished to resurrect. Moreover, there is considerable evidence that theoretically a unitary, coherent state still exists. First, the whole administration is structured in rational pyramidal hierarchies with almost all formal powers in the hands of those at the top. Second, there is excessive legalism: in France very little is left to discretionary choices by individual civil servants for almost everything is determined by precise legal rules which senior civil servants draft in Paris and communicate to their subordinates by innumerable juridically-phrased circulars and instructions. Respect for these legal rules is enforced by hierarchical supervision, periodic inspection and the appeals of citizens to the administrative tribunals and the Council of State. Furthermore, there is legal provision for a unified financial control and for the fixing of many detailed technical specifications at the top level of the administration in Paris. Finally, note that many writers of studies of the French administration have been either lawyers, political opponents of the government in power or sociologists with more or less pronounced marxist inclinations. It is perhaps not surprising that they have all converged in treating the juridical theory as reality and thus in maintaining this myth of the all-powerful, unitary state apparatus.

The idea that the French state forms a single coherent unity distinct from civil society may have a theoretical attractiveness but it is a concept of very little use for the understanding of administrative action. In practice the state is neither coherent nor united, nor has it even clearly defined frontiers with society. In addition to the conflicts between the different logics of the political, economic and administrative components of the state and to the traditional political clashes between parties and between the legislature and the executive, there are also ancient but on-going disputes over legitimacy within the administration. The French administration bears more resemblance to a battlefield than to an army and the competing forces constantly seek the support of allies in society or elsewhere within the state.

First, there are conflicts between ministries which inevitably result from the interministerial collaboration necessary in many policy areas. Hence, each year there are long and bitter struggles between spending ministries (such as Education and Agriculture) which seek to improve or extend their services and the Budget Ministry (formerly the Ministry of Finance) whose *raison d'être* is the control or reduction of public expenditure. In a similar way, the public order preoccupations of the Ministry of the Interior lead it into frequent conflicts with the Ministry of Justice and, in recent years, with the Ministries of Education and of the universities. Such interministerial disputes may be considered to form part of the 'checks and balances' of the system. In practice, they may prevent the adoption of policy or simply create long delays.

A second type of conflict invariably arises between ministries and the interministerial agencies. Hence, the 'excessive legalism' of the Council of State and the 'book-keeping mentality' of the Court of Accounts and the financial inspectorate are widely resented. The more recent 'missionary administrations' (e.g. the Planning Commissariat and the Regional Action Delegation) are also disliked: unlike the traditional 'control' agencies, however, they do not try to prevent action but rather to provoke and guide it and this is equally irritating to many within traditional ministerial offices.

The internal organisation of the ministries is another source of disputes. Clashes inevitably arise between the different divisions of each ministry, between the various corps in which senior administrators are grouped, between 'specialist' and 'generalist' corps, between senior and junior civil servants and between those in Paris and those in the provinces.

All public administrations suffer from similar problems but in France they are especially acute and permanent. The French system traditionally gives equal prestige, influence and rewards to both 'technical' and 'administrative' corps. It also posts some senior civil servants into the départements, whilst in some ministries certain posts are reserved for members of specific corps. The results are that coordination is difficult and delays are frequent. The administration cannot act as a corporate entity and behind the facade of state unity the effective power of the administrative branch of the state is fragmented and dispersed.

THE INSTITUTIONAL FRAMEWORK

The Constitution of the Fifth Republic was drafted in haste during the summer of 1958. The drafters included General de Gaulle himself (who wished to strengthen the Presidency he was about to assume), Debré, his Minister of Justice and future Prime Minister (who sought to reinforce the executive) and several members of parliament (who strove to maintain the prerogatives of the legislature). The resulting compromise, in spite of the efforts of legal experts, was a constitutional text which is confused, ambiguous and in places, contradictory. This did not prevent its adoption after 79 per cent of the voters had approved it in the September referendum. One of the major flaws in this Constitution is that it does not make clear whether it is the President of the Republic or the Prime Minister and government who should rule France. Whilst the Prime Minister is 'in general charge of the work of the government', which 'directs the policy of the nation' and is answerable to parliament, it is the President — not chosen by parliament — who appoints the Prime Minister, can dissolve the National Assembly (the lower house) and holds other powers essential to the functioning of the government. The text thus provides for the creation of a twin-headed executive: the powers both of the President and of the Prime Minister and government are greatly reinforced but the government is still responsible to parliament. The use, abuse, misuse and disuse of the present text by subsequent Presidents, Prime Ministers and parliamentary majorities indicate that they, at least, have believed in presidential supremacy, and the electorate has not disowned them for this belief.

The Presidency

The greater strength of the President arises in part from the fact that he is no longer the choice of parliament as during the Third and Fourth Republics. The 1958 Constitution established an electoral college of about 80,000 to elect the President. The referendum of October 1962, however, changed this and since then the President has been directly elected by universal suffrage. Although the 1962 reform gave him no new powers, it enabled subsequent Presidents to claim a mandate direct from the people — a legitimacy equal, if not greater than, that of the National Assembly.

The Constitution also provided for a more influential presidency by not only retaining all the traditional presidential prerogatives but also adding new ones. Thus, like their predecessors of the Fourth Republic, Presidents still preside the Council of Ministers, promulgate laws and sign decrees, appoint senior officials, grant pardons, and negotiate and ratify international treaties. In the past these were formal powers in theory and practice and because they are still formal powers today the countersignature of the Prime Minister and any other minister concerned is required. Inherited from the Third Republic are the powers of appointing the Prime Minister and dissolving the National Assembly before the end of its official five-year term (but it cannot be dissolved again in the next twelve months): as in both previous Republics, the President can also ask parliament to reconsider a bill or address a message to either house (or to both). No ministerial countersignature is needed for the exercise of these powers. The new powers of the President in the present Constitution are four-fold: (1) 'Arbitration' to ensure 'the regular functioning of the organs of govrnment' — this formulation has been sufficiently vague to allow the interpretation that the President should play a large and dynamic role in policy-making; (2) the right to refuse or grant a request from the government or parliament for a referendum; (3) the right to submit bills to the Constitutional Council; and (4) the right to assume full powers in an emergency situation — this has been used only once, from April to September 1961 after the attempted coup in Algeria. Whilst this collection of powers made the constitutional position of the Presidency much stronger than it had been in previous regimes, it is the practice of successive Presidents which had greatly extended the scope of the office. Since 1958 the Constitution has been stretched, changed and even violated, so that the President is no longer merely the Head of State but also the effective head of the executive and the most active politician in France.

In addition to the time-taking formal duties as Head of State (e.g. national ceremonies, receptions for visiting foreign statesmen, trips abroad and visits to the French provinces), the main presidential concerns are political leadership and policy-making. Even the seemingly formal power of appointment has been used politically — to reward the faithful and to punish the wicked. Presidents have not only chosen their own Prime Ministers (which was their constitutional right) but also dismissed them and played a major role in choosing the other ministers (which were not). Public speeches, television appearances and press conferences by the President are devoted to defending the policies of his government. Furthermore, the President is not only the chief manager of his parliamentary coalition (he defines its limits and organisation) but he also plays a key role in parliamentary elections (by dissolution he can decide the date, but he may also lead the campaign and determine the tactics of his supporters). In short, the President acts increasingly as if he were the head of government and parliamentary leader.

The scope of presidential policy-making has also expanded steadily since 1958. De Gaulle interested himself mainly in four policy areas — foreign affairs, the Common Market, defence, and colonial and French Community questions — and made all the key decisions in these fields. Pompidou, whilst retaining this presidential 'reserved domain' created by de Gaulle, also intervened continuously in economic, financial and industrial policy choices; and Giscard d'Estaing has added social and environmental questions. All three Presidents also intervened in other areas when, for example, the government was deeply divided or when a decision was particularly politically sensitive. Presidential policy-making is most visible in the field of foreign affairs, for here it is clearly the President who makes all major choices. Note that at European summit meetings it is the French Head of State who attends whilst all other countries are represented by their heads of government. Recently one ex-Prime Minister (Chirac) has complained that he was not even consulted over major foreign policy choices, notably over the French decision to support direct elections to the European Assembly.

Whilst the French President has no Executive Office at his disposal and normally deals with the administration indirectly through the Prime Minister and various ministers, he is assisted by a small staff of assistants located in the Elysée Palace — the official residence of the President. This staff is subdivided into a number of units of which the most important politically is the General Secretariat (until its abolition in 1974 the Secretariat for Community and Malagasy Affairs also played a large role). Composed of a small group (fifteen to thirty) drawn mostly from the top ranks of the civil service, the General Secretariat is the President's chosen team of personal advisors. Under the Secretary General, who coordinates the work and is in daily contact with the President, its members are given specific fields and ministries to cover. Each member has to provide the President with ideas and with information on the work of the ministry. He will often be present at meetings between the President and the minister and take part in interministerial committees. It is rare, however, for the President to delegate an area of decision-making to one of his team or to allow direct intervention in the work of a ministry. (Although Foccard under de Gaulle, and Juillet and Garaud under Pompidou, seemed at times to be 'super-ministers'.) In most areas of policy-making, the General Secretariat staff are his closest advisors but the ministers are his principal collaborators.

The Government

In theory the 1958 Constitution shifted power from parliament to the government and Prime Minister. In practice, these have worked under the President and with the support of the presidential majorities in the Assembly since 1962. In theory, too, the government remains collectively responsible to parliament, whilst in practice its members are increasingly individually accountable to the President. The power of the Prime Minister to choose the size and shape of his government is shared with the President who has the final word over both the choice of ministers and the competence of the ministries. The weekly meeting of the Council of Ministers (the equivalent of the British Cabinet) has been reduced to a formal session for the exchange of information. It is presided by the President who also fixes its agenda and timetable. The real policy discussions take place in three other forums: (1) informal meetings between the President and a minister sometimes with the Prime Minister and always with the relevant member of the President's staff; (2) *ad hoc* meetings of groups of ministers and their advisors to discuss specific problems, usually chaired by the President; and (3) interministerial committees — regular meetings under the President or Prime Minister of the ministers involved with particular policy areas to plan and coordinate action.

This presidentialisation of policy making nonetheless leaves the Prime Minister with certain important responsibilities. He can decide policy in areas where the President has no interest; he supervises and coordinates the work of his ministers; he controls the administrative services in his office; and he is responsible for liaison with parliament and for good relations with the parties of the presidential coalition. The influence of the Prime Minister thus depends on his personality, interests, political weight and above all on his working relationship with the President. The individual minister, too, can play a considerable role: he has direct control of his ministry and can be the main policy initiator in the area of its competence. His importance, however, depends not only on those factors which determine the influence of the Prime Minister but also on his relationships with the Prime Minister and on the prestige and power of his ministry.

The number of ministers and the structures of the ministries have varied considerably since 1958. Normally there have been less than fifty ministers serving in fifteen to twenty ministries. In 1978 the government included the Prime Minister, nineteen full ministers and eighteen junior ministers — called Secretaries of State.

Ministries, April 1978

Prime Minister's Office
Justice
Interior
Foreign Affairs
Health and the Family
Defence
Labour and Participation
Cooperation
Economy
Budget
Environment and Quality of Life
Education

Universities
Agriculture
Industry
Transport
Commerce and Crafts
Foreign Trade
Youth, Sports and Leisure
Culture and Communications

There are also two independent 'secretariats' — minor ministries (Posts and War Veterans) headed by Secretaries of State rather than full ministers. In addition there are sixteen Secretaries of State associated with the full ministries; these, however, look after particular functions within their ministries and do not act as general assistants to their ministers as is often the case in Britain. All ministers attend the weekly meeting of the Council of Ministers — or Cabinet — each Wednesday. The Secretaries of State, including the two heads of the secretariats, do not attend these meetings unless specifically invited for discussion of problems within their competence. Since 1974 they are informed of the discussions of the Cabinet in regular briefing sessions given by a senior minister (in 1978 the Minister of Justice). The variations in the numbers and functions of the ministries since 1958 have reflected the changing political and administrative preoccupations of the government.

The Ministries

Only the ministries of Foreign Affairs, Interior, Justice, Defence, Agriculture, Posts and War Veterans have remained more or less constant in titles and responsibilities since 1958. The constant changing of the division of functions between the other ministries may be attributed to a number of factors. The first of these is the political desire to have a specific ministry to deal with a major policy area. It was for this reason, for example, that early governments of the Fifth Republic normally included a Minister for Algerian Affairs: he disappeared when Algeria was given independence in 1962 but a new ministry — for repatriated citizens from Algeria — was then created, only to be abolished in 1964 when the major problems of integrating the former Algerian settlers were solved. A second governmental preoccupation affecting the number and size of ministries has been that of attempting to create the most administratively efficient organizations for the different policy areas. In France, as in Britain, this led to experiments with 'superministries' in the late 1960s, e.g. *Equipement* ('Infrastructure' — a new policy aim — which grouped the former Ministries of Public Works and Transports and Construction) and Health and Social Affairs. In the 1970s, however, this same preoccupation has led to the division of some of the bigger ministries into smaller units: in 1978 the Ministry of Finances was split into a Budget Ministry and a Ministry of the Economy, whilst the Equipement Ministry separated into the Ministries of Transport and Environment. In many cases both political and administrative reasons are important. Certainly, they were both significant in the decisions to set up the Ministry for Administrative Reform (in existence 1962-67 and 1972-74) and to divide the Ministry of Education by transferring all functions relating to higher education to a separate Ministry of the Universities. It should be noted that all these modifications result in considerable administrative upheaval within the services concerned.

Staff employed by Ministries, 1975

Education	832,652
Posts and Telecommunications	361,642
Finances	166,332
Interior	126,410
Equipement	83,408
Transport	12,131
Quality of Life	28,543
Culture	7,916
Justice	30,287
Agriculture	27,034
Labour and Health	19,116
War Veterans	5,122
Industry, Commerce and Crafts	4,893
Foreign Affairs	2,231
Prime Minister's services	2,207
Cooperation	703
Overseas Territories	289

There are not only differences from time to time but also from ministry to ministry. In the first place there are differences in size. Whilst the table is somewhat misleading (school teachers, postmen and policemen are included in the appropriate ministerial totals), it does demonstrate the enormous differences in numbers. One Minister of Education is said to have remarked that only General Motors and the Red Army employed more people than he did. There are also big differences in organisation. Most ministries are divided into divisions called directorates or general directorates which in turn are split into sub-divisions. The directors or directors general are thus the official heads of the ministry (except in Foreign Affairs which normally has an overlord — Secretary General), and they and their sub-directors are the points of contact with the ministers and the members of their *cabinets.* In some cases, small but specialist 'services' exist outside the directorates and are answerable to the minister through their own heads. Several ministries have separate inspectorates which again deal directly with the minister. The precise organisation of the ministry depends very much on the wishes of the minister and on general government policy. Since 1958 there have been frequent changes in the internal organisation of the different ministries and some ministries (e.g. Education and Interior) have been reorganised several times.

One other difference between ministries is in the relative importance of their field services in the provinces. Some ministries (e.g. Industry) perform almost all their functions in Paris and hence group all their civil servants in their central office. Others, however, provide services to all citizens, so have relatively few people in their Paris headquarters. The Ministry of Finance, for example, in 1975 had 118,000 of its 166,000 employees in its field services, whilst the Ministry of Posts had only 17,000 of its 361,000 employees in its central office. The 100,000 policemen (Interior) and 750,000 teachers (Education) are also distributed throughout France.

The Prime Minister's Office is exceptional in that it is more a collection of common services than a ministry. It includes: the General Secretariat of the Government, which looks after the work of the Cabinet; the general directorate for the administration and the civil service; the General Secretariat of National Defence; and a number of specialist agencies for scientific research, atomic energy, economic planning and regional policy. From time to time these agencies may be transferred to the responsibility of another ministry despite their interministerial functions. There is, then, neither unity nor coordination in the office of the Prime Minister. Note that the Prime Minister's *cabinet* and the General Secretariat of the government (working in close cooperation with the President of the Republic as well as with the Prime Minister) do play important roles of coordinating the work of the government as a whole.

The Prime Minister and each of the ministers has a small private staff of his own choice, termed a *cabinet*. Whilst the Prime Minister may have thirty or more staff, the average minister's cabinet is less than half this size. The majority of members are high-ranking civil servants, usually quite young, who are on temporary loan to the minister. The cabinet of the Prime Minister, like that of the President, assists in policy making and in coordinating ministerial action. The other cabinets, however, provide their ministers not only with ideas and advice but also with assistance in running the ministry, in negotiations with other ministries and in dealings with Parliament. How a cabinet operates depends on what the minister wants. In some cases different groups of members will oversee different divisions in the ministry. Elsewhere staff will deal with particular problems which affect several divisions. Almost invariably there is some tension between the cabinet and the directors as the minister relies on his personal staff to pursue his line at all times, if need be against that of his ministry. During the Fifth Republic there was a clear tendency for ministerial cabinets to grow in size, until President Giscard d'Estaing felt it necessary to impose limits on the memberships of all staffs except his own and that of his Prime Minister. It has been argued that this development has allowed the cabinet of the Prime Minister to play a more important role in both policy initiation and coordination, as members of ministerial cabinets (now smaller in size) have to spend most of their time on the internal concerns of their ministries. Finally, note that the loaning of senior civil servants to posts in cabinets is possible because of the relative freedom of these civil servants to take open political stances (although not all are chosen for the identity of their views with those of their ministers) and because of the security and flexibility afforded to members of the *grand corps* of the service, examined below.

Functional Decentralisation

One of the innovations of public administration in post-war France has been the creation of small, dynamic, single-goal administrative agencies outside the traditional ministerial structures. The idea of these agencies (known as *missions*) is not that they should themselves administer a policy but rather that they should inspire, encourage and coordinate the actions of those already holding power in existing structures both within and outside the administration. The best known have dealt with economic planning, regional policy and tourist development in certain areas.

The first of these agencies was the Planning Commissariat, set up as a small team (about thirty in number) of young, competent civil servants to organise and direct consultative economic planning of France's post-war reconstruction. The first five-year plan appeared so successful that the Commissariat, its consultative procedures and its five-year plans have become normal features of the French governmental system. The Commissariat, outside traditional state structures, seeks to 'concert' (to bring into harmony) private and public economic decision making through consultative planning procedures. In practice, this means it organises committees of industrialists, bankers, trade unionists, civil servants and economic experts to exchange information and to work out, for the different sectors of the economy, the implications of the forecasts from INSEE (the national statistics institute) and the policy intentions of the government. From the conclusions of the various committees and the government's instructions, the Commissariat drafts a five-year plan which is both a market forecast and an 'indication' of the government's policy intentions. The 'partners' who have partici-pated in the preparatory processes are then expected to collaborate in the implementation of the plan. Established at the Liberation and led for ten years by Jean Monnet, the first Planning Commissio-ner, the Commissariat gave itself much of the credit for France's post-war economic miracle. In the last decade, however, it has lost much prestige. The present seventh plan (1976-80) has been almost forgotten in the successive attempts of the government to control inflation and unemployment. Nonetheless, the Commissariat con-tinues to activate its committees which still group several hundred decision-makers from all parts of the economy and administration and there is still a useful exchange of information and opinions.

Another major 'missionary' agency is DATAR (Delegation for Regional Action) established in 1963 to stimulate industrial decentralisation to the poorer regions and to organise the articulation of regional interests into the economic planning processes. Like the Planning Commissariat, it is a small group of young senior civil servants essentially concerned with getting others to act rather than involving itself in any kind of detailed administration. In a discreet way, DATAR encourages the regional administrative field services and (since their creation in 1973) the Regional Councils to take initiatives and to cooperate with it in planning regional economic growth patterns and the organisation of industrial decentralisation. It also attempts to find industrialists to invest in France's poorer regions (it has even opened offices in the USA and in other European states to this end) and gives subsidies or grants to attract such developments. DATAR claims, however, that its successes reflect its ability to encourage, coordinate and inform rather than its use of such (in any case limited) funds.

At the core of the vast sector of the economy owned or controlled by the state are the fully nationalised concerns. These include coal, gas, electricity, the railways, civil aviation, tobacco and matches, the largest banks and insurance companies, the major shipping companies, the credit banks and specialised lending agencies, the Renault car firm and Aerospatiale (the aircraft construction firm). Some are virtually state monopolies but not all are profitable. In 1976, over 7 per cent of the budget was spent subsidising the 'lame ducks'. In fact, the lameness does not always result from natural causes for the government uses its nationalised industries as policy instruments in ways which may prevent profitability. Air France, for example, like British Airways, is obliged to buy and operate Concorde. There is also pressure to keep factories open in areas of high unemployment. Over one million people are employed in these industries (over 250,000 in the railways alone) and in some areas they are the major employers.

The main fully nationalised industries (notably coal, gas, electricity and Renault) are organised as *établissements publics*. While the term may be translated as public corporations, their legal status is rather different from that of their British counterparts: in law they are merely state agencies carrying out specific functions on behalf of the state. Hence, all important decisions are subject to ministerial approval; chief executives are appointed by the government (usually they are chosen from the senior ranks of the civil service); all financial dealings are subject to supervision similar to that exercised in the ministries; and, in some cases, employees have statutory conditions of employment like those in the civil service. Whilst each of these concerns has a representative board (comprising representatives of the consumers, the workers and the ministries), real power is concentrated in the hands of a chairman, a managing director, his departmental executives and the minister responsible. The juridicial similarity of these different industrial organisations is misleading, however: the extent of governmental intervention varies considerably from industry to industry and from time to time.

Apart from these corporations there are some fully nationalised undertakings which have retained the legal status of companies, e.g. the banks, and there are also many firms in which the state has effective control through more or less large share-holdings. Many of these concerns have been re-organised as mixed-economy companies (*societés d'économie mixte*), which means they are companies with both private and public shareholders carrying out state functions subject to state regulation. Companies of this kind include the SNCF (French Railways), Elf-Erap and CFP-Total (the two petrol companies which together supply half the French market), the shipping firms and most of the toll-motorways. There are also many ordinary companies in which the state owns shares. Such companies in which the state owned over 30 per cent of all shares numbered 800 in 1975. It has been calculated that the state now controls over half of all industrial investment.

The size of the public and semi-public sectors does not, however, imply that there is effective and coherent governmental control through them of the whole economy. Indeed, the government is not always successful in imposing its wishes on its nationalised industries despite its technical supervision (most through the Ministry of Industry), its financial control (through the Ministry of the Economy) and its power of appointing the senior personnel of these firms. Renault is a notable example of a public corporation with considerable independence from governmental interference, whilst the SNCF, in contrast, is a 'mixed-economy company' which is subject to very tight ministerial supervision.

Geographical Decentralisation

In France there are three levels for decentralisation: the 36,383 communes and 96 départements created at the Revolution, and the 22 regions created during the Fifth Republic, by decree in March 1964 and law in July 1972, which are not yet either full local authorities or universally accepted field service areas but merely territorial public corporations.

The traditional key figures in local government are the Prefects who originally wielded all powers decentralised from Paris. There is still one Prefect in each département and since 1964 the Prefect based in the most important département of each region also acts as Regional Prefect. The twenty-two Regional Prefects coordinate and direct those actions of the departmental Prefects and heads of regional field services which affect the economic development of the region and also act as executive officers for their regional councils. The departmental Prefects serve as official representatives of the state and as delegates of the government in the département (in which capacity they supervise the specialist field services); they head the field services of the Ministry of the Interior (police, fire service, political information, control of the legality of local authority decisions); and they act as executive officers of the departmental councils. This means that they are in constant contact with their 'own' staff in the prefectures and police headquarters, the directors of the field services and the local councils.

Almost all the main ministries have field services in the départements and these provide services directly to the public, work in cooperation with the local councils, or both. Throughout most of the Fifth Republic the heads of the field services of the Ministries of Finance and Equipement have been especially influential as they have checked the financial and technical aspects of local authority projects. In practice most French civil servants are employed in field services. Education and police, which are mainly local authority functions in Britain, have always been provided by field services of ministries in France, under the supervision of the resident representatives of the government — the Rectors and Prefects.

The councils of the local authorities work closely with the Prefects and field services. In fact, the regions are not full local authorities but are organs 'for the concerted action of the constituent départements' in the field of economic development. They can undertake studies, participate in state investment projects and execute their own projects, although their funds are very limited. Decisions are made by the regional council which is composed of all the deputies and senators and representatives of departmental and communal councils and which is advised by an economic and social committee composed of interest group representatives. The Regional Prefect executes its decisions.

The members of the departmental councils are elected for six-year terms, half being renewed every three years. The councils meet in full for only two short three-week sessions but elect permanent standing committees to oversee the activities the Prefects carry out on their behalf. Much of their spending is on roads and certain school and welfare services, although they can initiate projects in other areas and take part in joint ventures with communal councils.

The communal council, elected every six years, has a limited number of mandatory functions and the right to act in any other area not precluded by law. In practice, its most important function is to elect the mayor who, as official representative of the state and executive officer of the council, is the strong man of his commune. For the state he acts as registrar of births, marriages and deaths and is responsible for public order. For his council he implements its decisions, directs its employees and supervises its accounts. In the thousands of small communes being mayor is a part-time hobby but in the towns and cities it is a full-time and extremely powerful post. Mayors such as Defferre in Marseilles and Chaban-Delmas in Bordeaux have thousands of local government officers and massive budgets under their control (by 1970 there were over 700,000 local council employees and the number was growing rapidly). Until recently, however, the normal practice for most local councils was to 'hire' the services of central government field services. This was especially true for civil engineering and construction projects, and in all but the main cities it was normal for the Equipement services to play an important role as consultants and executive agents for the local council in almost all public building work. Other field services also provided services to the councils in their appropriate areas.

Also involved in local government are the trade associations and interest groups. Chambers of agriculture, of trade and industry and of crafts exist in every département and in all large towns and are frequently consulted by local politicians and administrators. Furthermore, in the prefectures, field services and town halls there are many consultative committees where local interest groups are represented. It is rare for any local action to be taken without prior negotiation with the groups concerned.

Local structures are still archaic and fragmented despite recent efforts to reduce the number of communes by mergers and to create the regions, and Paris still interferes obsessively (it can even veto a local choice for the name of a street). The Prefects check the legality of all local council decisions, there are national technical controls on all building and councils are very dependent on Paris for their finances (through grants and loans). Nonetheless, the system is not as centralised as all this suggests. First, the government looks increasingly to the people in the local administrations, councils and pressure groups for ideas and projects to solve unemployment and promote economic growth. Second, local councillors and mayors, through accumulating national and local offices, are often far more powerful than they appear. Third, the officials in the field services are themselves involved in their local communities and often see themselves as servants of the local interest as well as agents of the state. Ironically, this is also the case for the Prefects whose careers are dependent on their abilities to work smoothly with the local councillors. Moreover, it is not unknown for councillors and local civil servants to conspire together against Paris and to exploit differences between ministries or within ministries in Paris. Finally, urbanisation has made the mayors of the large towns into extremely important decision-makers in their own right.

Since 1958 there have been a number of attempts to reform local government institutions (in addition to the regional reform of 1972). In 1964 there was an internal reorganisation of the prefectures and a redistribution of tasks between prefectoral services and specialist field services. A number of measures have been taken to facilitate cooperation between groups of neighbouring communes for the provision of joint services: in four major agglomerations the communes have been grouped into 'urban communities' and in other urban areas 'districts' have been formed. The 1971 law on local government created the means by which the number of communes might be reduced through mergers but in the face of considerable local hostility these means have been little employed: mergers have in fact reduced the number of communes by 2,000. Finally, there has been a massive expansion of local government staffs, especially in the large towns. Instead of relying on the field services, the city councils have built up their own teams of economists, engineers, architects and administrators. If these posts in local government still do not rival those in the technical corps or grands corps in prestige, they are extremely lucrative and influential and, in some cases, are occupied by former or 'borrowed' civil servants.

The other distinct local government reform has been that of Paris and its region. In 1966 a first stage of reorganisation involved the creation of five new départements and a regional authority, but this reform still left the Paris region as a 'special' region managed by a government-appointed Delegate General and the city of Paris under the domination of two Prefects — the Prefect of Police and the Prefect of Paris (responsible for everything except police) — as it had been since the abolition of the post of mayor and limitation of council powers after the Paris Commune of 1871. In 1975 and 1976 the Ile de France region was reformed and now has institutions and powers similar to those of other regions. The following year

Numbers of Staff in Public Employment

Civil Servants (permanent posts)		2,080,000[1]
Schools and university teachers	750,000	
Armed forces (career officers) and gendarmerie	250,000	
State police	105,000	
Postal workers and telecommunications	350,000	
Manual workers	121,000	
Non-permanent Civil Servants		600,000[2]
Local Authority Employees		740,000
Includes prefecture staffs	16,000	
Public Enterprise		900,000[2]
Total		4,320,000

1   *Annuaire statistique de la France* 1977
2   Estimates for 1975

the commune-département of Paris was also restructured so that today it has a mayor (Chirac) who leads its municipal council and presides its departmental council (in fact the same body but at separate meetings). There are still two Prefects in Paris but whilst the Police Prefecture retains most of its functions, the functions of the Prefect of Paris have been so reduced that this post has been merged with that of Regional Prefect of the Ile-de-France.

THE CIVIL SERVICE

Organisation

According to the budgetary statistics, the civil service in 1976 numbered about 1,800,000 permanent posts of which nearly two-thirds were located in the Ministries of Education and Posts and Telecommunications. This figure, however, does not represent the total number of civil servants for it does not include non-permanent posts — which may be temporary, part-time or contract-based. Estimates of the number of these posts vary considerably but in the early 1970s it was calculated that the number of people employed in these ways in Equipement alone was 40,000 and that the total for all ministries might exceed 500,000.

The permanent posts, however, are almost all structured into four classes, known as A,B,C and D. The highest class, A, includes about 20 per cent of all posts; B, 30 per cent; C, 25 per cent; and D, 15 per cent. The other posts are mainly those of policemen and labourers. Within each class civil servants are grouped into corps according to the type of work, the service or division and the ministry. Within the corps there are steps (*echelons*) which effect the nature of each post and its hierarchical rank.

There is a further complicated differentiation within the 330,000 posts in class A. Two-thirds of these civil servants are university and senior secondary school teachers. Of the rest, a large majority are members of the top technical corps (e.g. Roads and Bridges, Agriculture, Mines and Telecommunications) or the specialist administrative corps (e.g. tax collection and customs). There are also 'generalists' — the 'civil administrator' corps in many ministries. Finally, class A includes the top generalist corps, the *grands corps* which thus form only a small fraction of this senior administrative category. These grands corps include the diplomatic and prefectoral corps, the Court of Accounts, the Council of State and the *Inspection générale des finances*. They are relatively small in size (the prefectoral corps has about 600 members and the Council of State under 300) but extremely influential. This influence arises in part from the importance of their administrative functions and in part from the abilities of their members and the facility with which members may either be loaned to occupy key posts outside the corps as directors of ministries and in cabinets, for example, or may temporarily move into politics or the public and private sectors of industry. The basic functions of the prefectoral corps have been described above, whilst those of the Court of Accounts and general financial inspectorate (audit and control of all public spending) and of the Council of State (the supreme court of the administrative court system) will be examined in a later section.

The civil service is thus highly stratified and fragmented, especially in its top ranks. The sole attempt (in 1946) to create a single generalist corps of civil administrators was doomed from the start and only the unified recruitment and training system for the grands corps remains. In theory, the competitive entry examination is the normal method of recruiting civil servants for all types of work and at all levels. In practice many in non-permanent and part-time posts are recruited directly and even for many class C and D posts (notably postmen, typists and porters) there is little competition except in areas of relatively high unemployment. The competitiveness is much greater for the class A and B posts and especially for the higher teaching posts, the technical corps and the senior administrative corps.

The competitive recruiting procedures for the technical corps really begins in the lycées. The very best students in mathematics and science stay on after the baccalauréat (which qualifies for university entrance) in special classes in a limited number of schools to prepare the entry examinations for the *grandes écoles*. Those seeking posts in the top technical corps aim for the most prestigious of these, the *Ecole Polytechnique* and, failing this, for one of the others. The Ecole Polytechnique was established by Napoleon to train military engineers and its students are still formally officer cadets. Those who come within the top 25 per cent in the final examination at the Ecole Polytechnique and a handful of the very top graduates from other grandes écoles are offered further training and posts in the technical corps. In practice this means that most of the civil and mining engineers have had two years of scientific training at the Ecole Polytechnique and a further two years of advanced engineering at the *Ecole des Ponts et Chaussées* or the *Ecole des Mines* (as trainee civil servants) — and all this after two years of special classes at secondary school.

Since 1945 those wishing to enter the senior administrative corps must pass through the *Ecole National d'Administration* (ENA). There are highly competitive entry examinations for graduates and established civil servants and most students have prepared for these in special classes at the Paris Institute of Political Studies after undergraduate studies there or at one of the Paris universities' law departments. There is another competitive examination at the end of the two years' studies at the ENA and the result of this determines the subsequent administrative careers of the students. Those at the top of the results list choose the posts in the grands corps, those lower down are left with places in the civil administrator corps of the different ministries.

The students at the ENA do not actually get a great deal of theoretical education. After only three weeks at the school all the 140 students are dispersed for a year of practical work which is normally spent on the staff of a Prefect. Only in their second year do they actually study at the school — in one of two sections, general administration and economic administration. The concentration is on the methods of administration and especially on its legal and financial aspects. Students are also educated in the practice of negotiation: to this end they are given lectures in international relations and industrial relations and are sent on a short work *stage* in a private or public business enterprise. Finally, all the students have to learn a foreign language. The aims, methods and results of the ENA have been under constant debate since the creation of the school and a number of reforms have been made, notably in 1971. The original aims of the school were less concerned with training and more concerned to democratise recruitment to the higher civil service and to reduce the effects of compartmentalisation and fragmentation. In a sense the ENA may be regarded as a two-year process for selecting 'high fliers' suitable for the grands corps.

This system of competitive examinations and schools for the top technical and administrative corps has been and continues to be subject to a number of criticisms. Some, from within the grands corps, argue that the ENA graduates are not prepared for their specific tasks and need considerable training once they join the corps. More generally, it is alleged that by basing recruitment purely on intellectual prowess demonstrated in examinations (and especially in orals) the system demoralises the lower grades of the administration who no longer have any prospect of 'promotion through the ranks' to senior posts in the ministries. There is, then, a waste of talent both within the civil service and amongst those who, having failed the ENA entrance examinations, pursue careers in the private sector. A second problem is that this distinct recruitment pattern for members of the grands corps makes them even more differentiated from other civil servants. It sharpens 'communications barriers' between grades and hence weakens the effectiveness of the administration. Furthermore, it is pointed out that candidates from middle-class Parisian families and the top Paris lycées (and for the ENA from the Paris Institute of Political Studies and law departments) are far more likely to succeed than anyone else. Certainly, the results appear to support these allegations: the vast majority of the students come from the better-off and better educated sections of Paris society and, more particularly, from the families of middle and senior civil servants.

Finally, note that the ENA and the Ecole Polytechnique are only the tip of a massive structure of civil service training. Each year an average of some 100,000 civil servants take part in a vast number of specialised training schemes. Of these, about 80,000 are in preparatory classes for competitive examinations but 70,000 of that number are established civil servants aiming for promotion to higher posts. Specialist courses are available in the provincial Institutes of Political Studies, the Regional Administration Institutes, the Preparatory Centres for General Administration (often run by universities) and in such ministry schools as the Training and Preparation Centre of the Ministry of Finance. In short, there is a vast network of schemes by which 'outsiders' may prepare for entry examinations and civil servants may seek promotion. Nonetheless, it remains almost impossible for anyone to gain a senior post by working up from the ranks. Almost all the high-fliers enter very close to the top through the ENA or Polytechnique channels.

Conditions of Employment

The conditions of employment in the civil service were unified and codified in the civil service charter (*statut*) of 1946 which was amended in 1959. The salary structure was also reorganised into a similar single general grid in 1948, after massive negotiations, and it has been frequently modified since that time. In practice, however, there is still very little unity of conditions or salary as different ministries, divisions and corps have amended and adapted the basic rules to suit their own ends. In general, all civil servants in permanent posts have security of tenure and pension rights. Most civil servants can only be removed by a legal declaration of redundancy of their post (with adequate compensation) or for incompetence (after a long and complex disciplinary procedure) and in practice these rarely happen. Diplomats, Prefects and Sub-Prefects, however, do not have these guarantees and may be moved to or from particular posts at the discretion of the government (although they retain a basic salary even when not in a post unless disciplinary action is taken). In a similar way, the directors in ministries have tenure in service but not in their particular posts. All members of the grands corps retain their positions in these bodies whenever they are 'on loan' in posts elsewhere in the administration or in the public sector. Thus if, for example, a member of the Court of Accounts gives up a post (in, say a ministerial *cabinet*) he automatically gets back his job at the Court. For diplomats and Prefects, however, posts cannot be automatically re-created and the loss of an outside post may result in a period without a job (but still with a salary, albeit reduced). The minimum retirement age varies according to the nature of the post, from fifty-five (for school teachers and firemen) to seventy (for members of the Council of State). Pensions vary according to the number of years in the service. A minimum of fifteen years is needed to qualify and for a full forty years a pension of two-thirds of the final salary is awarded. One other benefit of all civil servants is an annual paid holiday of at least one month.

All civil servants are subject to a certain number of restrictions. In their work they can only do what the law and their superiors in the administrative hierarchy authorise. If they exceed their powers, this may result in a citizen bringing a case against the state in the administrative tribunals. If they reveal official secrets or defraud funds, they will face stiff penalties from the criminal courts. If they do not perform their duties in a satisfactory manner, this will be noted in the annual report drafted by their superiors, and, in extreme cases, disciplinary procedures will be taken. Special disciplinary committees exist to examine all cases and to ensure that no arbitrary actions are taken against civil servants and they may refer cases to the National Council of the Civil Service. If a case is proved, sanctions may be imposed which vary in severity from an official warning to dismissal. A civil servant may not receive payment for outside activities (except teaching and writing) and after leaving the civil service he may not enter a business which has close dealings with the ministry to which he belonged (to prevent corruption).

The rights of members of the civil service to take part in trade union and political activities are liberal. The 1946 charter gave civil servants the right to join unions and to strike, although this latter right is subject to a number of restrictions. Advance warning of strike action is necessary and in some cases a minimum 'public service' must be provided, whilst the 1948 legislation makes it illegal for higher civil servants and the police to strike at all. Civil service unions are highly fragmented, a reflection of the traditional divisions of the French labour movement which are rooted in their ideological differences and distinct historical traditions. There are three major 'working class' trade union confederations, the CGT, the CFDT and the *Force ouvrière*; a large number of small autonomous unions; and a large 'white-collar-middle management' federation of unions, the CGC (*Confédération générale des cadres*). Most unions are service-based but within a division or service there may be several separate unions, each allied to a different national confederation or independent. Many lower grade office workers belong to unions in the moderate socialist Force ouvrière, although in traditional Catholic areas the CFDT unions (socialist-Catholic) unions are strong and many manual workers are in unions of the Communist dominated CGT. The majority of teachers belong to unions in a separate giant teachers' federation, the FEN, which has over 600,000 members. Despite this fragmentation, civil service unions are quite influential, not only because they are willing to go on strike or 'work to rule' but also because they have skilled negotiators and considerable sympathy from their superiors.

In theory all civil service salaries may be calculated from a pay grid which allocates an index number to every post and grade. Every year the budget sets a base payment and each civil servant then receives in salary an amount equal to this base payment multiplied by his index number. Originally the index numbers varied from 153 to 778 but union action has gradually won increases in many indices so that the top index is over 1500. Theoretically, the ratio of the highest to the lowest official salary could be 10 to 1 but in practice there is virtually no-one in posts near the bottom of the scale. This surrealist world of civil service pay is further complicated by the fact that almost every job carries indemnities, expenses or travel allowances, some of which may depend on personal circumstances. At the highest levels salaries are virtually personalised so that it is impossible to make generalisations. The official salary of a Prefect, for example, will depend on his post and his seniority but his real income will include massive indemnities and entertainment expenses and a free house and car, so that in a rich and generous département (the Prefect at Nice is said to have an expense account as large as that of the French embassy in Washington) he may not spend any of his official salary. The income of a civil engineer of the Ponts et Chaussées is increased by the payment of a percentage premium on the value of the building projects he supervises. Almost nobody at the top of the scale would be receiving less than twice the amount indicated by this index.

In France most civil servants are allowed to join political parties and participate in their activities; they obtain leave to fight elections and, if elected, to serve in parliament. The result is that the civil service is overtly political in many respects. Many civil servants, at all levels, play active roles in party politics, several hold office as mayors or local councillors and 35 per cent of the deputies of the Fifth Republic have been civil servants (although many as teachers). Second, not all the posts to which the government has a discretionary right of appointment are given to conservatives, Gaullists or Giscardians: there are known sympathisers of the Left in prefectures, embassies and even in ministerial *cabinets*. Finally, the relative paucity of ENA graduates amongst the deputies of the parties of the Left may reflect the weakness of the Socialist Party until recent years: the leadership of the 'new' Socialist Party now includes a number of senior civil servants and of the ENA graduates elected in 1978 to the Assembly one-third were Socialists. The importance of hostile senior civil servants has been demonstrated by numerous 'leaks' of embarrassing information to the press and by the bitter attacks of Gaullists (notably against members of the Council of State and the finance inspectorate). The other major factor is that the lower ranks of the civil service are predominantly sympathetic to the parties of the Left (and especially the Socialist Party).

Senior civil servants are not anonymous in the way which the British tradition of neutrality enforces. Relatively few posts are subject to restrictions on the rights to publish and take part in public debates on controversial issues (although senior military posts are exceptions).

The Control of Administration

Internal Controls and Administrative Courts

The activities of civil servants are supervised by a mass of internal administrative controls. In the first place, almost all branches of the administration are hierarchically structured. Orders and instructions, often written in formal legal terms, pass from senior to junior civil servants. One task of all heads of offices, field services, central divisions and prefectures is to make annual reports on the performance of their subordinates, and these reports may determine career prospects. There are also special inspectorates whose officers visit all parts of those branches of the administration for which they are competent. When there are allegations of misconduct, a special investigation may be carried out by a member of the relevant inspectorate or, in certain cases, by members of the intelligence service (*Service des renseignements généraux*). All this information may be used for disciplinary proceedings or simply, in most cases, for deciding promotions between different ranks within a class and corps (annual rises of échelon are almost automatic and simply bring a salary increment).

A second type of internal administrative control is that of public expenditure. In France there are both *a priori* and *a posteriori* financial controls. *A priori* controls are two-fold. The first is that of proposals for expenditure. Attached to each ministry is a financial controller, an official of the Ministry of the Budget whose task is to check the regularity of all spending plans and his approval is needed before the ministry can commit itself to any action that will involve expenditure. The second control takes place when payment is imminent. All actual payments are made by the treasurer-paymaster general of the département on warrants issued by the local officer of the ministry concerned. The treasurer and his accountants make a full check of the regularity of each payment.

There are also two types of *a posteriori* controls, the examinations of the finance inspectorate and the annual audits of the Court of Accounts. The former supervises all financial services of the state, of local councils and of semi-public bodies (including social security funds). It operates by sending (theoretically without prior notice) a team of inspectors to carry out a full audit. The inspectors investigate not only the accuracy of the accounts but also the efficiency of the administration under examination. All public accounts are also inspected annually by the Court of Accounts which, like the Council of State, is organized as an investigatory tribunal. It examines not only the regularity of accounts and also the efficiency of the administrative service. Its lengthy reports may criticise not only abuses and inefficiency but also defects in governmental policy, and proposals for reform may be made. Whilst these financial controls appear impressively rigorous, they are not always very effective. Two of France's most recent massive money-wasters, Concorde and the vast and unused abattoir-market complex at La Villette in Paris (shortly to be demolished, at further expense, and replaced by a park) were criticised by the Court only after long and detailed public and parliamentary scandals.

There is also a specialised control of the legality of administrative actions, a control exercised by the network of specialised administrative courts and the administrative tribunals under the Council of State. As the 'supreme court' of the administrative legal system, the Council of State determines the way in which the other administrative courts operate. Apart from its role as expert advisor to the government on the form and legality of decrees and regulations, the Council also rules on disputes between branches of the administration and on complaints by citizens who have suffered as a result of official acts of civil servants. An individual administrative decision, a local by-law made by a Prefect or even a decree issued by the government may be challenged before it. However, it does not only make a judgement (formally, it expresses 'advice' to the government), it also investigates the full details of the complaint by the citizen. Furthermore, it may declare an administrative action invalid not only because the legal powers of the administration have been exceeded (*ultra vires*) or correct procedure has not been respected, but also on the grounds that administrative powers have been used for purposes for which they were not intended. This last possibility allows the Council to investigate the motivation behind administrative (and government) acts which apparently respect the letter of the law. It may not, of course, make rulings on the constitutionality of laws voted by parliament (this has been the function of the Constitutional Council since 1958). Within its sphere of competence, however, it can be an extremely powerful check on civil servants for it can not only quash decisions but also award damages against the state.

In recent years, however, this administrative judicial system has come increasingly under attack, in part as a result of its lengthy delays but also because the judgements of the Council of State are not always respected. One attempt to improve the system was the establishment in 1972 of the office of Mediator (*médiateur*), a weak French version of the Ombudsman, to deal with both minor cases and those complaints alleging unfair (rather than illegal) administrative action. Whilst it must be admitted that these internal controls have not prevented instances of flagrant illegality, large-scale financial profligacy or the wrecking of beautiful and historic towns by wild administrative tower-building, it should also be pointed out that the very existence of these controls may keep most average civil servants from abusing their powers.

External Controls

The activities of civil servants are closely observed by many involved in politics and in particular by ministers, members of parliament and pressure groups. Since 1958 many ministers (although not all) have held their offices for relatively long periods and, unlike their predecessors of the previous regime, have not had to spend most of their time in parliamentary battles for the survival of the government. They have had more time and energy to get to know their ministries and to exercise an effective supervision over the activities of their civil servants. Furthermore, civil servants, realising that their political masters were unlikely to change in the short term, have been unable to employ the delaying tactics sometimes used during the Fourth Republic when a civil servant's proposal met hostility from his minister.

There is no doubt that the power of the French parliament as a controller of the government declined dramatically in 1958. Parliament is only permitted to meet for five and a half months (in two sessions), the nineteen specialist committees of the Fourth Republic have been replaced by six large and less specialised committees and the government effectively controls the time-table and agenda of both houses. Furthermore, the law-making scope of parliament is limited by the Constitution and further restricted by the possibility of a veto by the Constitutional Council. The financial powers of parliament are greatly reduced (the government may veto private members bills which increase spending or reduce taxes and, in certain circumstances, could introduce its budget by ordinance) and even parliament's abilities to amend laws and to defeat governments are strictly limited. In practice, of course, many of these constitutional restrictions have not been needed because since 1962 there has been a stable majority coalition loyally supporting the President's government. Moreover, most of the time the deputies and senators have been either unwilling or unable to use those powers which they still hold to check or control the executive. Nonetheless, governmental backbenchers may demand and obtain concessions from the government on its legislative proposals; parliamentary questions about the administration may embarrass a minister into controlling the excesses of his civil servants and even the large and unwieldy committees may investigate and arouse public opinion about such issues as civil service salaries or the inadequacies of the telephone system.

The other external influence on administrative behaviour is that exerted by the pressure groups. Every branch of the French administration works in a constant symbiotic relationship with its client interest groups. If the groups demand services which only the state can provide, the state in turn is dependent on the groups for both their expertise and their legitimising influence. In practice, interest group representatives continuously advise and watch administrative activities through a vast network of committees and commissions. Over four thousand of these committees are attached to the ministries in Paris, whilst even in a small département the Prefect has to deal with a hundred or more local committees in which interest groups are represented. At the local level in rural areas farmers' associations are especially influential and often operate in close cooperation with the Prefect and the Ministry of Agriculture's services. The existence of such semi-corporatist institutions does not necessarily mean that groups can take over the parts of the administration with which they are in close contact (nor does it imply the opposite) but it does indicate that administrative actions are under a continuous and not always sympathetic scrutiny.

CONCLUSION

In France civil servants not only control the massive administrative machine but they also occupy key positions at all levels of decision making — in politics and in both private and public sectors of the economy. Some civil servants have moved over into politics to become mayors, deputies or ministers. Others play important advisory roles through their membership of presidential and ministerial staffs. There are also those senior civil servants who are involved in politics as advisors to interministerial committees. Finally, there are many important administrative posts where political decision making is unavoidable: this is the case notably for Prefects, planners and regional policy specialists.

Civil servants have also permeated the managements and boards of directors of many public enterprises and private firms. This movement from the administration into business, now a well-established tradition, is known as *pantouflage*. In the public sector industries three-quarters of top executive positions are occupied by former civil servants and in the nationalised banks it is virtually unknown for anyone who is not from the top ranks of the civil service to reach any of the key posts. Private sector firms compete with each other to gain the managerial talents of former civil servants. Members of the prestigious technical corps are to be found as directors and managers of almost all large private companies and members of the administrative grands corps are in growing demand.

There is, however, no permeation in the opposite direction of industrialists and business managers into the senior administrative corps, although civil servants who have moved across into industry may subsequently return to their original civil service corps. One effect of this civil service permeation is to make senior posts in the administration extremely attractive to talented young people at the start of professional life. A place in the Ecole Polytechnique or ENA, far from confining a student to a bureaucratic or technocratic life, opens up almost limitless possibilities of interesting, responsible and lucrative careers. A further effect of this permeation is that it creates a network of personal contacts which may facilitate negotiations. Some critics of the French administration further assert that it creates a coherent ruling class which occupies all the summits of power in French society. It is difficult to prove or disprove this assertion, although there is evidence that some former civil servants in industry rapidly adopt the norms of their new environment and use their knowledge of the administration against the state (in many cases they are recruited precisely for this purpose), whilst others remain only titular holders of their managerial positions, leaving major decisions to be made by their subordinates, the professional businessmen. In any case, the members of the top technical and generalist corps are deeply divided by differences of expertise, rivalry for posts, clashing roles, personality conflict and profound political disagreements.

The governments of the Fifth Republic were by no means the originators of the idea of continuous administrative reform. The provisional government after the Liberation had made sweeping changes and even during the Fourth Republic there was a steady output of minor reforms. As the state machine has grown, governments have become increasingly interested in its internal organisation. The leaders of the Fifth Republic, however, have been quite explicit about their intentions of improving the administrative structures of the state. Throughout the Fourth Republic Debré argued that France needed not only a constitutional change but also a reformed administrative system to complement it. One of his early actions as Prime Minister was to send a circular to his colleagues about the urgent need for administrative reform. Pompidou, if less radical in his approach than his predecessor, was more constant: the governments he led, both as Prime Minister and President, included Ministers for Administrative Reform. President

Giscard d'Estaing has continued this process, his most recent measures being the division of the Ministry of Finance and the creation of a Ministry for Feminine Affairs. The aims, methods and results of this 'permanent revolution' in administrative organisation merit a brief examination.

The goals of administrative reforms since 1958 have been laudable but also inconsistent and incoherent. On the one hand, the governments have wished to strengthen and rationalise the administration in order to make it more efficient. On the other hand, however, they have wished both to improve the effectiveness of governmental control and to create new means for effective citizen participation and consultation. They have sought to decrease the duplication of tasks and the amount of red-tape — but to improve coordination and to make legal, financial and technical supervision more effective. In practice, the priorities have varied considerably depending on the minister responsible, the political circumstances and the administrative service under consideration. In short, there has been no consistent approach to administrative reform during the Fifth Republic.

The preparation of administrative reforms has been approached in an interesting variety of ways. Reports on problems and proposals for change have been made by permanent committees (the central committee on the cost and efficiency of public services and the permanent mission for administrative reform are two examples), by individual ministers (the university reform of 1968 was very much the work of Edgar Faure) or by experts (the 'three wise men' approach). In some cases there have been experiments with different measures in different branches of the same administration (the 1964 local government reforms were preceded by a series of local experiments in 1963), whilst in other cases there has been large-scale consultation of those concerned (the questionnaire on local reform sent to all mayors in 1977 is one example of this). In general, the actual drafting of a particular reform has been the work of a special committee under the supervision of either the Prime Minister, the minister concerned or the Minister for Administrative Reform and staffed by those with detailed knowledge of the administrative service to be reformed. In practice, this has meant that most reforms have been drawn up by precisely those civil servants whose lives would be most affected by their results.

The effect of this confusion of aims and methods is that reforms tend to be long delayed and relatively ineffective. There is no doubt that there has been a vast output of reforms since 1958. Ministries have been created, disbanded, restructured and renamed with alarming frequency, local structures have been rationalised (if not simplified), new 'missionary' administrations have been established (of which DATAR and the tourism development 'missions' of Languedoc and Aquitaine are perhaps the most successful) and computers, public relations services, and RCB (the French equivalent of PPBS) have appeared in every branch of the administration. All this does not mean that the basic problems are in any way resolved. Coordinating bodies and 'missionary' agencies often simply further complicate existing decision-making patterns. There are many who argue that the creation of regions has simply added an extra level of administrators between ministries and local government or field services, which in practice means extra expense and longer delays. Both inside and outside the administration there are critics who insist that too much money and effort is wasted on the processes of preparing and carrying out reforms and that the services for the consumer are thereby reduced rather than improved. Given the ways in which reforms are made, however, it appears that administrative reform will be a never-ending process.

One of France's most popular conspiracy theories is that there is a 'state within the state'. The precise meaning of this slogan varies considerably, as does the identity of the inner — and presumably all-powerful — body. Recent writings have identified this 'inner state' as the now-divided Ministry of Finance, the former Ministry of Equipement, the Polytechnique 'mafia', the electricity corporation or even the Communist Party. Most frequently, however, the 'state within the state' is the 'techno-bureaucratic elite'. One of the themes of this examination of the French administrative system is that the power of these top civil servants is potential rather than realised — and this is in part the result of there being no unity amongst the very different and distinct technocratic and bureaucratic elites.

The French administration is vast, complex, unwieldy and divided in outlook. If the competence and dynamism are the legendary qualities of the grands corps, inefficiency and delay are the equally renowned characteristics of many of the lower levels. If many senior civil servants are politically sympathetic to the present government alliance, their subordinates give massive support to the opposition. Technicians and generalists are in constant and barely-muted conflict for power and for privileges. Ministerial divisions wage continuous, gentle wars with each other, with the field services, with the *cabinet*, with the Budget Ministry and even sometimes with their client pressure groups. Many civil servants, at all levels, would sooner react than initiate. There is a very real danger that the growth of the state has not, in practice, created a united all-powerful administration but rather led to increased fragmentation and thus to greater susceptibility to domination by interest groups.

CHAPTER FOUR

Germany

THE BACKGROUND

Germany attained a form of national unity with the foundation of the German Empire in 1871 round Prussia, its historically dominant component. A republican constitution was drafted at Weimar in 1919 but the new Republic perished of internal weakness compounded with external pressure and was replaced by the National Socialist dictatorship in 1933. Defeat in the Second World War led to the dismemberment of Germany in 1945: the territory to the east of the Oder-Neisse rivers was annexed by the Soviet Union and Poland, the remainder divided into three western zones of occupation (American, British and French) and a Russian zone. The occupying powers were at first only prepared to allow the revival of political activity at local and regional level, and the zones of occupation were divided into state units which were given the historic name of *Land* (plural, *Laender*) but in March 1948 the three western zones were combined into a common economic area. In July, as fear of German revival was replaced by alarm at Russian expansion, the Western powers resolved on political unification also and empowered the heads of government of the Western Laender to convene an assembly composed of members of Land parliaments to draft a common constitution. Anxious that the new state should not seem to exclude the possibility of a subsequent reunification of Germany, the constituent assembly called the document it produced a Basic Law (*Grundgesetz*), not a constitution. This came into force on 23 May 1949 and the Federal Republic of Germany began life on 21 September 1949.

The West German state established in 1949 has three levels of government: national government at Federal level; state government at Land level; and local government within the Laender. The essence of federalism is a division of power between two levels of government — Federal and state — and a paramount written constitution is required to protect this division: the prerequisite of federalism is the notion of law being binding on government. This was the principle on which earlier forms of German federalism were based and in its formal characteristics the West German federal system conforms to the traditional features of German federal government. The legal source of government powers is the Basic Law, which in turn seeks to anchor the constitutional system in immutable values. There is a catalogue of basic rights which are binding on all organs of government. These basic rights, the federal system and the participation of the Land governments in the legislative process are declared to be incapable of revocation. Thus the units of the federation enjoy a constitutionally guaranteed autonomy.

In a system based on the supremacy of law, all lawful power is exercised according to the constitutional distribution of power. The residue of power not specifically assigned must be located somewhere in the system and in German federalism that is the Laender. In practice, this principle is largely negated by another that Federal law overrides conflicting Land law in areas of joint competence. Taken to its extreme this rule could virtually destroy the federal system itself. To safeguard against this the 1871 constitution provided for a second chamber (*Bundesrat*) of the national parliament which consisted of delegations of state governments and had power to veto measures passed by the popularly elected house (*Reichstag*). The drafters of the Basic Law revived the Bundesrat and gave it extensive powers to prevent any fundamental change in the division of power in the federal system.

The revival of a new style federalism in 1948-49 constituted the ratification of developments since 1945, being less the result of policy than of inertia. The western zones of occupation had been divided into eleven Laender plus West Berlin. With the exception of Bavaria, Bremen and Hamburg, these were new creations with little cultural or historic identity. Nevertheless, they quickly became a vested interest: Land politicians were not going to legislate themselves out of existence. Federalism, however, had wider support: because the Nazis had abolished it, it was self-evidently right to revive it; it offered a safeguard against overmighty central government; the Western allies, sharing this view, ordained that the new Constitution should be constructed on a federal basis. The

Basic Law did make special provision for the amalgamation of three small and contiguous Laender and after an arduous and protracted campaign these were united to form Baden-Wurttemburg in 1952. In 1957 the Saarland returned to Germany to form the tenth Land of the Federal Republic. Since 1949 there have been many proposals for rationalising the number and size of the Laender. Political arrangements, however, exist to embody interests, not to conform to symmetrical patterns, and vested interests defending the existing Land boundaries have been sufficient to prevent any change. Nor would greater symmetry necessarily produce any human or political benefits. The untidiest feature of the whole arrangement is the anomalous position of West Berlin which under international treaty remains a special zone of occupation and is not formally part of the Federal Republic. Though integrated with West Germany politically and administratively, its representatives in the Bundesrat and Bundestag can only vote in committee, not in plenary sessions.

Laender: Population, Area, Resources

Land	Population 31.12.77	Area (km²)	Net Tax Yield 1976) (million DM)	Above/below Average Tax Yield 1977 (DM per person)
Schleswig-Holstein	2,587,000	15,700	4,700	− 115.38
Hamburg	1,680,000	750	5,690	+ 381.49
Lower Saxony	7,224,000	47,420	13,010	− 118.17
Bremen	703,000	400	1,880	− 187.32
North Rhine-Westphalia	17,030,000	34,060	37,200	+ 23.84
Hessen	5,541,000	21,110	12,240	+ 38.64
Rhineland-Palatinate	3,639,000	19,840	6,710	− 99.48
Baden-Wurttemberg	9,120,000	35,750	20,390	+ 100.01
Bavaria	10,819,000	70,550	21,330	− 30.73
Saarland	1,081,000	2,570	1,900	− 184.57
West Berlin	1,927,000	480	3,330	−

The Basic Law pledges the state to uphold and maintain 'the traditional principles of the career civil service'. Three times this century — in 1918, 1933 and 1945 — the German career civil service has survived as an institution and in its personnel the overthrow of the political order. This example of political discontinuity combined with administrative continuity reveals the dominant influence of the Prussian model on the development of the public service in Germany. The modern professional civil service was a peculiarly Prussian creation of the reforms of 1807-11 and constitutes a historical tradition which has endured to the present day.

The Prussian reformers sought to modernise the monarchical Prussian state and to assimilate its development to that of the more liberal states to the west. In Germany the modern state administered by a permanent civil service arose in the enlightened despotism of the eighteenth century. By the turn of the century the notion of authority had become depersonalised, so that civil servants were regarded not as servants of the crown but as servants of the state (*Staatsdiener*). By virtue of their service to the state, civil servants came to enjoy a special position. In the first half of the nineteenth century it became accepted that they could not be dismissed except by a highly judicialised disciplinary procedure; appointment carried with it the right to an incremental salary, automatic promotion, payment during illness and a pension. The subjection of civil servants to a code of disciplinary law heightened both their restrictions and immunities. The notion of public service became inseparable from the existence of a special category of salaried employee. Institutions did not matter as such: they were invested with a plasticity which mirrored the political transformations first of Prussia, then of Germany. What was important was the status of the personnel who staffed the organs of the state. Public administration revolved round the concept of the career civil servant (*Beamter*).

The Prussian reformers made civil service status dependent on educational qualification and gave schools and universities the function of training state servants. The four modern classes of civil servant were established and the point of entry to each class was linked with a grade of educational attainment. The training of the higher service was of special significance. In the eighteenth century entrants received an education in cameralistics, a vocational subject comprising elements of public finance, agricultural economics, estate management and law. In the Prussian reform era the growing scale of public services led to the development of the idea of general administration over and above technical administration. At the same time state activity became indissolubly linked with the notion of law, so that law alone was regarded as providing the appropriate education for the higher service. This subject was made obligatory in 1846, thereby confirming the *Juristenmonopol* — the requirement that entrants to the higher civil service should have a legal training.

The Prussian reformers also gave the organisation of public administration an enduring form. They wished to construct a centralised modern state in imitation of the Napoleonic system. Prussia, however, lacked a natural capital in the way that Paris and London have established a tradition of metropolitan dominance in their respective countries, while extensive concessions had also to be made to the particularism of the Prussian provinces. The system of Prussian administration combined functional and regional specialisation. Five classic central departments were established in Berlin — Interior, Finance, Justice, Foreign Affairs and War — and constituted 'upper tier authorities'. With the exception of tax offices, there were in principle no specialist administrations below the upper tier, the central departments worked through generalist officers at middle and lower tiers instead. Prussia was divided into administrative districts (*Regierungsbezire*) headed by a District President (*Regierungspräsident*) and into subdistricts (*Kreise*) of which there were two types, urban and rural. The former developed their own elected organs of government, headed by an *Oberbürgermeister*; the latter remained units of state administration ruled by the *Landrat*, a generalist field official, and were further subdivided into municipalities (*Gemeinden*) headed by a *Bürgermeister* who was not a state official. This hierarchical system of administration divided all the territory of the state into geographical units and established a tradition of unified decentralisation which gave sovereignty to the central power but devolved administrative functions to intermediate and lower levels of authority.

Public administration thus came to be defined in terms of the state. In Britain, because Parliament seized sovereignty from the Crown, there was no need to develop a theory of the state as something apart from and superior to the monarch. In Germany, however, where monarchical rule endured much later, constitutional progress assumed the form of the subordination of the monarch to the state and the definition of the state in terms of law. The state was — or should be — the expression of legal order. Such a state was a *Rechtsstaat,* a system of power deriving from and observing clearly promulgated rules. It followed that civil servants, in executing part of the authority of the state, were engaged in a legal exercise. Therefore a legal education alone could equip the administrator to discharge his function in the Rechtsstaat. In applying the law, moreover, the administrator was not engaged in a purely executive function, because the particular form which the separation of powers doctrine assumed in Germany placed in the hands of the civil service an extensive power to make law.

British legislation seeks to maximise precision and concreteness. In Germany legislation establishes general principles, while detailed regulation is left to those who have the responsibility of applying rules. This extends far beyond the statutory authorisation of the executive to issue delegated legislation (*Rechtsverordnungen*): the real law-making power of the administration consists in its inherent capacity to issue administrative regulations (*Verwaltungsvorschriften*). While all dealings between the administration and other persons or bodies must rest on law, within the administration there is a law-free zone. Higher organs in the administrative hierarchy can give directions to lower ones based on the power of command and duty of obedience. Administrative regulations are internal measures applicable to civil servants, determining how statutes and delegated legislation are to be applied. Given the general terms in which these are formulated, much of what a law means in practice is determined by administrative regulations which require neither parliamentary authorisation nor, in general, are liable to scrutiny by the courts.

By the middle of the nineteenth century state activity had come to extend over the whole range of economic and social life. To free policy-makers from executive functions and detailed supervisory work, and to distinguish primary from subsidiary exercises of state power, statutory bodies were set up to carry out designated functions on behalf of the state.

The law of the state and its organisation is public as distinct from private law. Under public law there are a number of legal devices which any level of government can use for the purpose of delegating tasks to subordinate agencies. These public law agencies are equipped with the sovereign powers of the state, i.e. the capacity to make rules and impose penalties, and matters concerning them are in general subject to the jurisdiction of the administrative courts as opposed to the ordinary courts. They are given functions by law but left free to choose how to accomplish their task subject only to limited supervision. Ordinary government departments are supervised by the courts to check that their actions are within the law and that they use their discretion wisely; public law agencies are supervised only for the former.

Public law agencies are referred to as organs of 'self-administration'. The whole of German public administration is permeated by the distinction between 'state administration' (*Staatsverwaltung*) and 'self-administration (*Selbstverwaltung*). However, the latter term is confusing, so the alternative formulation of 'direct state administration' as opposed to 'indirect state administration' will be used here. The three leading examples of the provision of services by means of government agency are local authorities, the funds which administer pension and insurance schemes, and public utilities — gas, water and electricity.

In the early nineteenth century Prussia moved from monarchical to bureaucratic absolutism. The administrative apparatus and powers of the modern state preceded the rise of representative institutions and the German parliament came to coexist alongside the civil service. Constitutional theory sought to reconcile the *Beamtenstaat* with the *Parteienstaat* by invoking the separation of powers doctrine. Executive and legislature were seen as taking different and coordinate roles in a functionally divided system of government.

The civil service could not be cast in the role of the agent of the government, because it was the government. Civil servants came to stand in what the Basic Law calls 'a special relationship of service and loyalty to the state' and were entrusted with a monopoly over 'the exercise of the sovereign powers' of the state. They traditionally engaged in politics in the sense of policy making, judging what was in the interest of the state by the light of standards administered by themselves. They had an alternative and higher loyalty to that which they owed to particular monarchs, ministers or Cabinets. Governments came and went: the state abided and its continuity was embodied in the civil service. Because of this 'political' responsibility for policy, it was early recognised that the principle of irremovability from office was inappropriate for officials who held leading positions. Hence in 1848 a special category of political civil servant was introduced who can be removed from office at will and placed in temporary retirement contrary to the general rule. The other side of the coin is that civil servants in general have always been free to engage in party politics and in principle all enjoy the right to be elected to Federal, Land or local assemblies.

The task of elected bodies is not to control executive government directly. German liberals never demanded the political or parliamentary responsibility of ministers. Parliament legitimises the executive by providing the legislative framework within which it works, but this the executive fills out with administrative regulations. Public administration is defined by German writers as the residue of power which belongs neither to the legislative nor to the judicial branch of government. Thus the distinctions between policy making and advice and between policy and technical functions, which have played such a large role both in British constitutional theory and the structure of the British civil service, were wholly inappropriate to German circumstances. Those who have risen through the party hierarchy take part in government on equal terms with those who have come up through the civil service hierarchy. According to the German view, constitutional government requires the separation, not the fusion, of executive and legislature. Hence the Basic Law's article which guarantees the existence of the professional civil service follows from that which ordains that the state is based on the separation of powers.

Thus the 'traditional principles of the career civil service', which the Basic Law enshrines without specifying, extend to the heart of German tradition and the West German political order. In the first place these principles entail that there shall be a distinct category of employee, found in a wide range of institutions, known as the career civil servant. Their position is characterised by material rights — irremovability, non-contributory pension and social insurance — which have been extended to other categories of employee both within and beyond the public service. The special character of the public service is preserved by the ban on strike action and the requirement of a special loyalty to the state. Civil servants, moreover, are regarded as in some sense exercising a part of the state's authority. The state's authority differs from other forms of influence in that it is peculiarly associated with the rule of law. This does not require an apolitical bureaucracy which operates exclusively by logical deduction from general rules — the civil service is a fully political factor in the state — but that each political organ should have specific rather than general functions and that power should be distributed by law between executive and legislature, between Federation and Laender and amongst myriad public law institutions. As the Federal Constitutional Court has expressed it, the Basic Law, drawing on the tradition of German administration, regards the career civil service as an institution which, based on specialised knowledge, technical competence and loyal discharge of duty, guarantees stable government and thereby represents a balancing factor in respect of the other political forces which shape the life of the state.

More generally, the existence of the career civil service is bound up with what may be called — in a convenient but inaccurate term — all the values of middle-class society: the tedious virtues of a respectable occupation; education as an instrument of social differentiation and entitlement to an adequate income; scorn of irregular perquisites; the realisation of personal ambition in socially acceptable forms. In a word, the civil service, with all its manifold ramifications, is part of what German writers call *Kultur* and it survived the political transformations of Germany because the sort of society which valued the things with which it was associated also survived.

THE INSTITUTIONAL FRAMEWORK

The Party System

In West Germany the principal units of administration are the Laender. It has been suggested that West Germany does not have a truly federal system, simply a form of administrative decentralisation. This proposition would be tenable if political power were concentrated in national parties which dictated policy to the Federal and Land governments, thereby rendering nugatory the separation of functions of the federal system. Since 1969 a marked trend towards polarisation between two national parties has been detected in West Germany. Nevertheless, the two-party system has never taken root in Germany and the struggle for power is conducted in a different mode from that of British politics.

To all intents, there are three national parties: the Christian Democratic Union (CDU), conservative with an autonomous Bavarian wing called the Christian Social Union (CSU); the Social Democratic Party (SPD); and a small liberal party, the Free Democratic Party (FDP). Since 1949 governments have remained coalition-based. All the parties have at some time somewhere been in coalition with each other. Even if a single party has an absolute majority of seats in the elected house (Bundestag), this would be inadequate for the conduct of essential government business for several reasons.

First, because the Basic Law contains much detailed regulation it has been found necessary to amend it frequently to carry through political changes (thirty-four times between 1949 and 1977). This requires a two-thirds majority in both houses of parliament which can only be secured if government and opposition vote together (unless, as in 1966-69, the CDU/CSU and SPD form a Grand Coalition). Each Land also has a constitution which has to be adapted to changing circumstances. The system requires government and opposition to cooperate in this respect. Second, all major legislation requires the approval of the upper house, the Bundesrat. Because the Bundesrat and Bundestag are constituted by different means, their political composition diverges. To a certain extent the constitution institutionalises conflict between the two houses, hence the Federal government has to compromise with the Bundesrat to secure the enactment of its measures. Thirdly, the Federal government has to cooperate with the Land governments, not only because they are parties to the legislative process through the Bundesrat but also because they are leading elements in the administrative process. The opposition in Bonn will invariably be in government in some of the Laender. At any time all the parties will be in power somewhere. Hence party differences have to be subordinated to some extent to the common interest in carrying on the government of the republic. Thus there exists a traditional preference for a broad cross-party measure of agreement, and this runs through the whole system of public administration.

Powers of Federation and Laender

Because public administration is regarded as a branch of law, it is to a unique extent organised and conducted according to rules. National rules originate from the Federal goverment but have to be approved by the Land governments. These express their consent through the Bundesrat, which is an appointed not an elected assembly and consists of delegations from the Land governments. Including four West Berlin delegates who can only vote in committee, the Bundesrat consists of eleven delegations with between three and five members depending on size, making a total of forty-five members, and votes are cast en bloc in plenary sessions.

Constitutional amendments are the most formidable measures to pass into law, followed − in declining order of difficulty − by laws requiring consent, ordinary laws, decrees and regulations. The general rule is that all bills passed by the Bundesrat are subject to a suspensive veto or amendment by the Bundesrat but the latter can be overridden by a corresponding majority in the Bundestag. 'Consent laws', however, require assent of the Bundesrat. The distinction between these and ordinary laws is nowhere defined in the Basic Law but sections scattered throughout the Constitution state that laws on a particular subject require consent. In general, they affect the powers, interests and activities of the Laender. By 1973, 55 per cent of all laws were consent laws, the most important group flowing from the broad interpretation given to the article which deals with Federal regulation of Land arrangements for implementing Federal law. In each case it is up to the Bundesrat to decide whether or not to treat a bill as a measure requiring its consent. It can be challenged in the Federal Constitutional Court but few such occasions arise as in cases of doubt the Bundesrat prefers to use its power, exercisable in respect of all bills, to refer a measure to a Mediation Committee composed of an equal number of members of both houses to seek an agreed version of a bill. Agreement is much easier in committee because Bundesrat members vote individually and are not legally bound by the instructions of their governments. In this committee, as in all other Bundesrat committees, Land civil servants normally take the place of their ministers, further illustrating the fully political role of German civil servants.

The Federal government and Federal ministers have extensive powers to legislate by decree delegated to them by individual statutes. The parent law must fix the content, aims, extent and limits of such decrees and the latter can be declared invalid if the parent law is too imprecise. A decree which, if it had been a statute, would have required the consent of the Bundesrat, also requires such approval, as do all decrees based on consent laws. Federal authorities also issue administrative regulations which must have the consent of the Bundesrat if directed to Land ministries.

As far as the respective powers of the Bundesrat and state parliaments (*Landtage*) are concerned, the Basic Law distinguishes between the exclusive, concurrent, framework and — by implication — reserved (i.e. residual) spheres. A list of subjects is enumerated on which exclusively the Bundestag can legislate. In a further — concurrent — list the Laender have in principle the right to legislate, but where a matter is inappropriate for regulation on a Land basis the Federation may pass laws which then override Land law. The Federation also has power to issue framework laws *(Rahmenvorschriften)* in specified areas, of which the most important are public service law and the general principles of university education. All matters not specifically assigned in these ways belong to the reserved sphere in which the Landtage alone can legislate. In practice these distinctions are of little importance. Federal powers are so broadly constituted and constructed that Federal legislation almost wholly displaces Land legislation on matters of substance. In German federalism it is the function of the national government to make laws and there exists a high degree of Federal legislative uniformity as a result. The powers of the Landtage are restricted to the reserved sphere — the police, the organisation and functioning of local government, broadcasting and cultural matters, and education up to university level — and the enactment of Land legislation to implement Federal law. The importance of the Bundesrat in national legislation is the counterpoise to the weakness of Land parliaments.

As far as the Federation and Laender are concerned, there are five types of public administration: Federal administration; Land administration of Land laws; autonomous Land administration of Federal laws; Land administration of Federal laws as agent; and administration by government agencies. The field of direct Federal administration embraces foreign affairs, defence, the armed forces, the Federal police, the railways, the post office, inland waterways, air traffic and the collection of certain taxes. For these tasks the Federation has its own administrative apparatus and there are no equivalent Land ministries. Federal administrative networks are organised on a three tier basis: Federal ministries or offices whose competence extends over the whole country, districts and local offices. Different agencies have created different units (for example, the Federal Railways has ten districts while the Federal Post has eighteen). Nor do district and local units correspond to political divisions.

Education forms the largest single item of Land and local authority expenditure and school organisation varies from Land to Land. Radio and television belong to the sovereign power of the Laender, as a leading decision of the Federal Constitutional Court confirmed, and, singly or jointly, they have established broadcasting agencies. Each Land has its own police force under the ultimate authority of the Land Minister of the Interior but relative uniformity of organisation is achieved because the Federal government gives subsidies in return for conformity with federally determined standards and because the Police Administration Laws in all the Laender have a common basis in earlier Prussian legislation. Federal police powers are restricted to the Border Guard, a central information office in Wiesbaden and the coordination of measure against subversion; in special cicumstances Land police can be put under Federal orders. Local government is also a matter for the decision of Land government and assumes a wide variety of forms throughout Germany.

The Laender are also responsible for administrating Federal legislation in the many fields for which there is no Federal administration. Much of this involves independent Land administration. The administrative autonomy of the Laender is laid down as the general rule in the Basic Law, leaving the Laender free to decide how Federal measures should be enforced. There is provision for various forms of Federal supervision and take-over in the event of Land contumacy, but these powers have not so far needed to be invoked.

A higher degree of supervision is provided for in the field of delegated administration, however, where the Laender act as agents of the Federation. The vital distinction between independent and delegated administration is that the Laender pay for the former while the Federation pays for the latter. Though the Basic Law originally restricted the Federal tasks which might be delegated to the Laender (with motorways the principal item), the constitutional amendments of 1968-9, which lay down that whenever the Federation provides 50 per cent or more of the costs of the programme the Laender shall be its agents, virtually give the Federation a general power of delegation.

Both levels of government make extensive use of agencies. Indirect Federal administration is carried out by public law corporations, of which the principal ones are for health and social security. Compulsory insurance for medical treatment, loss of earnings, accident, unemployment and retirement covers the whole employed population: contributions are paid to and benefits administered by a multitude of different Insurance Funds. Medical treatment, for example, is paid for by Sickness Funds of which there are some 1,850: if a fund draws its contributors from within one Land, it is supervised by the Land Social Minister, if it draws contributors from more than one, it is supervised by the Federal Insurance Office which is a branch of the Federal Ministry for Labour and Social Affairs. Within Laender the prime agencies to which administrative tasks are delegated are the local authorities.

Financial System of Federation and Laender

It is a fundamental principle of Land autonomy that the greater part of the financial costs of services are met out of the general allocation of funds to the Laender rather than by specific grants from the centre. An entire section of the Basic Law is devoted to this question. After substantial revision, something like finality was achieved by the Tax Reform Law of 1955. The system adopted by the Bonn Republic represents a compromise between the two previous methods of adapting public finance to federalism. In Imperial Germany all taxes were — with minor exceptions — collected by the states, which paid grants to central organs. In the Weimar Republic, by contrast, all taxes were collected by the Federal government and the Laender were compensated with grants in aid from the centre. In the Bonn Republic different shares of a common tax revenue accrue to Federal and state governments, while the yield of other taxes is assigned exclusively to one or other level, the basis of allocation regulated by the Basic Law. All taxes can be classified as 'mixed' (yield distributed between more than one level of government) or 'exclusive' (yield assigned wholly to one level of government): two-thirds of tax revenues are mixed, the remainder is raised by divided taxes.

The Federation has exclusive legislative competence over customs and excise, and concurrent power over taxes which accrue to it in part or where the need for regulation on a federal basis exists. In practice, determination of taxes is exercised by the Federation to avoid unacceptable variations in the incidence of taxation in different parts of Germany through Land or local authority action, such variations being specifically prohibited by the constitution. Wherever the yield of a tax is assigned wholly or in part or to the Laender or local authorities, however, Bundesrat consent to Federal legislation is required.

The principal yield is from income and corporation taxes, the latter on company profits. The 1955 law fixed the Federal share of these at 35 per cent and the Laender share at 65 per cent, subject to biennial revision. Local authorities complained bitterly that they were dependent on the bounty of Land governments for a share in these revenues. The 1969 reform conceded that local authorities should receive 14 per cent of the income tax collected in their areas: the balance was to be divided equally between Federation and Laender, giving each 43 per cent; corporation tax revenue is divided equally between the Federation and the Laender. As *quid pro quo* for giving the local authorities a share of income tax, it was agreed that the Federation and Laender should each receive 20 per cent of the tax on business premises which had hitherto flowed exclusively to local authorities and which still remains the principal source of their income. Thus what was given with one hand was taken away with the other. The purpose of this reallocation of tax revenues was to safeguard the financial balance between levels of government, which would be upset if one tax proved a more dynamic source of revenue than another. Value-added tax, previously a perquisite of the Federation, was in 1969 brought into the share-out because the Federation could only secure a higher fixed proportion of income and corporation taxes at the price of giving the Laender a share in VAT: since 1976 the Federation gets 69 per cent, the Laender 31 per cent.

West Germany wishes to combine a federal system of autonomous regions with uniform incidence of taxation and uniform levels of social provision in all parts of the country. The apportionment of taxation between different levels of government, though complex, is simplicity itself when compared to the financial equalisation system which redistributes revenue from rich to poor Laender and from rich authorities to poor local authorities. The actual tax yield in each Land is weighted by its population, resources and requirements: this calculation shows whether it has an above average tax capacity and so contributes to equalisation, or a below average capacity and so receives equalisation. In 1977 four Laender were contributors (Baden-Wurttemberg, Hamburg, Hessen and North Rhine-Westphalia), while the remainder (Bavaria, Lower Saxony, Rhineland Palatinate, Bremen, Schleswig-Holstein and Saarland) were beneficiaries of the system. Land governments are responsible for conducting financial equalisation among local authorities.

The distribution of revenue among the various levels of government is based on the different functions which they discharge. The principal items of Federal expenditure are defence and the balancing of social security funds which are in a state of perpetual deficit. Though the bulk of government services are paid for by the Laender and local authorities, Federal funds flow freely to the Laender and local authorities by virtue of the provisions concerning delegated administration and by the general constitutional provision that any Federal programme which places undue burdens on them should be defrayed by Federal subsidies.

The collection of taxes raises special problems. When the Basic Law was drafted the Western Allies, in accordance with their requirement that West Germany should be established on a decentralised basis, forbade the revival of a national fiscal administration. Taxes which accrue solely to the Federation (customs and excise) are collected by the central government. All other taxes are collected by the Laender but where the yield is shared with the Federation they act as its agents: the principal revenue authorities are thus effectively joint Federal-Land agencies. The Laender can in turn delegate the collection of local taxes — notably the business premises tax — to local authorities. Thus the device of delegated administration enables administrative cohesion to be reconciled with the integrity of the different levels of government.

Federal-Land Cooperation

The federal system in West Germany has been characterised as 'executive-legislative federalism' on the grounds that the Federation makes law which the Laender implement; the political power of the Federation is thus balanced against the administrative power of the Laender. This division of functions is not and cannot be clear-cut: through the Bundesrat the Laender play an extensive role in Federal government; through delegated administration, which has been extended far beyond the narrow ambit conceived by the constitution, the Federation plays a major role in the administrative process. The elaborate formal modes of dividing functions must break down in practice, because governmental functions as a rule embrace more than one level of government so that national and state governments share in most tasks of government except defence, foreign affairs, the post and railways.

When the functions of government were more restricted, Federation and Laender could behave towards each other rather like sovereign states. This tradition has not wholly disappeared. From 1949 to 1969 the Federal Cabinet included a Minister for the Bundesrat and Laender Affairs who in theory acted as the channel of communication between the two levels. The Laender still maintain permanent delegations in Bonn, headed by a Plenipotentiary who acts as an ambassador to the Federal government. The common affairs of Federation and Laender are extensively regulated by an infinite number of legally enforcible treaties and administrative agreements whose exposition forms a constant preoccupation of the Constitutional and Administrative Courts.

Since 1945, however, the characteristic means by which governmental cooperation has been pursued consists in permanent conferences of Federal and Land ministers. The chief of these is the Conference of Minister-Presidents (Land heads of government) which meets once or twice a year. Eleven others, dealing with finance, justice, education, the interior and other major fields of administration, meet more frequently and in turn have spawned countless committees with civil service participation. Their aim is to secure common policies on the basis of exchanged information and views (e.g. standardisation of school terms, school examinations and teacher training).

The great virtue that is claimed for the German federal system is that it enables national policies to be adopted to local needs. Taken to an extreme, however, its decentralisation could lead to a fragmentation of decision making which would preclude real decisions. The Laender, indeed, frequently give the impression of being bureaucracies intent on maintaining their existence rather than instruments of national policy. The arrangements of German federalism are also highly contrived. The system of public finance, for example, resembles an endless series of transfers of money from the left to the right pocket. In practice, the deleterious effects of federalism are offset by the influence of the party system. The parties which are required to work together are national parties which have shown readiness to place national considerations above regional interests and governmental considerations above political differences.

The Federal Chancellor

In the Empire established by Bismarck in 1871, the Chancellor was the sole minister. One by one offices were established, each headed by a civil servant of State Secretary rank who was accountable to him. In the absence of a collegiate government the Chancellor had the responsibility for coordinating these departments, with power to lay down rules of policy binding on all government departments ('guidelines competence'). The weakness of the Imperial Chancellor was his exclusive dependence on the Emperor. The fathers of the Weimar Constitution made the Chancellor dependent on and dismissable by parliament. A collegiate government was established ('Cabinet principle') but the Constitution also declared that each minister conducted his department 'independently and under his own responsibility to the Reichstag' — the 'office principle' of departmental autonomy. The Chancellor was overshadowed by the President who had an independent position, being elected by universal suffrage for seven years, and secure powers of his own.

When the Basic Law was drafted, the Federal government was strengthened at the expense of the President and Bundestag. The Bonn Republic finally killed the Kaiser by reducing the President to solely formal and representative functions. According to the

Basic Law 'the Federal government consists of the Federal Chancellor and Federal Ministers' but the pre-eminence of the Chancellor was maintained. He alone is voted into office by the Bundestag and can only be removed by a vote appointing a new Chancellor (the 'constructive vote of no confidence'). His appointment requires an absolute majority of members and so he must in practice be the leader of the dominant party in parliament. He embodies the Federal government and is the connecting link between executive and legislature. The Chancellor's formal supremacy continues to be symbolised by the guidelines competence which takes the place of collective responsibility in the British system of government. Whatever the government does is assumed to be the expression of the Chancellor's policy and all members of the government are bound to support it as long as they hold office. The purpose of the guidelines competence is that the head of government should serve as a counterweight to the centrifugal pull of party loyalties and departmental particularism. To enable the Chancellor to unify government policy, he has at his disposal a ministry of his own.

The Office of the Federal Chancellor is the linear successor of Bismarck's Chancellery established in 1878. Once a collegiate Federal government based on party coalitions was established in 1919, it became the hub of government. A key to its powers was the fact that the head of the Chancellery acted both as chief adviser to the Chancellor and as Secretary of the Reich Cabinet. The Chancellery formed the nodal point of government and administration in that the Chancellor communicated with departments through the Chancellery. It was re-established in 1949 and from 1952 it became known as the Office of the Federal Chancellor, the shift of name revealing that the office had developed into the personal instrument of the Chancellor. The circumstances of the foundation of the Federal Republic heightened the importance of the office and made it centre on the Chancellor rather than the Cabinet.

The changed party system after 1945 made government much more stable. The first Federal Chancellor, Konrad Adenauer, held office for a period (1949-63) equalling the life of the Weimar Republic, during which there had been fourteen occupants of the office. While the chancellorship was stabilised, Cabinets remained coalition-based, a circumstance which inhibited the development of the Cabinet into a homogeneous committee. Hence the Cabinet was a body acted upon rather than acting.

Adenauer neglected fields of government of peripheral importance. However, he installed as head (State Secretary) of the Office
a trusted associate, Hans Globke, a born eminence grise with a
genius for exercising authority in the guise of diffident self-
effacement. He ensured that the Chancellor's guidelines permeated
the whole range of government activity. A system of rotating civil
servants between the Office and the other ministries was established,
so that it had agents and ambassadors throughout the government
machine. Globke also exploited the Chancellor's right to information as a means of controlling other ministries and coordinating
policy. The Rules of Procedure of the Federal Government state
that the Federal ministries must inform the Chancellor of 'matters
significant for the determination of the guidelines of policy and the
conduct of the business of the Federal government'. The Office has
divisions, each responsible for the supervision of certain ministries
and areas of policy. Ministries send in monthly reports which are
annotated and submitted to the Chancellor via his State Secretary.
It was also made responsible for monitoring the legislative process
in the Bundestag and for negotiating with parties and parliamentary
committees to overcome obstacles to the progress of the government's legislation.

In its modern form the Office of the Federal Chancellor has
become the place where all the threads of government run together.
It prepares and executes the decisions of the Federal government,
coordinating the departments in the exercise of the Chancellor's
guidelines competence. It directs foreign and defence policy. The
State Secretary is the best informed man in government: he channels
information to both the Chancellor and Cabinet and as senior State
Secretary he presides over the informal cabinet of State Secretaries.
Like other Federal ministries, it has a number of 'subordinate
offices' attached to it, including the Intelligence Service and the
Press and Information Office of the Federal Government. The
latter is an enormous publicity apparatus at the disposal of the
Federal Chancellor and its head — known as the Government
Spokesman — is a leading figure in government.

In 1969 Horst Ehmke (SPD) was appointed to the Cabinet as
ministerial head of the Chancellor's Office. Rather than adopt the
discreet tactics of Globke, Ehmke sought by means of structural
changes to integrate within the Chancellor's Office the planning

and overall direction of the government as a whole, so that other ministries would respond to initiatives of the Chancellor's Office, rather than vice versa. Greater and mightier ministers than Ehmke, however, were not prepared to accept such dictation and this innovation was discontinued in 1972 when the Office returned to the hands of a State Secretary. It has retained a planning division, however, which works in conjunction with planning sections in the ministries.

The Federal Government

The number and functions of Federal ministries are determined by the Chancellor according to political and administrative requirements. Cabinet ministers are appointed and dismissed by the President at the Chancellor's behest. Cabinets have varied in size from nine to twenty members. When the Grand Coalition of the SPD and CDU/CSU was formed in 1966 there were too few government offices to go round and to remedy this the office of 'parliamentary state secretary' was introduced in 1967 whereby a member of the Bundestag was appointed to assist each departmental minister. While this office has been retained subsequently, the real deputy ministers are the civil servants of State Secretary rank: the larger ministries have two (Chancellor's Office, Foreign Affairs, Interior, Finance, Economics, Defence) while the others have one. They constitute the 'ministerial bureaucracy' and are effectively part of the government.

Federal Government and Ministries, 1978

Federal Chancellor (Office)
Foreign Affairs
Defence
Interior
Justice
Finance
Economics
Food, Agriculture and Forests
Labour and Social Affairs

> Transport, Post and Telephones
> Inner German Affairs
> Environment, Building and Town Planning
> Youth, Family and Health
> Education and Science
> Economic Cooperation
> Research and Technology

The ratio of government posts to Bundestag members is low: one in seventeen compared to about one in six in the British House of Commons. A minister does not have to be able to perform well in parliamentary debates because plenary sessions are unimportant in the Bundestag in comparison with committee work. This situation reinforces the separation of legislature and executive. Because ministers are recruited from Land politics or from outside politics as well as from the Bundestag, Cabinet members lack the common background of a political training in parliament. As Cabinets are coalition-based, they also lack a common party allegiance. Most of the Cabinet's routine business is dispatched without discussion: draft decisions are circulated to ministers; if within a narrow time-limit none request that the matter be put on the agenda, it is formally approved. Ministers are busy people who know that other ministers, like themselves, resent the questioning of one department's decisions by another, hence over a wide field of business the Cabinet ratifies rather than decides.

In view of its weak collegiate character, instead of becoming internally specialised through the development of a Cabinet committee system of the British type, the Cabinet has taken the road of external expansion to embrace a wider range of participants. At Cabinet meetings parliamentary and official State Secretaries regularly take the place of their ministers. Because of the partial separation of legislature and executive, the parliamentary leaders of the governmental parties are not members of the Cabinet, though they frequently attend it. Outside experts, such as the head of the national bank, are called in for consultation. Cabinet committees - on matters such as economics, defence, foreign affairs, education and the environment — are conferences of experts rather than sections of the Cabinet to which it delegates decisions.

From the nature of the Cabinet it follows that ministers are concerned with the running of their departments rather than the integration of departmental policies into a general government programme. Rather than a unified central administration, there is a loose confederation of ministries. Ministers work in isolation from each other and do not regard themselves as personally involved in the coordination process.

With the exception of Defence and Foreign Affairs, Federal departments have relatively few executive responsibilities. Hence they tend to be all generals and no soldiers. Those tasks which are not performed by Land ministries are often devolved on semi-autonomous subordinate offices. The Transport Ministry, for example, is formally responsible for weather-forecasting but this work is actually performed by the German Meteorological Office in Offenbach. The responsibility of the Ministry of Labour and Social Affairs for supervising a wide range of Insurance Funds is discharged by the Federal Insurance Office in West Berlin. Where the bulk of administration is performed by the Land counterparts of a Federal ministry, the latter's role is restricted to the drafting of legislation, the allocation of money and the coordination and supervision of the work of Land governments. This, in turn, means that several Cabinet posts are of relatively minor political importance, which reduces the significance of the Cabinet as a whole.

The Basic Law states that within the Chancellor's 'guidelines' each minister conducts the affairs of his department independently and under his own responsibility. Their autonomy, however, is limited by the powers of the Ministry of Finance. Though management of the economy is the task of a separate Ministry of Economics, the Finance Minister's powers over the budget, anchored in the Basic Law, ensure it a central role in government and it reinforces the coordinating role of the Chancellor's Office.

In preparing and implementing the budget the Finance Ministry acts as controller of public expenditure. In the 1960s, however, financial control of public expenditure through annual budgets fell out of favour in West Germany, as elsewhere. It was criticised for concentrating on candle-ends and ignoring macro-economic factors. To supplement traditional budgetary methods, medium-term financial planning based on estimates of economic growth was advocated and in 1966 the Finance Ministry was given responsibility for drawing up a five-year plan, containing budgetary projections of revenue and expenditure in the light of macro-economic assumptions and targets. A Cabinet committee was established, known as the Finance Cabinet. Because Land governments and local authorities are responsible for some 40 per cent of public expenditure, a consultative Financial Planning Council was set up with the Federal and Land Finance ministers, four local authority representatives and a representative of the national bank.

As a result of these changes the Finance Ministry gave up detailed financial scrutiny in return for control over the totals. The need to relate public expenditure more closely to projected economic growth brought the Finance and the Economics Ministries closer together, and in 1971 they were merged, only to resume their separate existences in 1972, partly because both coalition parties wanted a minister concerned with economic affairs. The result of financial planning has been an increase in unplanned deficits. Economic planners characteristically overestimate growth and underestimate expenditure. Germany's conversion to financial planning came after the rate of economic growth had passed its zenith, and two decades of growth without planning gave way to planning without growth.

The Basic Law guarantees the budgetary autonomy of the Laender and the Laender in turn confer a similar freedom on local authorities. The infallible result of this arrangement is that spending always exceeds the level which the Federal government regards as desirable. To secure greater Federal control over public expenditure a constitutional revision was undertaken in 1969. In the face of Bundesrat opposition, however, the result was a compromise formula stipulating only that Federal and Laender budgeting 'shall be adjusted to the requirements of macro-economic equilibrium'. No institutional means have been provided for turning this aspiration into reality.

Land Government

North Rhine-Westphalia, Bavaria, Baden-Wurttemberg, Lower Saxony, Hessen, Rhineland Palatinate, Schleswig-Holstein and the Saarland each have a Cabinet headed by a Minister-President and consisting of ministers supported by State Secretaries. The three city states of Hamburg, Bremen and West Berlin have, instead, a Senate and senators, led in Hamburg and Berlin by a Chief Burgermeister, in Bremen by a Senate President. Their civil service heads of departments are known as State Councillors.

All Laender have ministries of the Interior, Finance, Economy, Transport, Labour and Social Security, and Education. The key minister is the Minister of the Interior who in the Prussian tradition is head of the general internal administration, has command of the police and is responsible for all matters for which no specific ministry is named. Land ministries also have a number of autonomous operational units attached to them. In the city states the Land government doubles as the major local authority, but elsewhere there are a number of political and administrative units below Land level.

(1) The government district has been retained as a unit of decentralised administration in the six larger Laender (North Rhine-Westphalia, Baden-Wurttemberg, Lower Saxony, Hessen, Bavaria and Rhineland Palatinate). The District President is a very senior 'political' official, appointed by the Minister-President and under the control of the Minister of the Interior. He serves as the agent of Land government in matters delegated to him and is the principal executive institution within the Land, bringing the threads of government in a district under a single roof. The District President controls Land police in his district. He supervises for legality the activities of local authorities and public undertakings. The schools inspectorate and audit office report to him. His office administers Land funds for education, roads and housing, whether directly expended or paid to local authorities. It also has an extensive administrative law function: giving legal opinions to local authorities and hearing appeals from individuals aggrieved by their actions. It supervises industry and commerce, with power to issue warnings and impose fines for breaches of law, appeal from which lies to the ordinary courts.

(2) The Kreis as a subdivision of the Land has been adopted throughout Germany. In 1831 the Stadtkreis (county borough) was given corporate status and government was vested in a local chief executive, the Oberburgermeister, and elected councillors. The characteristic 'double role' of local authorities was established at the same time. For certain purposes the Stadtkreis remained a unit of state administration, and in performing these tasks the Oberburgermeister is the agent of the state and acts under instructions. In performing the tasks which had been allotted to local government, however, he is the officer of the corporation. When acting in

this capacity, the District President has no power to issue directives to him and the corporation itself is subject to supervision only for the legality of its actions. Stadtkreise are now generally towns with a population of 80,000 or above.

(3) The Landkreis was given corporate status and an elected government in 1872, the Landrat remaining an officer of the state administration for certain purposes and became the officer of the corporation for others. The Landkreis (one may think of an English county) is further divided into municipalities. The principal difference between the two as local authorities is that the municipality has universality of competence, whereas the Landkreis only has those functions given to it by law: in general it performs those tasks which are either beyond the financial capacity of the former or cannot properly be performed in a local framework. In its capacity as an agent of state administration the Landkreis is, for example, the housing and highways authority. As an autonomous corporation the Landkreis administers savings banks, hospitals, secondary education, vocational training, public assistance and the provision of gas, water and electricity. The organisation of Landkreis government varies from Land to Land but always contains three elements: an elected Council, an executive committee and the executive officer, variously named Landrat, Kreisrat or Oberkreisdirektor: in Saarland and Rhineland Palatinate he has remained a state official but in all other Laender he is a local official.

The Landkreis finances itself by a levy on the tax receipts of municipalities in its area. The Stadtkreis is not divided into municipalities and so receives all the revenue which would normally be due to them. Certain tasks of Kreis government are beyond the capacity of all but the largest cities. The commonest solution is for Kreise jointly to form public undertakings for specific services, e.g. the supply of gas, electricity or water. Alternatively, the Land government can establish multi-purpose territorial corporations at the intermediate level between Land and Kreis and vest the administration of larger projects in them, thereby extending the principle of indirect state administration.

(4) The functions of municipalities (*Gemeinden*) can likewise be classified as 'delegated' and 'autonomous'. They are multi-purpose authorities, responsible for everything not assigned to other authorities. As in the case of the Kreis, single tasks can be delegated

to joint undertakings. The Burgermeister is as a rule appointed for a fixed term by the council and his role varies according to the constitution of the municipality. In the last decade there has been a sharp reduction in the number of municipalities, from 24,282 in 1968 to 8,991 in 1974. The creation of larger municipalities by process of amalgamation, together with the rapidity of communications and the centralisation of Land politics through the political parties, have led local leaders to deal directly with Land ministries, thereby diminishing the importance of the Landkreis government and — where he exists — the District President. The vested interests of appointed and elected officers in district and Kreis government, however, have hitherto prevented any reduction in the layers of government between municipality and the Land. Thus an individual can be subject to up to five levels of administration: Federal, Land, district, county and municipality.

THE CIVIL SERVICE

Structure of the Civil Service

One of the leading features of German public administration is the enormous breadth of the civil service concept. The civil service is not only everyone who wields state authority but also every policeman, judge, person in the armed forces, school teacher, university professor, postman, train driver and every public sector employee. The reasons for the relentless diffusion of the notion of public service go to the roots of German development. In Britain wide areas of social life — education, local government, religion, health and welfare — have traditionally been conducted by independent corporations and institutions. In Germany such activities have been carried on through the state and in forms determined by it. The status of official is also highly prized, in the past for its social prestige and security of employment, now perhaps more for the generous non-contributory pension rights and social insurance which accompany it.

For all its institutional diffusion, the public service remains highly unified. In Prussia the civil service was a body of state servants distributed over a wide range of autonomous bodies but all employed on the same terms and subject to the same conditions. The corporate identity of civil servants overrode institutional divisions. The pattern set by Prussia proved influential throughout Germany. Even before 1871 the principles of the Prussian civil service had been widely adopted by other German states; after 1871 they were generalised throughout Germany by the Civil Service Law of 1873, whose successor is the Federal Civil Service Law of 1953 (revised 1977). Of the subjects on which the Federation may issue framework legislation in order to ensure proper regulation in the interest of the whole country, the first on the list is 'the legal relationship of the persons employed in the public services of the Laender, municipalities and other corporations in public law'. The Federation thus has power to lay down general regulations on appointments, training, conditions of service and legal responsibilities of all public servants, including those in indirect state administrations and those in unpaid offices. When a Land government sought to raise judges' salaries unilaterally, the Federal government, fearing that public service pay would rise unpredictably if scales varied among Laender, secured a constitutional amendment which brought the regulation of pay and pensions into the catalogue of concurrent powers, thereby filling in the gaps in its framework powers. Hence there is a homogeneous body of public service law.

The term 'public service' (*öffentlicher Dienst*) is a broader term than 'civil service' (*Beamtentum*) as not all people in public employ have the status of official. The historical division of the personnel of the public service into 'officials' (*Beamten*), 'employees' (*Angestellten*) and 'workers' (*Arbeiter*) has been retained. Of the total public service (excluding the armed forces), 42 per cent are officials, 34 per cent employees and 24 per cent workers. The official alone is entrusted with the exercise of the sovereign powers of the state, enjoys a special position in public law, is required to have a special loyalty to the constitutional order, must obey orders from his service superior, cannot lawfully strike, and is entitled to non-contributory pension and social insurance rights. The official alone is subject to disciplinary law and claims which he has against his employer are referable to the Administrative Courts. As a result of the Prussian reforms all officials must have prescribed educational qualifications on entry to the service. Employees and workers are employed on contractual terms subject to the jurisdiction of the Labour Courts, perform work less directly connected with the exercise of state power and have contributory pension and insurance schemes. In practice the categories overlap to a considerable extent in terms both of formal status and of the types of work done.

The triparite structure of the public service is mirrored in trade union organisation. Officials belong to the German Federation of Officials (the most influential — with 800,000 members a pressure group of formidable strength), employees to the German Employee's Union and workers to the Public Service, Transport and Communications Union; school teachers, particularly those of more radical persuasion, often belong to the Education and Science Union. Only the first draws its membership exclusively from the public service and this homogeneity reinforces its pre-eminence.

Personnel and Public Services, 30 June 1976

Federation		
Federal Ministries	299,000	
Railways	405,000	
Post	417,000	
		1,121,000[1]
Laender		
Central Administration	106,000	
Finance	117,000	
Police	186,000	
Administration of Justice	115,000	
School Teachers	479,000	
University Staff	223,000	
Medical Personnel	66,000	
		1,292,000
Local Authorities	870,000	
Social Insurance Funds	198,000	
Public Utilities[2]	423,000	
		1,491,000
		3,904,000

1   Excludes armed forces and border guard
2   Gas, water, electricity

The annual salary increases agreed for officials have set a standard for the whole economy and to some extent served as a form of indirect incomes policy.

The institution of industrial co-determination (*Mitbestimmung*) has not been introduced to the public service but elected committees provide consultation and advice on conditions of work. These Personnel Councils, which resemble the British Whitley Councils, are a medium by which the unions disseminate their influence in the public service.

The scale of public sector employment has always been very considerable. In 1976 there were — excluding the armed forces which contain a large number of conscripts — four million people employed in the public service out of a working population of 27 millions, i.e. 15 per cent. To this may be added half a million part-time staff and over a million pensioners. In so far as the proportion of the working population employed in the public service has significantly increased in recent years, this may largely be ascribed to teachers and others employed in education.

Within the framework of Federal law each Land makes inde-pendent provision for the civil service. Within Laender civil servants are classified either as direct or indirect Land officials, depending on whether they are employed by the Land or by a government agency (e.g. a local authority). While there is variation in such matters as training, this is not sufficient to impair the overall legal unification of the public service. Amongst other things, this enables people to transfer easily from one Land to another or to the Federal service.

The unity of the public service is most strikingly realised in the grading of all official posts in the direct state administration — including the railways, post offices and armed forces — according to a uniform scale of ranks and salaries. Posts are divided into those with incremental salaries and senior posts with fixed salaries, graded from A1 to A16 and B1 to B11 respectively. Within each grade are grouped a number of posts each with its own title, in many cases untranslatable because they only make sense by reference to the point which they constitute in the civil service hierarchy. Trad-itional German society has long been regarded as attaching excessive importance to titles of office holders and this characteristic owes much to the influence throughout society of the civil service rank structure. What matters, however, is not the title itself but the fact that it gives a precise indication of the holder's salary, educational attainment and social status.

According to the entry qualifications required, there are four 'career groups' of officials, each providing a self-contained career structure. They are:

Higher Service (*höherer Dienst*)	A13-B11
Executive Service (*gehobener Dienst*)	A9-A12
Clerical Service (*mittlerer Dienst*)	A5-A8
Basic Service (*einfacher Dienst*)	A1-A4

The points of entry to the different classes dovetailed with the traditional school system. Though the modern school system varies from Land to Land, in principle all children proceed from primary school to one of three types of school: intermediate (normally leading to trade school), secondary or grammar. The hallmark of the grammar school (*Gymnasium*) is that it alone can award the *Arbitur*, the certificate of fitness for university established in 1788. Secondary school pupils who wish to work for this exam can transfer to a grammar school. Entrants to the higher service must have studied at university for three years; entrants to the executive service must have attained the Arbitur; entrants to the clerical service must have passed the secondary school certificate; entrants to the basic service must have passed the intermediate school certificate. The key division is that between A8 and A9: all entrants to A9 upwards must have been awarded the Arbitur and commissioned ranks in the armed forces begin at A9.

An official must also complete the period of in-service training prescribed for his class. Although appointed as an official at the start of this training when he also takes an oath to the Constitution, it is only when he has completed his in-service training and probationary period, and has reached the age of 27, that the appointment is made for life.

The Higher Service

On the administrative side of the higher civil service the hierarchy roughly corresponds to the British services as follows:

Permanent Secretary	*Staatssekretär*	B11
Deputy Secretary	*Ministerialdirektor*	B9-B10
Under Secretary	*Ministerialdirigent*	B5-B7
Assistant Secretary	*Leitender Ministerialrat*	B3-B4
Senior Principal	*Ministerialrat*	A16-B2
Principal	*Vortragender Rat*	A15
Administration Trainee	*Assessor*	A13

The peculiarity of the training of entrants to the higher service is that they have traditionally undergone the same training as lawyers. When in the nineteenth century it was established that administrators required a legal training, it followed naturally that they should have a common education with judges and lawyers. There is a two-stage process consisting of a First and Second State Examination, with an interval of practical training between them.

Examinations which afford qualifications for careers are organised by the state and are conducted by boards consisting of professors and other civil servants. There are various ways in which students can qualify as candidates for higher service posts, but the general rule is that entrants must have studied for at least three years at university and have passed the First State Examination in Law and Social Sciences. Examinations are conducted in each Land by a Legal Examinations Office (with appeal from the examination board to the Land Minister of Justice). The candidate then applies to the President of a Land Court of Appeal to be admitted into government service as a Referendar (again with appeal to the Minister of Justice). Once admitted he becomes a probationary civil servant and spends about two years in practical training: for one-third of the time he is attached to government offices, for the remainder he works in law courts and with public prosecutors. This makes him eligible for the Second State Examination in Law and Administrative Studies, and only after this stage is successfully completed do the paths of administrators, judges and private practice lawyers diverge. The administrative civil servant applies to a government department for admission as an Assessor. Once appointed he is then bound to reach the rank of A16 (Ministerialrat) by regular promotions.

The aspirants to posts above this normally extend this period of education and training by completing at some stage a university doctorate in law or a related subject (note that the German doctorate requires less research than the English; candidates for university posts must complete a much more substantial work, the *Habilitation*). The academic character of German in-service training is enhanced by the fact that Referendars and Assessors can spend six months or a year at the High School for Administrative Sciences in Speyer which was established in 1947 on the model of the Ecole Nationale d'Administration in Paris and has the status of a university. It is maintained by the Rhineland-Palatinate government but the Federation and other Laender contribute by paying fees when they send trainee civil servants to attend courses. The influence of the Speyer school can be said to have confirmed rather than modified the academic and legal bent of the higher service.

Students who have equivalent qualifications in other subjects, combined with requisite practical experience, can be exempted from either or both State Examinations. Diploma students of a Technical University can be admitted to the Second State Examination after two and a half years' professional training, while those qualified in the pure sciences can apply for admission to the higher service after four and a half years' appropriate work. However, Germany does not have anything like the Scientific Civil Service in Britain. The work of the latter is by and large carried out by government agencies which — as institutions of indirect state administration — do not have the uniform rank structure and system of entry which binds together all units of the direct state administration. Therefore there is little incentive for those with technical and scientific qualifications to apply for posts in the administrative higher service. Thus in the absence of a distinction between policy and technical functions, or of parallel hierarchies of administrators and specialists such as exist in Britain, lawyer-administrators hold sway in the higher posts of government.

Estimates of the number of lawyers in the higher administrative service depend on definitions. A jurist in Germany is anyone who has had a legal training but the requisite academic study includes a wide range of social science subjects, while the practical training is common to a number of professions including administrators, practising lawyers, judges and tax accountants. Thus 'lawyer' is a protean description. The Federal Post is a government department and the Federal Railways are legally part of the Ministry of Transport: engineers fill many leading posts in both but they are different types of organisation from ordinary ministries and it may be misleading to regard them as part of the administrative civil service. Given the large number of subordinate offices performing technical functions which formally constitute part of ministries, such examples could be multiplied. Hence estimates of the number of lawyers in the higher administrative service vary from 46 to 85 per cent.

The education and training of higher civil servants reflects the whole ethos of administration. In Germany administration is considered as a formal art, not an exercise in pragmatic wisdom, and administrative acts are justified by reference to law rather than by invoking practical reason. It is axiomatic that civil servants should be educated in subjects appropriate to the formal, juridicial character of administration. While the utility of this training is undoubted, its wider effects are more controversial. In its classic nineteenth-century form, German administrative law fostered the notion that administrative problems could be solved by the application of law alone. From this it was inferred that the task of administration was to find the correct legal solution to problems and that administrative solutions were more objective, more reasonable, less self-seeking than political solutions. From this derived the traditional bureaucratic ethic which stressed the political neutrality of the state, its superiority to social interests and the organisations embodying them, the value of obedience and authority as opposed to debate and partisan activity. These notions are now much scorned as devices to conceal and advance the interests of social groups anxious to maintain the governmental status quo. The real criticism, however, is that they overlooked the active role which civil servants played in parliamentary politics as soon as representative institutions were called into existence alongside the apparatus of the bureaucratic state.

Socialising effects are also attributed to the prescribed education of higher civil servants. German university students are dispropor-tionately middle class in origin and half the entrants are recruited from families of civil servants. The system confirms existing social divisions and is according to Dahrendorf the expression of 'the real inner continuity of German officialdom'. The shared background leads to a distinct caste identity which − it is argued − makes officials hostile to social change: 'Lawyers' . . . conservative education tends to make them into defenders of the social status quo, their origin predestines them to identify the interests of the middle and upper class with those of the whole community'. Such observations may be regarded as sociological hyperbole. The civil service is and should be a source of stability in society, devoted to upholding the constitutional order. That order also contains an in-built capacity for continuous change, and political change goes hand in hand with social change. Hence political attitudes cannot be reduced to being simply for or against some unspecified thing called the established order.

Appointments and Promotion

While uniform entry qualifications and standards of training are laid down by law, the actual system of appointment is highly fragmented. Though the Federal Ministries of the Interior and Finance have certain responsibilities for the civil service as a whole, there is no centralised recruitment agency corresponding to the Civil Service Commission in Britain. Each ministry, each local authority, each government agency goes about selecting staff in its own way. For entrants to the higher service, the prestige Federal ministries — the Office of the Federal Chancellor and the Foreign Ministry — organise a series of tests and interviews which last for a week and closely resemble the procedure of a Civil Service Selection Board in Britain. In others, such as Youth, Family and Health or Economic Cooperation which appeal to those who prefer a secure niche in the civil service to the risks and rewards of competition, the same procedure lasts half an hour.

The great bulk of promotions take place automatically. Within ministries and agencies the power to promote is vested in internal commissions and — in the absence of a centralised management of the service — civil servants tend to make their whole careers in the same department. When a post in the administration is advertised — as when a municipality seeks a new Burgermeister — officials with the appropriate educational and service qualifications may apply for it. In practice the political parties often decide which official is to be appointed to such a post. Indeed, the rotation of officials by political parties to some extent takes the place of the rotation of officials by a central personnel department. This is especially true of the highest appointments, which are made by ministers or by the Federal or Land Cabinet as a whole.

From B7 all civil servants are 'political', i.e. they can be pensioned off at the minister's discretion. In filling such posts ministers may appoint someone from outside the department who may not necessarily have the ordinary civil service qualifications. In the past it was rare to go outside a department, let alone outside the service, to fill these senior posts but in the changed circumstances of the Bonn Republic about one-third of appointees to these posts are outsiders. As a result, the leadership of the civil service has become heterogeneous in composition and administration has been assimilated to politics. The most remarkable single example was in August 1978 when the Federal Building Minister (SPD) appointed the 32-year old Burgermeister of Regensburg as State Secretary of his ministry. In the appointment or displacement of political officials the party affiliation of the individual invariably plays a role. Instead of outright removal, an official may be moved from a key to a marginal post and the bulk of displaced political officials secure reappointment within the same ministry. The possibility always exists, however, of being placed in temporary retirement on reduced pay. This prospect has never deterred anyone from accepting promotion out of B6. In the first five years of temporary retirement the official receives 75 per cent of his salary, an income which in the 1st Earl of Durham's phrase is 'such a one as a man might jog on with'. Moreover, officials of this level of seniority can normally find employment outside the civil service, particularly if they are able to present themselves as the martyrs of political faction.

'Temporary officials' are officials appointed to a post for a limited period, the most common example being a Burgermeister. If at the end of their term they are unable to secure another appointment, they too can be placed in temporary retirement.

The traditional system of organising the civil service is subject to two general criticisms. First, it is said to produce excessive departmentalism. The Federal civil service lacks any elite group which can transcend departmental loyalties. Most civil servants make their careers within a single department, which unduly narrows their vision and flexibility. There is no provision for rotating them which would give them, as Lord Bridges has observed, 'a wide and synoptic understanding of the problems of government as a whole'. Second, because of the rigid educational prerequisites for entry to a particular career group, it is very difficult to transfer from one class to another. In the days when civil service classes dovetailed fairly closely with established social structures, this was generally accepted but now it is regarded as an unjustifiable handicap to aspiring merit.

The Berufsverbot

The 'traditional principles of the career civil service' require a fundamental loyalty to the state on the part of the official. This is the 'special relationship of service and loyalty to the state' specified in the Basic Law, which is as old as the career civil service itself. The West German state established in 1949 was particularly sensitive to this need, firstly because in the Weimar Republic the civil service was widely regarded as lacking in basic loyalty to the state, secondly because West Germany was particularly exposed to subversion from East Germany. Against this background, the Civil Service Law of 1953 incorporated the requirement that the civil servant should be an active defender of the democratic order.

In the late 1960s sections of German university students experienced a wave of left-wing rejection of West German society. They advocated the overthrow of parliamentary democracy by non-parliamentary means (hence their name APO — Opposition Outside Parliament). When this failed, without reversing their goal, they changed their method to the 'long march through the institutions', i.e. subversion from within. Whether or not this phenomenon was of long-term political significance, the Federal and Land governments had to deal with its immediate effects as candidates of extreme views came forward for appointment to administrative and judicial posts, and new teachers in schools shocked parents by substituting their own form of teaching for what they regarded as bourgeois indoctrination.

In view of both public reactions and what was perceived as a real threat to the integrity of the public service, the Federal and Land governments issued the 'Radicals' Decree' of 1972 (a misnomer: it was not an administrative regulation but a circular, agreed by the Chancellor and the Federal and Land Ministers of the Interior, reminding public authorities of the democratic order clause in the civil service laws). As a result government offices began to investigate candidates for the civil service in order to exclude those whose fundamental loyalty to the state was suspect. This administrative practice was widely challenged before the administrative courts but was ultimately upheld by the Federal Constitutional Court in 1975, which held that it followed from 'the special duty of loyalty of the official that he must unambiguously distance himself from groups which oppose the existing constitutional order'.

This overt political scrutiny of applicants to the civil service has been named by its critics the 'vocational ban' (*Berufsverbot*). In proportion to the numbers employed, the number adversely affected by the ban has been very modest — about a thousand people have either dismissed or denied appointments. Against this figure must be set the very much larger number of cases investigated by the Office for the Protection of the Constitution — over 700,000. Besides raising important matters of principle, the ban is unwieldy in operation because of the great breadth of the public service.

Recently some SPD governments, in particular the Senate of the city state of Hamburg, have announced their intention of confining this scrutiny of public service applicants to key areas: the police, internal administration and the administration of justice. Formidable legal and political obstacles stand in the way of such a modification of the current practice. Moreover, public authorities have to move within the limits set by the relatively narrow political consensus which prevails, whose defensiveness ultimately derives from the German sense of the enemy at the gate.

Political Activities

Administration in Germany has traditionally been regarded as the application of law not the exercise of discretion. Civil servants regarded themselves as a supplementary source of leadership to party politicians because they were servants of the state which stands above politics. To be 'political' in German usage meant to engage in party politics. In the broader sense of engaging in the leadership of the state, the German civil service has always been political. Hence there has never been any distinction between policy making by elected ministers and policy advice by officials. Officials have also long been political in the limited sense of engaging in party politics. From the beginnings of German parliamentarism they formed the largest single occupational group of deputies. Since 1949 party affiliation has become the prerequisite for a wide range of public appointments and in the sphere of political posts outsiders have frequently ousted career civil servants. The result has been called an enmeshing (*Verfilzung*) of career patterns and styles of behaviour which has integrated parties and bureaucracy.

The Basic Law confirms that officials may be candidates in elections but allows restrictions to be placed on this freedom. For example, Kreis officials cannot as a rule be elected to the Kreis Council which they serve or municipal officials to the municipal council. In general, there has been a luxuriant growth in the parliamentary representation of officials who now comprise some 43 per cent of the membership of the Federal and Land Assemblies. Such figures, however, can be misleading. Teachers form the largest occupational group among officials serving in parliament; administrative officials constitute 18 per cent of parliamentarians, a less striking but not inconsiderable proportion.

A leading factor has been the very favourable financial arrangements for those combining an official with a parliamentary career. Until 1975 an elected official was placed in temporary retirement and received 60 per cent of his former salary, with regular promotion and increments. As a member of parliament he received a considerable salary and expenses in addition. He qualified simultaneously for a civil service and a parliamentary pension, and was entitled to return to the public service at any time. If he could also practise a profession, he could at the least double or treble his income. A judge could receive 60 per cent of his former salary, his parliamentary salary, his outside earnings as a lawyer and qualify for two pensions without giving up the security of his official post. To cap all this, parliamentarians have a vested interest in raising civil service salaries as their remuneration is geared to civil service rates: the elected official might thus have the agreeable duty of voting himself a double set of salary and pension increases. Vested interest prevented the Bundestag from modifying this disagreeable spectacle. It was a situation ripe for remedy by the Constitutional Court which in 1975 went out of its way to hold that a civil servant elected to a salaried representative office could not simultaneously receive a pension as a temporarily retired official. According to the draft Law on Deputies his civil service post is suspended without pay from the day of his election to six months after the expiry of his mandate, though in other respects the position remains unchanged.

While this has removed one anomaly, the career interest of civil servants in party politics remains strong. Once a sizeable number of officials develop and express party affiliations, it is no longer possible to decide personnel matters without reference to the party to which individuals belong. From this it is only a short step to a system in which the holding of the correct party-book is the prerequisite for appointment.

In the sphere of political posts (B7 and above) it has always been accepted that the ruling parties should appoint civil servants of their choice. From 1949 to 1969 the long CDU/CSU hegemony in national government led to the permeation of the higher reaches of administration with overt or covert CDU/CSU appointees. Since the SPD-FDP coalition assumed office in Bonn in 1969, there have been extensive personnel changes in Federal ministries as officials belonging to the SPD and FDP have been appointed in their place. The domination of civil service personnel policies by considerations of party allegiance extends far beyond the narrow scope of political posts, however. The great goal of political competition between the parties has become control of patronage and a party elected to power at any level is obliged by the expectations of its supporters to favour candidates of its political colour in matters of appointment and promotion. Hence an SPD government will try to appoint SPD headmasters and CDU administration will as a rule appoint CDU public health officers. The concomitant of this process has been the flood of civil servants into the parties: it is estimated that almost 9 per cent of officials belong to political parties and something like 15 per cent of party membership consists of officials.

To the English this is all redolent of the spoils system. In a German context, however, the intermeshing of public service and party politics helps secure the proper subordination of the appointed to the elected branches of government. Political parties are instruments for filling offices and competition between the parties in a democratic society enables a measure of equity to be preserved in the distribution of the fruits of office. The facility with which leading civil servants can move into politics overcomes the institutional barriers between the administration and political leadership. If administration is inherently a political activity, then — it can be argued — it is better that this should be taken into account rather than concealed by constitutional fictions.

In Britain government is controlled in part by the institutionalised rivalry which exists between the permanent administrators —

whether in national or local government — and the elected representatives of the people. In Germany, civil servants and politicians are overlapping, not exclusive, categories; moreover, rivalry between the parties is limited by the overall preference for a consensual rather than an adversary mode of politics. Adam Smith long ago observed that people of the same trade seldom meet together without their conversation ending in a conspiracy against the public. To the outsider, it may seem that party politicians have colonised the state, shared out its rewards and organised its affairs to their own advantage, an impression which can only be strengthened by the favourable financial terms on which it is possible to combine political and civil service careers. It is partly because of this weakness of in-built controls of government that the German system has come to lay such emphasis on legal control.

THE CONTROL OF ADMINISTRATION

The Rule of Law

In Britain, because of the sovereignty of Parliament, legal means of controlling the administration have been eclipsed by political means, embodied above all in the doctrine of ministerial responsibility to Parliament for all acts of the administration. In West Germany parliament is subordinate to the constitution, and in consequence the rule of law takes priority over the claims of parliament.

While sharing many of the formal elements of the British Parliament, the substance of the Bundestag is very different. Because civil servants, far from remaining anonymous, play a vigorous part in political life, they have no need to hide under their ministers' skirts. The Bundestag's preoccupation with law making in committee rather than with confrontations between Government and Opposition in plenary debates attenuates the parliamentary role of ministers. In 1952 Question Time on the British model was introduced to supplement parliamentary scrutiny of ministers but this institution cannot in Germany attain the importance of its British equivalent because it does not have the additional function of providing a testing ground for ministers and future ministers. Indeed, German ministers normally send their State Secretaries — official and parliamentary — to deal with parliamentary questions. Ministerial responsibility is to the Chancellor rather than to parliament, and the real meeting ground for ministers and members of parliament is in the specialised committees of the Bundestag where legislation is made. In these committees civil servants regularly take the place of ministers and participate on the same terms as parliamentarians. The function of the German parliament is to legislate: administration is a legal activity, properly left to the supervision of the courts. To the British no matter is more fundamental to the control of government than scrutiny of public expenditure; in Germany the auditing of public expenditure is conducted by a judicial body independent of both Cabinet and parliament, i.e. the Federal Court of Accounts.

The specialist committees of the Bundestag also provide a focal point for consultation between interest groups and government departments. The electoral system enables interest groups to nominate through the political parties representatives directly on to the committees of the Bundestag dealing with their field of activity. Hence the Economics Committee of the Bundestag is dominated by the Federation of German Industry, the Agriculture Committee by the German Farmers' Union and the Home Affairs Committee by the German Federation of Officials. Interest groups have similar close links with government departments which are fostered by the recruitment of civil servants to posts in the Bonn headquarters of interest groups. The intimacy of the links between the administration, parliament and interest groups makes it difficult to discern who is controlling whom. Therefore one must ultimately turn to the courts for an objective scrutiny of what the administration does.

In Britain there is, as Dicey pointed out, no special body of law applicable to acts of public authorities and, where answerable in law, the latter are subject to the ordinary courts of the land. In continental systems there is a separation of administrative courts and ordinary courts. This feature has always been regarded as an essential characteristic of the Rechtsstaat. In the past remedies against the administration through the administrative courts were confined to cases specified by law; other cases went elsewhere or had no legal redress at all. As the functions of the state increased, the citizen's scope for appeal was steadily widened. The Basic Law stated that whenever a citizen was injured by an act of public authority he should have legal redress and if no administrative court had jurisdiction, then the ordinary courts would hear the case. The jurisdiction of the former was extended by a decree of 1960 which made them competent for all legal disputes involving public authorities, provided that these were not of a constitutional nature or assigned to special courts.

'Administrative jurisdiction' is concerned with the resolution of disputes between citizens and the administration, or between different units or levels of administration. The administrative courts decide such cases on the basis of law but statute law may itself be challenged for conflict with the higher law of the constitution. German theorists had long debated whether or not the courts did or should have the power to review the constitutionality of statutes. The Basic Law settled this question on favour of review: a Federal Constitutional Court was established at Karlsruhe with the power of determining the constitutionality not only of enacted but also of proposed laws. Its scope is very wide because the Basic Law enshrines fundamental rights which are made binding on all organs of government including the legislature. All citizens prejudiced in their fundamental liberties by actions of the state have access to the Court. In conjunction with the constitutional guarantee of legal redress, this means that anyone who believes he has an action against public authority and is rejected by the administrative and the ordinary courts can proceed to a constitutional complaint. In addition, each Land has a constitutional court empowered to declare Land laws invalid because repugnant to the Land constitution.

The influence of the Federal Constitutional Court permeates the whole system of government. Because all administrative acts are subject to challenge, the statute laws on which they are based must be drafted in a manner consistent with the constitution, and subordinate legislation must respect both the parent statutes and meet the tests of equity and reasonableness expressed in the general principles of German administrative law. It should not be thought, however, that the administration is perpetually hamstrung by the need to cite precise authority for every act it undertakes. The assumption underlying administrative law is that of the superiority of the state to the citizen and other social interests. The administration also acts on its own initiative as the repository of the inexhaustible and imprescriptible duty of government to safeguard the community. To reconcile this paramount duty with the principles of the Rechtsstaat, German legislation makes general grants of power which in effect provide the administration with a discretion to act in what it holds to be the national interest.

Administrative Courts

Control by administrative courts evolved naturally from the hierarchical organisation of Prussian administration, for its origins lie in the appeal to a higher authority against the decision of a lower authority. To this day a citizen must first seek an 'informal legal remedy', as it is called, within the administration before he can go to a court. The first stage is simply to request the decision making authority to reconsider and it is bound by law to answer. If this does not satisfy the citizen, he may complain to the supervisory authority. Every unit of administration is subject to supervision by a designated superior authority, among whose tasks is the hearing of administrative appeals. For example, the Landkreis supervises the municipality and complaints against the latter are taken to the former's legal committee composed of the Landrat and two councillors. If the complainant is still not satisfied he can appeal to the administrative courts.

The general administrative courts operate on three levels. District-based courts of first instance hear cases in divisions consisting of three professional and two lay judges. Appeals go to a Land court and may then be taken on matters of Federal law or general principles of administrative law to the Federal Administrative Court established in West Berlin in 1952, both sitting in senates of three professional judges. The Federal Court also hears disputes of an administrative nature between Land governments or between the Federation and a Land.

In order to relieve the burden of these courts, special administrative courts have been established for certain matters. In 1965 appeals against the decisions of tax authorities were transferred to a new set of Revenue Courts operating at Land level, with a Federal appeal court in Munich. Disputes involving social insurance matters — an ever growing source of litigation — have likewise been devolved since 1953 on a separate set of Social Insurance Courts at district, Land and Federal level, the latter in Kassel: all cases are heard by panels of one professional and two lay judges. Disciplinary courts — courts-martial and courts which deal with breaches of civil service regulations by officials — are also classified as special administrative courts. It is a testimony to the comprehensive jurisdiction of the general and special administrative courts that, outside them, there exist hardly any administrative tribunals of the type which have burgeoned in Britain.

The jurisdiction of the administrative courts extends generally to all 'administrative acts'. This is a term of art but essentially means a decision of an authority, taken in an individual case in the field of public law and affecting a member of the public. It is thus narrower than the corresponding concept in French administrative law which embraces general regulations as well as individual decisions. The determination whether or not there has been an administrative act is of crucial importance, because this alone grounds the jurisdiction of the administrative courts. German law recognises that if the administration carries out an activity of a private character, such as owning property or entering into a contract, it is governed by private law. Public law is applicable where the administration has the power to impose unilaterally obligations on individuals or where the public interest governs relations between the administration and the private individual. German law has never been burdened with any of the conceptual or practical difficulties which accompanied actions against the Crown in Britain before 1947. In its private capacity the state has a separate legal personality (the *Fiskus*) and can sue and be sued in the ordinary courts in the same way as anyone else. In individual cases it may be extremely difficult to decide in which capacity the state is acting.

The judges of the administrative courts enjoy full judicial independence. They are appointed after the standard legal training of all entrants to the higher civil service and thereafter pursue a career in a particular branch of administrative jurisprudence. Neither the Constitutional Court nor the Federal Administrative Courts gives legal advice to the government in the manner of the French Council of State. Contact between the administration and administrative courts, however, is fostered by the practice of appointing some administrative civil servants to them.

Law and Procedure

Administrative law is not codified and so has no central point of reference. Its sources are a multitude of individual enactments and the general principles of administrative law developed by the courts, which enforce on public authorities a set of procedural rules analogous to the rules of natural justice in Britain. The Administrative Courts' Decree of 1960 sought to establish a uniform set of rules governing administrative remedies and in general the same procedures apply however a particular course of action arises. To ground the jurisdiction of the courts there must have been an administrative act, and to give a plaintiff *locus standi* he must show that his rights have been injured, either directly or indirectly. (For example, if a local authority gives A permission to extend his house and this adversely affects B's property, then B can use the normal administrative law remedies to challenge that permit.)

The grounds on which an administrative act can be impugned are — very generally — that it contravenes some legal norm or that it constitutes an improper exercise of discretion. Once it has been established that a plaintiff has a *prima facie* case, the court takes over the burden of investigating the facts and law of the case, assisted by a state attorney. The plaintiff — in theory — sits back and lets the court do the work. Below Federal level there is no requirement to be legally represented and proceedings can be informal, especially in the Social Insurance Courts. These features make it easier to bring a case than under adversarial procedures — like the British — where the plaintiff must assemble his own case. It is also because of the investigative function of the courts that German judges spend their careers working in one branch of law and increase in specialisation as they rise in rank. The sovereign ease with which senior English judges move from one branch to another is a source of amazement to Germans — but German judges have to perform the work of both counsel and the bench in England. The first stage of the court's work is a preliminary investigation intended to settle a matter cheaply and expeditiously if possible, which must generally be instituted by the plaintiff within one month of the administrative act complained of. If this fails to settle the matter, he brings a suit to annul the decision, to clarify his rights, or oblige the administration to do or not to do some act. Within one month of the verdict either party can appeal. In Social Insurance Courts all proceedings are free, but elsewhere the general rule applies that the losing party must bear the full costs of the case.

The scope of German administrative jurisdiction is very broad and its procedures are not intimidating. The criticism is nevertheless made that redress through legal procedures only draws in a limited number of the cases where an individual believes that an administrative decision should be different from that with which he is confronted. It has been argued that what is needed is a yet more extensive and flexible review procedure, of the sort carried out by the Ombudsman, but this has so far been decisively rejected in Germany. Decisions — the argument runs — are either legal or illegal; questions of legality are to be determined by the courts; to introduce a third category of administrative acts is to erode the distinction between legal right and legal wrong and thereby undermine the Rechtsstaat itself. In the case of the armed forces a Military Ombudsman has nevertheless been introduced because when the armed forces were re-established in 1955 memories of harsh discipline were live: he hears individual complaints and makes an annual report to parliament.

CONCLUSION

The intermeshing of politics and administration has become one of the leading characteristics of German public administration. No official who cares for his job can work without regard to the political parties. For example, a Burgermeister whose term of office is about to run out must canvass the party secretary to know what his next appointment is going to be. By the same token those who want posts in the public service can approach them through the medium of party. Whatever advantages in terms of political responsiveness this overlapping of politics and administration may bring, it also produces the impression that the state is a gigantic vested interest serving the personal enrichment of politicians and administrators. In the public service there has been a multiplication of highly paid posts with cast iron security, so that a German ministry characteristically has more Deputy and Assistant Secretaries than office cleaners.

The overlaying of administration by politics has also led to the diffusion of responsibility. In the days when party involvement was a rarity among civil servants, responsibility for particular decisions could be ascertained by tracing the hierarchical line of command to their source. It was a matter of honour in Prussian administration to decide as much as possible at every level of government without reference higher. Hence responsibility was ascertainable and civil servants were prepared to take responsibility. Once the vertical hierarchy is subject to the horizontal pull of parties, it is no longer clear who is deciding what. Paradoxically, the old official ethic of administration being a matter of applying law without regard to political considerations, and law as embodying a general interest apart from the particular interests of the parties, still survives and is influential. In many a German Burgermeister two souls struggle in one breast, that of the official and that of the party politician. The German official has both to implement policy and justify what he does politically, and in moments of stress longs to be where the wicked cease from troubling and weary are at rest.

Legal rules remain the vital unifying factor holding the German system together. German arrangements constitute a mean between theoretical clarity and practical confusion. In theory the system is rendered transparent by rules, in practice it is opaque. The complex, multi-layered federal system has successfully solved the problem of devolution but lacks a clear institutional centre to settle the great issues of the day. On the outbreak of the First World War the Austrian Foreign Minister Berchtold complained: 'Who is in charge in Berlin?' The same question might be asked of the Bonn Republic, for the sedulous pursuit of consensus, the wholly admirable desire to settle questions by negotiation rather than by exercises of will, the dispersal of authority rather than its concentration, lead to inanition at the centre.

Modern accounts of German public administration take it for granted that its more traditional elements are in urgent need of reform. It is normally, however, a prior condition of reform that the system which it seeks to replace should be discredited and the German civil service has in consequence suffered many unjust criticisms. The Bonn democracy had to rebuild an impoverished, exhausted and divided country and to merge the heritage of the past with a parliamentary system modelled after other West European states. The resultant success has been achieved because of rather than in spite of the continuity with the past, and the modern shortcomings of the administrative system lie in the loss not the retention of traditional virtues.

CHAPTER FIVE

Italy

THE BACKGROUND

Italy has existed as a modern nation for little more than a century but in that time she has experimented with three different types of regime: the liberal state until 1922, Fascism between the two World Wars and the post-war Republican system formally promulgated in 1948. Like other European states with marked changes of regime, such as France and Germany, there are, nevertheless, important threads of continuity in the administrative tradition. Long-established patterns of administrative style tend to prove less easily challengeable than the formal appearance or public ideology of a regime, as both Mussolini and the politicians of the post-war era discovered.

This is not to suggest that Italian public administration has been unaffected by those developments which have affected central government in virtually all industrialised states: the great expansion of government intervention in the economy, the assumption of wide responsibilities for social welfare and the creation of special bodies, often outside the formal ministerial structure, to carry out these tasks. But these developments have occurred gradually and to a large extent independently of the nature of the regime. Many of the alleged drawbacks of Italian administration as it exists today, such as the high degree of centralisation, the problems of coordination and the relatively poor quality of officials, are thus long-standing features of the political system.

The problem of centralisation dates back to the period of unification. The very diversity of the new state — in language, culture, and economic life — led Italy's new rulers to suppose that only a strong and centralised system could create lasting national unity. They found a convenient model in the French administrative system — of which the whole peninsula had had experience during the Napoleonic invasion — and a suitable instrument for carrying it out in the Piedmontese state. National unification was, in fact, largely the work of Piedmont. Its ruler became first king of Italy and its constitution, the Italian constitution. Thus Italy adopted the Piedmontese parliamentary system, in which ministers were largely responsible to the legislature rather than the monarch, but also its highly centralised and often autocratic administrative structure of government departments. This system was aimed at removing regional differences and controlling, if not destroying, regional opposition. Former territorial divisions were replaced by a new and artificial system of provinces and communes along French lines in which central government exercised real power through its prefects.

This centralisation was in many respects counterproductive. For much of the population government remained at best remote and at worst arbitrary and oppressive, and as a result the new state failed to win respect in many quarters. The parliamentary system, furthermore, lacked disciplined political parties and operated on the unprincipled distribution of favours to individual deputies and their clienteles as a means of buying local support. Where this support could not be bought, it was obtained by coercion and civil rights were frequently suspended or ignored. The consequence was a marked contrast between the theory and practice of Italian government. In time the political elite felt secure enough to allow limited elements of local autonomy, and more effective systems of legal and financial control over the executive were established. But as the sphere of government activities gradually increased, this was counter-balanced by an accumulation of new powers at the centre.

During the Fascist era, although formally the constitution was retained, all respect for its principles disappeared. The Fascist drive for central control led to the suspension of most local autonomies and to further state regulation of economic life. Perhaps surprisingly, however, a second major feature of Italian government in the twentieth century emerged at the same time: the tendency towards a dispersal of power along functional lines. The extension of state control was dictated less by ideology than by the exigency of the economic crisis of the inter-war years. It led to the creation of IRI (the Institute for Industrial Reconstruction) and a whole series of agencies established to take over or to regulate sectors of the economy which were facing severe difficulties and in which the corporative demands of important interests had to be satisfied. These agencies were introduced on an unplanned, *ad hoc* basis and not in pursuit of a preconceived strategy leading to a completely corporate state. To a large extent each became an independent fiefdom acting as a law unto itself. This was facilitated by the fact that they were generally established as 'special agencies', i.e. outside the formal ministerial structure. In this way arose one of the paradoxical features of Italian government: a highly centralised state and yet one with major problems of coordinating the activities of its various branches. In practice, what minimally effective coordination there was, was provided not by institutional mechanisms but by the Duce and the Fascist Party and by the complex web of party contacts which infiltrated all areas of public life.

Post-war Italy therefore inherited an historical legacy of a complex and Byzantine structure of public agencies set alongside the apparently well-ordered and hierarchical pattern of the Napoleonic state. Both types of administration were infused with an outlook in which the distinction between the sphere of partisan politics and the impartial world of administration proper was extremely blurred. The post-war Republican Constitution was intended as a reaction against these tendencies, and in particular against excessive centralisation. It provided for a parliamentary regime and a territorially decentralised state in which substantial local autonomy was granted not only to the restored provincial and communal councils but more importantly to an intermediate tier of regional government.

The reality proved rather different. Except in the four (later five) so-called 'special' regions on the periphery, the regional tier of government was not established until the seventies. The high degree of territorial centralisation remained but so did the problem of coordination. The special agencies were not wound up, or absorbed into a more rational administrative system, but tended instead to proliferate. The central ministerial departments were not reformed either. There was virtually no purge of personnel after the war and the excessively formal, hierarchical and legalistic outlook of the civil service survived into the post-war era. One regime replaced another but the bureaucracy quickly settled down to a close working relationship with its new and equally durable political masters, the Christian Democrats.

To appreciate how this came about, it is important to understand the structure of post-war party politics. The party system has been dominated by two major parties: the Christian Democrats (DC) and the Communists (PCI). Around these two are clustered a series of smaller parties. On the extreme right are the Neo-Fascists and the Monarchists, while in the centre — moving from left to right — is a series of smaller parties: Socialists, Social Democrats, Republicans and Liberals. Because, until the seventies, the Communists were treated as an anti-system party, any government has had to be based upon the Christian Democrats who have formed the mainstay of every single government since 1945, although they have never has a workable parliamentary majority on their own. Initially, the ruling coalition was of the 'Centrist' variety: an alliance of the DC, Liberals, Social Democrats and Republicans. However, in 1962-63 this was superseded by the 'Centre-Left' coalition in which the Socialists replaced the Liberals. Since the early seventies this formula has also broken down as the Socialists have insisted that the increasingly moderate Communists should also be associated with government. As parliamentary arithmetic now prevents a return to the old Centrist coalition, the Christian Democrats, while still holding the reigns of government, have had to accept growing Communist influence, although the Communists are not yet formally in government.

The persistence of Christian Democrat rule and the strength of the allegedly anti-system Communist opposition were together responsible for the long delay in establishing regional government. The fear of giving the Communists a governmental base in their electoral strongholds of central Italy, together with a realisation that the Christian Democrats were stronger at national level than at the grass-roots, led successive DC governments to postpone decentralisation.

The longevity of DC rule has also caused the problem of policy coordination and the associated expansion of special agencies. Christian Democracy was originally built upon the twin pillars of Catholicism and fear of Communism but, with the decline of the former and the increasing moderation of the latter, the DC has come more and more to rely upon clientele relationships with certain groups — particularly in the underdeveloped South — to maintain its electoral support. The special agencies were especially useful as a source of patronage — through jobs in the public service and through the benefits they dispensed. For a time they were also a useful means of developing sectors of the economy in which private enterprise initially lagged.

The traditions established under Fascism were crucial for patronage purposes. Officials were brought up under a system where party infiltration of the service was the norm and where clientele links between politicians and constituencies or interest groups were an essential part of government. This system has become institutionalised in post-war Italy. The phenomenon of *lottizzazione* — the covert allocation of 'spheres of influence' in the public service, with the lion's share going to the ruling party — has become a feature of Italian government. Moreover, because of the Christian Democrat Party's long stay in power, and because of its internal factional divisions, the real distribution takes place within the party itself. Each faction has sought to establish its own sphere of patronage within the public administration, and especially within the special agencies, and the effect upon policy coordination is understandably dramatic.

The Institutional Framework

Italian public organisations can be divided up in a number of ways. A major distinction is made between active, consultative and controlling agencies. The present section discusses the first, while the functions of consultative and controlling agencies are examined later. The active administration can be divided into central government and the various levels of local government: regional, provincial and communal. Though we are mainly concerned with the central administration, recent devolution measures make it essential to consider also the administrative powers of regional government.

Central government consists of a wide range of organisations. Besides the central departments of the traditional administration there are a number of 'autonomous administrations', such as the state railways and the postal services, which are supervised by, but not part of, particular ministries. There is also an enormous category of organisations known as *enti pubblici* (public agencies), totalling nearly 60,000, which employ more people than the central departments and whose span includes social security, health services, commercial regulation, economic development and manufacturing industry.

The Cabinet

The Italian Cabinet — formally known as the Council of Ministers — has overall responsibility for the activities of central government. It is composed of the Prime Minister, departmental ministers and ministers without portfolio, of whom there are generally between four and six. On occasions, for reasons of coalition balance, there has also been a Deputy Prime Minister. Junior ministers (known as under-secretaries) are not, of course, members of the Cabinet. Given that changes in the structure of the departments of central government have been rare in post-war Italy, and relatively unimportant, the composition of the Cabinet tends to be fairly inflexible. The only variations occur as a result of the number of ministers without portfolio the Prime Minister chooses, or is constrained, to appoint. They are generally entrusted with specific tasks (e.g. relations with parliament or the regional governments, or Italy's role in the United Nations) or have charge of agencies attached for no very clear reason to the Prime Minister's office rather than to a particular ministry (e.g. the National Research Council or the Development Fund for Southern Italy).

The Constitution lays down the principles of collective ministerial responsibility to parliament for actions taken in the name of the Cabinet and individual responsibility for the activities of particular ministries. In practice, neither principle is fully operative. Collective responsibility is undermined by the fact that most governments are coalitions of parties and ministers are prepared to criticise implicitly, on occasions explicitly, the actions of Cabinet colleagues at the opposite end of the spectrum. This is reflected in the very high level of Cabinet instability; Cabinets on average last less than a year and tend to be brought down more by internal divisions than by their failure to maintain the confidence of parliament.

Individual responsibility tends to be an elusive principle in all parliamentary systems because of the impractability of holding ministers responsible for every single action carried out in their name. But it is also undermined by the fact that Italy has not the same tradition of a well-developed procedure for questioning ministers or debating the activities of specific ministries as Britain. The focus of parliamentary debate does not lend itself to policy accountability either; it tends to centre on broad ideological conflict between Left and Right or on very specific questions touching the interests of the clienteles of individual deputies. In recent years, however, there has been a slight tendency for debate to focus rather more on the intermediate policy level than in the past as the ideological tension within the political system has declined.

In principle, the functions of the Italian Cabinet are similar to those of most parliamentary regimes: it determines governmental policies and coordinates the activities of government departments in pursuit of these policies. To this end it collectively approves all draft government legislation to be presented to parliament and all 'legislative decrees', 'decree-laws' and major administrative regulations. (Most laws leave the government the task of filling out the details: this delegated legislation is known as legislative decree and requires no further ratification by parliament. Decree laws may be issued by the government in an emergency, such as a financial crisis, but require parliamentary approval within sixty days.)

The Cabinet is also responsible for resolving differences of policy and conflicts of competence between ministries. However, in a system where coalitions are the norm and where the dominant party is itself highly factionalised, it is a rather large and unwieldy instrument for effective decision-making and policy coordination. This would not be so serious if the Prime Minister were able to exercise some real degree of power, if there were an effective 'inner Cabinet' and if there were a well-developed system of Cabinet committees. Unfortunately none of these three conditions holds.

Italian Prime Ministers, even when they have survived in office for any considerable period of time, as De Gasperi (1945-53) or Moro (1963-68), have never enjoyed the degree of ascendancy over their Cabinet colleagues which would enable them to make a reality of their constitutional responsibility for overall policy coordination. There are various reasons for this. The office of the Prime Minister provides no specialist technical services to check upon the activities of different departments or to formulate long-term policy. Unlike Britain, the Prime Minister is not necessarily the official leader of his party; he is often no better known to the public than his most important colleagues, and within his own party the post of party secretary provides an important alternative source of authority. Thus individual ministers tend to resent any attempts to impose upon their own spheres of authority and regard a Prime Minister as enjoying his office on no more than an interim basis. As a result, the various attempts to introduce legislation strengthening the Prime Minister's office by the establishment of real technical services have failed.

It is, in any case, doubtful whether such a measure would by itself be very effective since a reorganisation of the complex and fragmented structure of central government would also be necessary. Many Italian ministers sit in the Cabinet as staunch defenders of departmental interests and the interests of the clienteles linked to their ministries. Probably the most serious problem lies in the sphere of economic policy, responsibility for which is divided between the Treasury, the Ministry of Finance and the Ministry for the Budget and Economic Planning. Even where the last of these succeeds in obtaining formal Cabinet commitment to a particular strategy for economic planning, that strategy has in practice been undermined by the inefficiency of the Ministry of Finance and the autonomous monetary policies pursued by the powerful Treasury Minister and the Governor of the Bank of Italy who work in close cooperation.

Interministerial committees do, of course, exist and are given a formal status either by decree or by law, with a fixed and publicly known membership. The most important are for Economic Planning, for Prices and for Credit and Savings, and certain decision-making powers are in fact delegated to them by the Cabinet. Other less important committees have also operated on a permanent or temporary basis, often to study particular problems and make proposals for Cabinet consideration. Available evidence suggests, however, that they have not been a great success as agencies of policy coordination and that, like the Cabinet, they have tended simply to ratify decisions taken elsewhere in the administrative hierarchy or in the special agencies.

Ministries

The division of the administrative functions of central government into ministerial departments, which was established in the middle of the nineteenth century, remains the basis of Italian administration. The number of ministries has, of course, gradually expanded: from seven at the start, fifteen between the wars, to the present figure of twenty. The number and organisation of Italian ministries is determined by law. In practice, the structure has been relatively inflexible. Unlike some other European countries, there has been no move to seek better policy coordination by the amalgamation of ministries in associated fields although recently there has been much discussion of such reform. Rather, over the years, those changes which have taken place have involved the creation of new ministries. Three were created in the fifties: State

Italian Ministries and their Personnel, 1976	
Foreign Affairs	7,079
Interior	99,647
Justice	40,745
Finance	104,381
Treasury	14,995
Defence	272,608
Public Education	1,008,062
Public Works	6,593
Agriculture and Forestry	10,451
Trade and Industry	1,720
Labour and Social Security	14,899
Posts and Telecommunications	2
Transport and Civil Aviation	5,007
Foreign Trade	484
Merchant Shipping	1,567
The Budget and Economic Planning	264
State Holdings	158
Health	2,331
Tourism and Entertainment	422
Cultural and Environmental Heritage	9,042
	1,604,086

The above figures include a number of categories which are not normally classed as civil servants in Britain: 863,600 primary, secondary and university teachers are employed by the Ministry of Public Education and 300,000 members of the police and armed forces are employed by the Defence and Interior ministries. Note that two 'autonomous administrations', are directly responsible to the Ministry of Posts and Telecommunications and employ virtually all the civil servants in this sector. Finally, the total includes some 3,600 officials employed in various agencies formally part of the Office of the Prime Minister (e.g. The Central Statistical Institute, The Development Fund for the South and the National Research Council)

Participations, in an attempt to strengthen political control and impose some order on the sprawling empire of the state's share in Italian industry; Health, bringing together functions formerly shared between the Ministry of the Interior and a State Health Commission; and Tourism and Entertainment, formerly the Tourist Commission under the control of a minister without portfolio. In the sixties changes were limited to expanding the functions of the Budget to include Economic Planning, and in the seventies a further ministry (Cultural and Environmental Heritage) was created in a belated attempt to protect Italy's cultural treasures from the ravages of flood, tide, vandals and foreign art dealers.

There is an increasingly urgent need for some rationalisation of the fragmented ministerial structure. The system has grown up in an unplanned way and many functions are divided between several ministries so that disputes of competence are frequent and economies of scale lost. Moreover, with the devolution of functions to the regions in the last two years, it has been argued that several departments no longer have any real role to perform and should either be wound up or merged with others. Tourism, Health, Public Works, Agriculture, Transport, Merchant Shipping, and Posts and Telecommunications have all been identified as ripe for amalgamation or at least drastic pruning. Certainly, neither the three independent ministries dealing with economic policy, nor the three dealing with Commerce and Industry, Foreign Trade and Merchant Shipping, seem justified by rational criteria. So far, however, the need to find enough ministries to satisfy all political factions has combined with the powerful entrenched interests of the bureaucracy itself to prevent necessary legislation.

The internal organisation of Italian ministries tends to follow a fairly standard pattern. Except in Defence and Foreign Affairs there is no equivalent of a British Permanent Secretary in overall charge of the department. Instead, the ministries are divided into a series of functional directorates, each headed by a Director General, the number varying from between two or three in the smaller ministries to up to a dozen in the larger ones. Each is subdivided into divisions and sections to create an organisationally neat but in practice extremely hierarchical structure in which decision making is marked by serious delays and by regular blockages at the top, caused by the unwillingness of officials at lower levels to take responsibility for decisions. To facilitate internal coordination, and to help the minister and his under-secretaries achieve a measure of control over the directorates, there is, as in France, a well-developed system of ministerial *cabinets* which are composed of outside advisers — often from other branches of the state service such as the Council of State and the Court of Accounts — and permanent officials of the ministry who may themselves be connected to the minister through personal or political ties. These offices also provide the link between the political and administrative roles of the minister and deal with his relations with the Cabinet and other ministries, parliament and the press.

Each ministry is flanked by a decentralised section of the Treasury's Central Accounting Office which plays an important role within the ministry. Its approval is required for all expenditure, giving it considerable powers of delay and, where projects do not fit the overall expenditure plans of the Treasury, an effective veto. Each ministry also has its own internal accounting offices and there are auditing controls exercised by the Court of Accounts. As a result of this extremely complex framework of controls over expenditure, there are serious problems of delay in implementing policy programmes in all Italian ministries. There is, moreover, a separation of financial accountability and control from the process of policy formulation and implementation which has provided a serious barrier to the adoption of much needed techniques of modern management.

In recent years considerable sums of money have as a result accumulated in the Treasury which represent revenue earmarked in the annual budget for certain purposes but for which authorisation of expenditure has not yet been granted. Almost invariably this is due to inefficient administrative procedures and the multiplicity of legal controls. These so-called 'passive reserves', which do not reappear in subsequent annual budgets, have built up steadily over the years and constitute an enormous discretionary power in the hands of the government. By slowing down or speeding up the eventual authorisation of these sums, it can effectively undermine any notion of parliamentary control over public expenditure.

Special Agencies

A wide range of special agencies has grown up on a piecemeal basis under Fascism and since the Second World War. The reasons why they were established varies from case to case. In some instances, it was because government intervention was intended to be temporary but in fact proved permanent; in others, it was because the close legal and political control exercised over the ministries was thought inappropriate. The variety of special agencies and the different types of relationship they have with central government make classification extremely difficult. However, at the risk of some over-simplification it is possible to identify three broad groups.

Autonomous administrations. There are six main agencies of this type. All derive a substantial part of their operating revenue from the provision of commercial services. Since the standard procedures for financial accountability and control in ministerial departments would interfere with efficient commercial management, they are given a degree of operational independence. However, despite their title, they remain under close supervision by the central departments. In the case of the two largest — the Postal Service and the State Railways — this is widely seen as one of the major causes of their chronic inefficiency and recurrent financial deficits, for although the Director General of each is formally independent of the corresponding ministry, the minister himself heads the administration's board and retains responsibility for its policy. As with British public corporations, it has proved extremely difficult to define a satisfactory boundary between general policy and day-to-day management, and ministerial intervention in the latter is frequent.

Autonomous Administrations and their Personnel, 1976

Administration of State Monopolies (Finance)	16,000
Independent National Road-Building Agency (Public Works)	13,000
Posts and Telecommunications Administration (Posts)	174,000
State Agency for Telephone Services (Posts)	14,000
State Railways (transport)	221,000
National Forestry Commission (Agriculture)	1,000
	439,000

The ministry to which each administration is attached is given in brackets. The Forestry Commission is being wound up as the state forests are transferred to the regional authorities

State Holdings. This system has been widely seen as an interesting alternative form of state intervention in a mixed economy to the nationalisation formula adopted in Britain. Instead of vesting control of a whole sector of industry in the hands of a public corporation responsible to a minister (along lines similar to the autonomous administrations), the state holdings formula is one in which state companies act much more as entrepeneurs, controlling only part of an industrial sector, competing with private enterprise and obtaining resources not just from commercial activities and government grants but also from domestic and international capital markets. It is not, of course, the only formula used since the war. Besides the autonomous administrations, Italy has on one occasion resorted to the public corporation approach: in the case of ENEL, the national electricity authority which is responsible directly to the Ministry of Industry.

The major state holdings are all responsible to the Ministry of State Holdings but the relationship between the commercial activities and the political authority is much more indirect than in the case of the public corporations. This has been achieved through formal structures and through informal practices. The system provides for three levels of organisation. At the top is the holding company which has direct contact with the ministry. There are six major holding companies, the two most important being IRI, which has a stake in a wide range of industries from steel and automobiles to air transport, and ENI, which is primarily concerned with hydrocarbons but has interests in textiles and chemicals. Other holding companies include EFIM (manufacturing industry in the South), EGAM (mining and the metallurgical industries), EAGAT (spas and thermal waters) and EGC (cinema and the film industry). Below the major holding companies are a series of financial holding companies which deal with narrower areas of industrial activity (in the case of IRI: steel, engineering, shipbuilding, shipping, etc.). Finally, at the base, are the operating companies themselves, the shares of which are owned either wholly or in part by the holding companies.

The political authority thus stands at considerable remove from commercial operations. The power of the minister is restricted to approval of the overall investment plans of the holding companies. In the fifties and sixties the state undertakings acted with a wide margin of independence and had a considerable degree of success in several fields. They expanded greatly and today employ approximately three-quarters of a million persons, representing a three-fold increase since 1950. They have also developed an extraordinarily able group of managers at all levels whose enterprise and flexibility (compared with the civil service proper) has been responsible for much of their success.

In the seventies, however, a marked change has come over the state holdings sector. Political control has increased as more and more senior appointments have gone to those with close party affiliations, particularly Christian Democrats. There has also been an increasing tendency to use the state holdings to take over ailing industries in order to keep down unemployment. As a result, the financial performance of the groups has suffered dramatically and they are having to draw increasingly on the Treasury-supported Endowment Funds.

Other Public Bodies While it is possible to identify the autonomous administrations and the state holdings as separate and important sub-groups within the category of special agencies, it is less easy to classify the other public bodies (enti pubblici). In all, there are nearly 60,000 of them, many operating at local level. Welfare assistance, health insurance, pension schemes and bodies providing grants and other forms of assistance to school and university students account for the majority; each of the 8,000 communes, for example, has a public welfare agency. Such services, which in most societies grew up in a piecemeal fashion and were provided by a variety of public, semi-public, charitable and private agencies, have in Italy still not been rationalised. Thus alongside the major national pension institutes and health insurance schemes exist a host of similar agencies — also considered as public bodies and subject to administrative law — which serve limited sectional groups such as sharecroppers, artisans, policemen, teachers and railway personnel. Other public bodies operate in the spheres of education, cultural activities, research, sport and tourism. There are also many other economic agencies apart from the autonomous administrations and state holdings. At local government level there are transport services and building consortia, for example, while in agriculture there are over 500 official organisations dealing with a variety of matters from veterinary services to commodity purchasing. Finally, the category includes a large number of national banks, finance corporations and savings banks.

There is an urgent need for a thorough reform of the various types of special agency, and in recent years governments have attempted to reduce their number and to simplify the statutes governing their structure and the conditions of employment of their personnel. It has been difficult, however, to draw up an inventory of the agencies or to determine exactly how much they spend, how many people they employ and whether they all still perform useful functions. Faced with these problems reforms have to date been modest. In 1975, sixty-seven special agencies were wound up, while in 1977 a further group were identified for investigation and possible inclusion within the framework of the new regional administrations. The latter group gives some idea of the range and specificity of Italian public bodies: it included the Bologna Home for Retired Actors, the National Agency for Aid to the Orphans of Italian Physicians, the National Agency for the Moral Protection of Children, the Committee for the Moral and Social Protection of Women and the National Fire Prevention Agency.

The special agencies constitute a central part of the network of clientele relationships built up by the Christian Democrat Party over the years — popularly known as the system of *sottogoverno* (literally, 'undergovernment'). They are the most politicised part of the state administration in that the majority are controlled by boards whose members are appointed, normally quite openly, on a party political basis. Their very specificity — often dealing with very limited sectional or territorial groups — and the fact that they are outside the framework of tight legal controls imposed upon the administration in the civil service proper makes them an ideal mechanism for the distribution of patronage.

Decentralised Services

Despite the considerable functional decentralisation described above, the Italian administrative system is quite highly centralised territorially in the sense that the powers of local authorities over important functions such as education have always been much more restricted than in Britain. However, many of the central departments have field services where much of their work and many — often the majority — of their staff are located. These are

generally based upon the territorial units of sub-national government: the regions, provinces and communes. In the seventies,
moreover, a new regional tier of government was introduced right
across the country and a wide range of administrative powers was
placed under the control of authorities at this level. Description of
decentralisation is complicated, furthermore, by the fact that the
implementation of regional governments has brought about a
marked change in the relationship between various levels and the
precise nature of the new pattern has yet to emerge.

Before we describe regional and local government, however, we
must look at the decentralised services of central government.
Virtually all government departments have field services of some
sort. The most important are Public Works (offices at regional and
provincial level), Finance, Education and Agriculture (all with
provincial level inspectorates) and the Ministry of the Interior
which has its agent, the Prefect, in each province. The Ministry of
the Interior is also responsible for police and fire services, over
which the Prefect has command at provincial level.

Formally, the government is free to appoint whoever it wishes as
Prefect and very occasionally individuals who are not members of
the career civil service of the Ministry of the Interior are appointed.
He can be removed at the discretion of the government and, as in
France, an individual's tour of duty in any one province is limited
to a few years. As in France, again, the role of the Prefect is crucial
to understanding how decentralisation operates. He is, in effect,
the chief representative of the state locally and, in addition to his
role as chief provincial officer of his ministry, has ultimate
responsibility for public order in the province.

Until the recent regional reforms he also had substantial powers
over the activities of provincial and communal councils. In this
capacity he could veto their actions on grounds of illegality and his
approval was required for all contracts they entered into (in this
case approval could also be withheld on grounds of expediency).
The Prefect could take over administrative functions where local
councils failed to meet their statutory obligations and ultimately
advise the government to dismiss the mayor, dissolve the council,
install a temporary prefectoral commissioner and hold fresh
elections. These powers traditionally gave him enormous political,
as well as legal and administrative, importance. There is little
doubt that, especially in the fifties, the prefectoral corps played a

major party-political role in arranging patronage for the government parties and in making life difficult for left-wing authorities.

In one important respect, however, the Italian Prefect has differed from his French counterpart. He is only responsible for the affairs of the Ministry of the Interior and not for the field services of all the other ministries as well. The latter communicate directly with their headquarters in Rome and do not work through the prefecture, although the Prefect may in actual practice play an important informal role in this chain of command

In recent years the power of the Prefect has been reduced considerably. This has occurred for two reasons. Since the early seventies the Communist Party has wielded substantial influence over the governing coalition and this has enabled it to reduce prefectoral pressure on local authorities. More importantly, the introduction of regional government has reduced the legal controls which the Prefect exercises over provincial and communal councils. Since 1972 a new body, the Committee of Control over the Provinces and Communes, checks upon the legality of their actions, can refer back any decision it considers inexpedient and, in certain cases, may take over any administrative function where a council fails to fulfil its statutory obligations. The Committee consists of three administrative experts nominated by the President of the region, a judge from the regional administrative tribunal and a fifth member nominated by the government's Regional Commissioner. The existence of a Regional Commissioner, a new agent of central government supervising the regional assemblies who has been superimposed upon the prefectoral structure, has also reduced the power of the provincial Prefect. The latter's supervisory role over local authorities is now largely limited to the local public agencies discussed earlier.

Regional Government

The 1948 Constitution envisaged the establishment of twenty regions to which a range of legislative and administrative functions would be devolved. Five were distinguished as 'special regions' with slightly wider powers: Sicily, Sardinia, the French-speaking region of Val d'Aosta, the partly German-speaking region of Trentino Alto-Adige and Friuli Venezia Giuli. While these were established (the last not until 1963), successive governments failed to introduce enabling legislation on finance and electoral procedures for the ordinary regions until the end of the sixties and it was not until 1970 that their first assemblies were elected. Since then a series of measures have gradually defined and widened the powers of the regions.

The experience of regional government has so far been rather disappointing. The original hope was that the regions would provide a more flexible system of administration than the old ministries. It was thought that they would integrate functions, previously divided between compartmentalised hierarchies, at a level where account could be taken of the specific needs of the area and where some genuine democratic control be exercised.

The regions were to have powers in three main areas. The first was social and community services, e.g. welfare relief, health, local transport, manpower training, libraries and museums, but excluding education (except for the provision of financial aid to schoolchildren and students). The second was land-use planning (including drainage and water supply), forestry and, most important of all, urban development. The third concerned economic activities of a specifically regional character, e.g. local commerce, agriculture, tourism, mineral waters, artisan crafts, hunting and fishing. Functions other than those specified in the Constitution could also be devolved. The national government, on the other hand, was to maintain control of those areas fundamental to the unity of the state, such as foreign policy, monetary and industrial policy, justice and education and would be responsible for general framework laws in the areas of regional competence.

While this separation of functions undoubtedly possessed a certain logical coherence, it tended to be undermined by the fact that the central government itself determines the exact extent of the administrative functions devolved to the regions, the precise limits of their legislative powers and the nature of their financial autonomy. Moreover, the Constitution gives the government substantial supervisory powers over the regions. Its Regional Commissioner must approve all regional legislation. In cases of dispute, the matter will be referred to the Constitutional Court if the proposed legislation is thought to be either unconstitutional or to conflict with the fundamental principles of national framework legislation, or to parliament if it is seen to conflict with the national interest or the interests of other regions. At the same time a

Commission of Control, presided over by the government Commissioner in each region, supervises the legality, although not the expediency, of regional administration.

However, the distribution of competences between central and regional government originally envisaged was upset most severely by the long period which elapsed between writing the Constitution and introducing the ordinary regions. The original distribution made sense at a time when the structure of government institutions was being reshaped, immediately after Fascism, but developments over the next two decades made decentralisation far more difficult. The failure to rationalise ministerial structures as government acquired new functions resulted in overlap and confusion of roles; the tendency to hive off many functions to special agencies continued; and both sectors became important repositories of party patronage. It became harder to establish a basis for devolving control of so many different agencies in a coordinated manner, while the dominant governing party was in any case very loath to relinquish its interests. For these reasons the transfer of powers to the regions, especially the ordinary regions, was far more limited than originally conceived.

The 1970 law on regional finance left it to the government itself to define by decree the precise range of government and special agency offices sited in the region which would be transferred with their personnel, and which would be retained to enable the government to carry out its general coordinating functions. Almost every ministry acted conservatively on this matter. In the field of agriculture, control of forestry and implementation of EEC legislation remained in the hands of the ministry, while for health a range of twenty-five functions, including public hygiene and preventive medicine, was reserved despite the establishment of regional health authorities. Similar limits were imposed in social welfare, urban planning and public works. Not only were the first ordinary regional councils restricted by slow and limited delegation but they also faced a situation of great administrative confusion. Power in a wide range of matters was not only fragmented at the centre but now also between centre and regions, with further wastage of resources and conflicts of competence.

It was therefore understandable that pressure should build up at regional level for a redefinition of the system on a much less restrictive basis. In particular, there were demands that parliament should not leave it to the government to define the area of devolution since the absence of strong Cabinet leadership meant that each ministry became arbiter of its powers and neither the bureaucracy nor the minister in charge could be expected to favour their reduction. The crucial turning-point came with the regional elections of 1975 and the general election of 1976 which marked a major shift to the left and especially to the Communist Party. After the general election, the parties of the Left, which strongly favoured a more radical devolution, exercised a substantial influence over government policy. The result was a new law in 1975 redefining the process of decentralisation. Like its predecessor, it also delegated to the government the task of defining precise areas of administration but this time the discretion was much more limited and the areas involved considerably broader. Health insurance agencies were now included, as was control over provision of public housing and the task of implementing EEC regulations at regional level, particularly in relation to agriculture. At the same time a Commission (under Massimo Giannini, a distinguished lawyer) was set up by the minister in charge of relations with regions to make proposals for the government decrees which would give substance to the 1975 law. Finally, after a long political wrangle and several false starts, the relevant decrees were promulgated in 1977.

By passing to the regions a further substantial range of administrative functions, the new decrees provide, at least in principle, a real opportunity to achieve the coordination of policies at an intermediate level which lay at the heart of the original conception of Italian regionalism. In the case of land-use planning, for example, the regions will no longer be limited to approving the urban development plans of the communes within their territory but will enjoy a series of complementary powers in relation to agriculture, the siting of local transport and the execution of public housing projects. In this way, it is hoped that a much more coordinated approach to land use in its widest sense and to regional economic development can be achieved. The same is true of the provision of social services. By linking more of the uncoordinated and disparate welfare agencies under one authority at regional level, it is hoped that many of the conflicts and much of the duplication can be avoided. How far these hopes will be turned into reality remains unclear. The pessimists fear that the problems which characterised central government may simply repeat themselves in each of the regions. This may occur if the regions fail to make use of existing services at provincial and communal level or if they seek to establish bureaucratic systems which undermine the process of collegial policy making in the regional executive. There are disturbing signs that this is in fact happening in some ordinary regions, just as it happened in the special regions.

Equally important will be the matter of regional finance. Here the crucial questions are whether the regions will dispose of sufficient resources to fulfil their new responsibilities adequately and whether their financial precedures will be sufficiently flexible to avoid the problems which result from the rigidity of budgetary procedures at the centre. The regions have only very limited powers to raise their own revenue and in 1974 a mere 8 per cent of their income came from this source; the remainder was provided directly from the centre and much of it was earmarked for obligatory services. This problem has become gradually more serious as inflation steadily reduces the real value of their own resources. New legislation on regional finance introduced greater flexibility into budgetary procedures in 1976 but the problem remains. If it is not resolved there is little long-term prospect that regionalism will achieve any real coordination of services and development policies. It will amount to little more than the decentralisation of a series of still uncoordinated administrative activities.

Local Government

Italy has two tiers of local government — the provinces and the communes — but neither enjoys the extensive powers of local authorities in Britain. The Italian authorities have exercised few of the powers of their British counterparts over education, housing, health and the police, and as a result they employ far fewer staff. Before the introduction of the recent devolution measures all three sub-national units of government put together (the regions, provinces and communes) employed little more than 500,000 people in all. The communes, in particular, have for long been chronically short of finance and many of the larger southern cities have run a permanent and increasing budget deficit. The result is that after discharging those functions which they have a statutory obligation to fulfil, the financial margin remaining to communal authorities for discretionary activities (nursery school provision, special transport services, recreational facilities, etc.) is very limited.

The administrative services of the commune which are, of course, distinct from the decentralised field services of central government departments, perform two types of role. First, they carry out the obligatory or discretionary activities of the commune itself: e.g. the obligatory provision of local traffic police, of public health, of refuse disposal services, cemeteries, public lighting and the maintenance of local roads, parks and buildings; the provision of certain types of basic social services, welfare support and health care for low-income families; and responsibility for urban development. Second, the communal administrations act as agents of the central government in certain regulatory matters, e.g. census data collection, registration of births, marriages and deaths, and military conscription. Here the mayor of the commune acts as an official of, and is responsible to, central government.

The provinces, like the communes, are for certain purposes self-governing territorial units with elected councils from which are drawn the executives (*giunte*) that assume responsibility for the various administrative departments of the province (as in communes). However, the powers of the provincial authorities are extremely limited and include little more than the provision of certain types of local roads, certain very modest levels of social services (care of illegitimate children, vaccinations, medical laboratories) and the maintenance of secondary school buildings. In recent years the utility of maintaining the provincial tier of local government has been increasingly questioned. While the provinces are important as the main units for the decentralised services of national government, the autonomous powers of the provinces as self-governing authorities are very restricted. With the establishment of regional authorities throughout the country, Italy now has four levels of government and the province would seem to be the obvious level to wind up, especially since there is an increasing tendency at the lowest level for communes to provide inter-communal consortia for the provision of certain services.

THE CIVIL SERVICE

The Scope of Public Employment

Total public employment in Italy accounts for approximately 4 million of the 19 million members of the active population. This is divided between central departments and the autonomous administrations responsible to them; local authorities (regions, provinces and communes); special agencies in the administrative and service sectors; state holdings and other special organisations engaged in financial and commercial activities. Precise and up-to-date figures are difficult to obtain because the Treasury only publishes figures for the employees of central government and the autonomous administrations, and because other data tends to be published rather late. There is, in any case, no comprehensive official source for the 60,000 enti pubblici. The figures in the table are therefore only approximations.

Total Public Employment

Central Government:	
Civil Servants	410,000
Teachers	865,000
Armed Forces and Police	300,000
Judiciary	7,600
Autonomous Administrations	440,000
Local Government	520,000
Special Agencies	600,000
State Holdings	800,000

Here we are chiefly concerned with personnel employed directly by central government departments and indirectly in the autonomous administrations. These have increased by 80 per cent over the last 25 years, during which period the size of the active labour force has remained virtually static. As a result, the proportion of the labour force employed by central government has risen from nearly 6 per cent to just under 11 per cent. Central government employment includes school and university teachers, and much the largest element of this increase has been due to the expansion of the educational sector: over the period 1972-76, the staff of the Ministry of Education alone expanded by 25 per cent from 800,000 to over a million. Central government employment also includes members of the judiciary (7,600) and the 'military' (357,000). The majority of this latter group (297,000) were career members of the armed forces and members of the police forces but certain corps in other ministries (Agriculture, Finance, Justice) are also considered as 'military'. A peculiarity of the Italian system, for example, is that the tax inspectorate (*Guardia di Finanze*) is formally defined as a military corps, largely for historical reasons rather than because the Italian state can only extract taxes from its citizens by the use of force. Excluding teachers, the judiciary, the police and the armed forces, but including the tax inspectorate, the 'civil service' in Italy therefore consisted in the mid-seventies of some 410,000 members engaged in various types of administrative activity, of whom approximately one-quarter were employed in Rome and the remainder in the various field services distributed throughout the country.

Civil Service Structure

Despite several attempts at reform contained in the most recent legislation, the Italian civil service is today still characterised by extreme compartmentalisation, rigid hierarchies and an excessively legalistic mentality. These features stem from the concept of the *stato di diritto* (the state based upon law) in which the exercise of public powers is subjected to a series of tight legal controls which are intended both to form a guarantee against arbitrary executive action and to give authority to the actions of even the lowest level of officialdom. The concept has two important ramifications. First, all administrative procedures have to be regulated by a complex series of laws, decrees and regulations and, as new functions have been acquired by government, the structure of administrative law has built up into a tangled web of well over a hundred thousand separate items. Second, it is implicit in the concept of the civil service that the relationship of the public official to the state cannot be a contractual one like that of employer and employee elsewhere because the public official both represents the state and is employed by it. To maintain the system of legal guarantees, it must be an authoritarian relationship in which functions, career grades, remuneration and other conditions of service are unilaterally determined by law and in which, in return for certain privileges such as security of tenure, the employee accepts conditions of subordination not applicable in other labour relationships.

These legalistic and hierarchical conceptions of public administration may have been appropriate in nineteenth-century liberal Italy when administrative activities were restricted to the fairly mechanical application of procedures laid down by the legislature. They are, however, quite inappropriate in a modern state with positive concepts of economic management and social welfare which require the civil service to gather information, engage in forward planning and manage a complex, changing society. They are equally inappropriate when labour relations in other sectors have changed from authority to bargaining relationships.

Formally, the Italian civil service is organised upon a four-fold career structure. At the top is the *carriera direttiva* (administrative career), members of which are responsible for policy formation and direct the administrative services. Since 1972 it has itself been internally divided to create an elite corps of *dirigenti* (managers) — effectively a new career level — above the remaining *direttori*. Below this is the *carriera di concetto* (roughly equivalent to the old Executive Class in Britain) which deals with routine administrative tasks. Third comes the *carriera esecutiva* — the clerical class (typists, secretaries, accounts' clerks, etc.). These three classes form the *impiegati civili* (literally 'civil officials'), while at the base of the structure are the *carriera ausiliara* (auxiliary personnel): the service's ubiquitous doormen, porters, chauffeurs, cleaners, etc. Each career is itself divided into a series of grades.

No clear distinction has until recently existed between generalists and specialists since formally all civil servants are classed in grades of the career classes. However, in practice the ministries — which are responsible for recruiting their own staff — recruit entrants according to functional needs. While the largest element will be general administrators, who merely require the general educational qualification for the career in question, there are a number of functions for which it is necessary to recruit specialists — doctors, engineers, statisticians, veterinary surgeons, town planners, scientists and so on. This is particularly the case in those ministries

Structure of the Civil Service, 1976

	Central Departments	Autonomous Administrations
Carriera Direttiva		
Managerial Grades: General Manager Higher Manager First Manager (after two years) First Manager	5,710	1,120
Other Grades: Inspector Generale Director of Division (1st Class) Director of Division (2nd Class) Supplementary Director Director of Section Administrative Councillor	29,620	1,980
Carriera di Concetto Chief Secretary Principal Admin. Secretary Administrative Secretary	45,920	45,230
Carriera Esecutiva Chief Assistant Principal Admin. Assistant Administrative Assistant	161,190	182,340
Carriera Ausiliara	76,550	173,930

which perform a large number of technical tasks, such as Public Works and Health, but within most ministries there are directorates which deal with at least some technical matters and, in these, specialists recruited into the career classes can and do reach the highest posts within the service.

One consequence of the practice of fitting specialist activities within the general framework of the service is the existence of enormous disparities between ministries, and even between directorates within a ministry, in the grades and pay of those who perform similar functions. This has also applied to generalist administrators and is one of the worst features of the tangled web of laws and administrative regulations governing personnel management in the service. The arbitrary upgrading of certain types of function and the *ad hoc* way in which functions have been assigned to various grades, and even career groups, over the years has created a situation in which there is no rational relationship between qualifications and work on the one hand, and grading on the other. The injustices generated and the damage done to morale, are readily understandable. This is one of the reasons, together with differences in the labour market for doctors or engineers compared with holders of 'generalist' qualifications (law graduates in particular), why it has been far more difficult to recruit specialists than general administrators. It has also meant that even where the civil service has been equipped with modern technical equipment — and with the exception of computer technology the service remains seriously underequipped — it has been impossible to use it adequately because qualified staff is often lacking.

Recruitment

The Italian Constitution stipulates that access to employment in the public service shall be through open competition 'except in those cases laid down by law'. This principle, which forms part of the philosophy of legal guarantees underlying Italian public administration, is based on the assumption that any other method of recruitment would not ensure selection of the most able and would be open to abuse. In reality, by no means all posts are filled through formal competition and in any case the system itself is seen as neither fair nor particularly efficient.

In many cases the competitive system has been abandoned for a large number of appointments. A decree of 1971 allows departments to draw up lists of aspirants to temporary posts and then select from these as required. In 1976 no less than 100,000 teachers and 10,000 postal workers were classified as temporary. These temporary staffs tend to prove remarkably permanent and naturally expect to become formally established. The result has often been the postponement of competitions to fill permanent posts or the temporary abandonment of competitive selection. At regional level the principle has been virtually dropped for auxiliary personnel and is limited to 45 per cent of the executive and clerical groups. Even at the level of the carriera direttiva in the central administration, it has not always been respected: between 1956 and 1961, 31 per cent of those entering this career class proved to have done so without a formal competition.

For each career access to competition requires the possession of certain minimum educational qualifications or, if the candidate is already in the service, he or she must have reached a certain grade in the career below that for which the competition is being held. For the carriera direttiva a university degree is required and for specialist posts also the appropriate professional qualification. For the carriera di concetto the higher secondary school leaving certificate (*maturità* – broadly equivalent to A-levels) is necessary, although in practice probably more than half this career class are also graduates. The lower secondary school certificate and the elementary school diploma form the requirements for the carriera esecutiva (for which proficiency in shorthand and typing may also be necessary) and the carriera ausiliaria.

The system of selection is extremely inefficient in practice. For each competition a separate examining board has to be formed and when, as is often the case, there are many candidates, this consumes the energies of large numbers of civil servants in the ministry concerned. The procedure for announcing and holding competitions is very involved and may be drawn out over months, or even years, during which time the posts either remain unfilled or are occupied by temporary staff – with the results referred to above. Examinations at all levels have until recently been extremely academic, often bearing little relationship to the abilities required. The process is also costly to candidates who generally have to spend some considerable period after graduation studying special subjects – almost invariably at their own expense – to prepare for the entrance exam and who run the risk that this expense may be wasted if they fail to secure a place.

Three features mark the type of personnel recruited into the Italian civil service. Firstly, the service is dominated by southerners. The significance of this is that the South, in contrast to the industrialised and technocratic North, is still characterised by the allegedly backward cultural patterns of a Mediterranean society: in particular, lower levels of educational attainment, hierarchical patterns of political relationships and a legalistic rather than managerial approach to administration. The southern element has increased over the years: from 56 per cent of higher civil servants in 1954 to 75 per cent by 1966. The figure is lower for other officials since more of these serve in field offices and are recruited locally, while a greater proportion of the carriera direttiva is concentrated in Rome and recruited nationally. A related feature is the prevalence of law graduates, who account for approximately half of all the higher officials. The civil service provides one of the few means of employing the enormous numbers of law graduates turned out by southern universities where science and technology tend to be rather poorly developed and unpopular. Finally, — and here the Italian situation differs less from that in other European countries — the higher civil service tends to be overwhelmingly middle class and to have a large proportion of entrants who are themselves children of civil servants, though a far higher proportion than usual seems to come from lower middle-class than from managerial and professional families.

The markedly southern nature of the service itself reflects the relatively low prestige attached to a career in the higher civil service in Italy compared to France or Britain. Posts in private and state industry are considered more prestigious, and certainly offer much better pay and better opportunities for rapid career advancement. Such opportunities are not so readily available, however, to those from the South as they are to northerners. It is probably also the case that the security of a post in public administration is a far more important attraction in southern society than in the North.

Whatever the reasons, it is clear that the social composition of the higher civil service has a profound effect upon the way the service operates. The patterns of legal authority and hierarchy, and the prevalence of administrative rather than managerial attitudes characteristic of the stato di diritto, are reinforced by the cultural background of those who enter the service. Moreover, this background is not mitigated by the socialising effect of prestigious institutions grouping entrants into self-conscious, cohesive and almost evangelical *grands corps* as in France. The majority of higher civil servants have received such professional training as was available on the job within their own ministries. The Higher School of Public Administration, set up in the early sixties, has only recently come to provide more than very short and badly organised in-service courses.

Career Management

The Italian civil service is characterised above all by its compartmentalisation. This is not only horizontal (by career class) but also
vertical, since recruitment is by individual ministries rather than a
unified civil service commission and most careers are pursued in
one ministry alone. Even within ministries the qualifications for
given directorates, divisions and services are often specified in
detail, so that in addition internal rigidity problems arise. In the
past there has also been compartmentalisation between headquarters
in Rome and the ministry's field offices, although this did not
apply to some sectors such as the prefectoral corps and has in any
case begun to break down with the transfer of personnel from
central to regional authorities.

However, this rigidity has had serious consequences. In the first
place, civil servants have little knowledge or experience of
administrative practices and problems outside their own ministries
or directorates. Compartmentalisation has thus contributed to
hostility and suspicion between departments, a lack of collaboration
and a determination to defend their own interests, in particular
against any break in hierarchical career progression through lateral
transfers of personnel. Second, it has created difficulties in
optimising the use of personnel in that civil servants cannot easily
be posted where they are most needed. Finally, it has encouraged
the development of permanent clientele relationships between
certain departments and the interest groups in their sphere,
particularly in the case of agriculture and industry.

It is important to add that the higher levels of each career group
are dominated by those who have spent their entire working life in
the service. There is little mobility between the civil service itself
and other areas of public or private employment. The only
exception to this rule is that many directorships of special agencies
— especially in the economic sector — are held by senior civil
servants, but this phenomenon is more important for the patronage
which it offers ministers who want the support of senior civil
servants in their factional battles than for any functional efficiency
created by the existence of 'interlocking directorates'.

Entrants to the service are appointed to the lowest grade within
each career group and, except for the narrow pay range in each

grade, they can in theory only obtain an increase by promotion to a higher grade. Promotion should only occur when there are vacant posts in the grade above. In practice, however, staff pressure to set this principle aside has been irresistible and 'supernumerary' promotion has been widespread. This has given rise to the existence of more directors of divisions and sections than there are divisions and sections to direct, and since it occurs department by department it gives rise to considerable disparities across the service. The practice lies at the root of the absence of a rational relationship between grading and functions noted above. An alternative technique has been to create new units and complexities within a ministry to accommodate promoted staff in new posts of responsibility.

Promotion is based upon a combination of seniority and assessment of ability (*merito*); more rarely, upon written and oral examination. 'Merit' may be 'absolute' or 'comparative'. In the latter case, once the list of those who qualify for promotion in absolute terms is established, promotion itself takes place in order of seniority. This system is particularly prevalent at lower levels of the service. The annual report on all employees below the level of *dirigente superiore,* which includes an assessment of efficiency and, significantly, 'attitudes to those in authority', is a major element in the system. The structure of career management is much criticised. It is widely thought to discourage initiative and favour obedience, and is in any case heavily weighted towards seniority since a disproportionately large number of employees end up with maximum marks on the annual assessment and are classed as equally promotion-worthy. Political considerations are also sometimes thought to play a role in assessment, although obviously this is impossible to prove. There is, however, substantial evidence that the majority of officials themselves see both the system of competition and the system of promotion as inefficient and unjust.

Even greater harm is probably done to civil service morale by the pay structure which has been described as a veritable 'earnings jungle'. The salaries that attach officially to each grade appear fairly low by European standards and Italian civil servants occupy a less favourable place in the earnings hierarchy than their counterparts in other countries. Civil servants also do less well than those in other sectors of the public service such as the special agencies — particularly the state holdings — and regional administration. However, the official pay levels often bear little relationship to real earnings because of an enormous and Byzantine structure of laws and regulations giving special allowances, expenses, overtime earnings and the like to particular individuals or groups. Their range defies classification. Some are insignificant, such as the few pence a month for employees engaged in 'strenuous or very strenuous work'. Others are more significant. In the early seventies it was reported, for example, that certain officials received special allowances ranging from £18 to £50 per month in addition to daily attendance allowances and expenses for acting as hospital auditors. At the very top levels of the service the allowances, directorships of other public agencies and special bonuses are thought to more than double certain salaries. To all these financial benefits a whole range of benefits in kind, such as travel permits, use of official cars and rent-free accommodation must be added.

Recently attempts have been made to rationalise these special payments and no less than 200 were eliminated through incorporation into official pay, particularly at the higher levels. Nevertheless, several hundred remain in existence, including the opportunity to supplement income through institutionalised overtime, for which there is ample scope given that most civil servants work the so-called *orario unico* from 8.00 a.m. to 2.00 p.m. There is no doubt that they make a considerable difference to pay levels although no one knows exactly who benefits most, or by how much. As in the case of career management, however, the effects are unequal and contribute to injustices and divisions within the service.

Reform

In the light of all these problems it is no surprise that the seventies have seen several attempts at reform. These have had three main objectives: to introduce much greater uniformity across the service by removing marked disparities in pay and career prospects; to break down compartmentalisation and promote staff mobility; and to encourage a more 'managerial' approach to administration at the higher levels of the service, thereby increasing efficiency.

Much of the pressure for the first of these objectives has come from the public service branches of the national trade union confederations. They have been especially anxious to establish a unified bargaining system for the whole of public sector employment and in recent years they have increased their formerly rather weak following among public employees. So far, however, they have been unable to break down two important barriers. The first of these is the existence of many independent unions and professional associations operating in the public sector — the most important of which is *Dirstat*, the association of the carriera direttiva. These unions tend to have an inbuilt interest in opposing a unified civil service and a single bargaining structure. Second is the fact that the public sector is regulated by administrative law and that agreements which the unions succeed in concluding have therefore to be ratified by the political authority. Not only does this draw the bargaining process out, it also leaves open the possibility that agreed reforms may subsequently be undermined by unilateral changes, as has occurred several times in recent years.

One of the most important reforms — at least on paper — has concerned the higher reaches of public administration. A Decree of 1972 created a new class of 'managers' (*dirigenti*) at the top of the service. This elite group was to take over many of the formal powers previously vested in the minister. The minister and his closest political aides would then be free to concentrate on setting priorities and forming long-term plans, while the dirigenti would have the task of implementation and coordination, including many of the formal powers of authorisation (e.g. for sums of money up to a given ceiling) which previously absorbed much of the minister's time. The new group would, therefore, enjoy much wider discretionary powers than the old *direttori*, circumscribed as they had been by tight procedural rules. In this way it was hoped to encourage initiative and increase flexibility. Significantly, the salaries of the new group were to be 'comprehensive'; special payments, overtime earnings and allowances were to be abolished or, more accurately, incorporated into the new pay scales. When the scheme was introduced in 1973 this led to the virtual doubling of official salaries of the new groups.

The intention, however, was not to establish a new career class but rather a particular type of administrative function — that of general management — to which members of the carriera direttiva would have access as and when they demonstrated their capacity. To this end the reform was accompanied by a reorganisation of the process of selecting and training higher civil servants. The academic character of the open competition is — very gradually — being modified to incorporate aptitude and personality tests and to include assessment by interview as well as written performance. More important, the Higher School of Public Administration was reorganised to undertake new training functions. It was to recruit graduates straight from university — thereby breaking the practice of recruitment by ministry — and half the new places in the carriera direttiva were to be reserved for such entrants. In this way, it is hoped eventually to create a more cohesive, less compart-mentalised group of senior administrators.

The School was also to provide mid-career management courses for members of the carriera direttiva who, having proved their worth at the level of section director, are chosen for inclusion in the new managerial group. These courses are to include a period of secondment in other ministries or outside agencies and the reports candidates make on this experience will form part of the final examination for the course. Implementation of these provisions has been slow. The new courses for entrants and for the managerial group are only just getting off the ground and it is therefore too early to assess their effectiveness although previous experience of in-service training at the school is not encouraging.

In any case, the experience of the new managerial group has itself proved extremely disappointing so far. Given that manage-ment courses would take several years to bring into operation, the new group was originally created en bloc, with senior members of the carriera direttiva simply re-designated 'dirigenti' within each ministry. Moreover, the group itself is extremely large — 6,000 in all — and has tended to turn into a new career class in the top half of the old carriera direttiva. There are now three grades of dirigente, the highest further divided into classes A, B and C. There are also signs that seniority, rather than merit, is becoming the effective criterion for appointment as a 'manager', with damaging effects upon initiative and morale. Finally, as recent reports by the Court of Accounts testify, the principle of a 'comprehensive' salary scale for all the dirigenti is being gradually undermined by a re-establishment of 'exceptional' payments to selected groups carrying out particular tasks.

The results of the reform have therefore been very limited. There is little evidence that the relationship between ministers and senior civil servants has changed; as one commentator observes, 'the ministers have not learned to plan, nor the managers to manage'. In fact, in some ministries the reform has added to administrative confusion, since the relationship between the dirigenti and the directorates they are supposed to manage has not been adequately defined. The 1972 decree specified only the number of 'dirigenti' to be attached to each ministry but not the directorates, divisions and sections to which they were to be assigned. The absence of any effective re-organisation of the internal structures of the ministries themselves, and the very large numbers of staff involved, have combined to ensure that the functions of the new managerial group are not substantially different from those of the former senior echelons of the carriera direttiva. Moreover, vertical compartmentalisation has not been broken down because, by and large, the dirigenti have remained tied to their particular ministries and horizontal compartmentalisation has in fact increased since they have tended to form an extra career class.

A more radical approach is now being sought. A first step was made in 1977. All personnel in directorates which were abolished as a result of regional devolution and who were not themselves transferred to the regions, were linked together in a new unified block of career groups, attached to the office of the Prime Minister and administered by a committee of senior officials and staff representatives. They are to be assigned new roles in the ministries 'for given periods on the basis of requests by the individual administrations and according to the need to strengthen the service in pursuit of government programmes'. Many hope that this is the first step towards the creation of a completely unified civil service administered by a single Civil Service Commission under the final authority of the Prime Minister.

It is too early to say how effective this will be. The development of Italian public administration has been characterised by the creation of new agencies of control sharing power with the pre-existing ones: partial reforms which have at times done more harm than good. Any new unified structure will have to overcome the resistance of the three agencies which presently share responsibility for personnel administration.

The first of these is the High Council of the Public Administration. It contains senior representatives from each ministry, trade union representatives and a number of outside experts, and must be consulted on personnel policies, management and the organisation of services in central government. Established in the 1950s, the Council represented a first, rather half-hearted attempt to introduce some uniformity into the civil service. It has never succeeded however; its advice is not mandatory on the individual ministries and it has come to function as a forum for departmental interests rather than as a genuinely collegial body.

It has failed, in particular, to impose its will on the second, and most important agency — the ministry, with its own personnel directorate which is advised by a Council of Administration chaired by the minister and containing staff representatives, including a large group from the independent unions and professional associations. It is at the ministry level that the real problems are created and it is here that attempts to unify the service will face their most severe test. The third agency which influences personnel administration, in the sense that it ultimately has formal control over the purse-strings and approves expenditure on personnel, is the Treasury's State Accounting Office. In principle, it could provide a means of coordinating personnel policy throughout the service but any Treasury Minister who used it in this way would soon find himself faced with the opposition not merely of the civil servants themselves but also of departmental ministers. Nevertheless, the key role of the *Ragioniere Generale*, head of the Office, has been recently recognised. He has not only been included in the committee responsible for overseeing the unified block created in 1977 but was also appointed by Prime Minister Giulio Andreotti to head his personal *cabinet*.

Conditions of Service

A law of 1957 regulates conditions of service and lays down an elaborate series of rights and duties together with the appropriate normally very involved-procedures by which rights are protected and by which discipline is invoked.

After a short probationary period, the civil servant enjoys four main rights. The first, tenure, is qualified in various ways. Judges of the Court of Accounts, for example, are virtually irremovable. Ordinary civil servants, on the other hand, can be removed from office at the discretion of the administration (subject to appeal procedures) if, for example, they take on additional employment outside the service, become destitute or are found to be grossly incompetent. Such action, however, is extremely rare. The remaining rights — to payment, career and pension — are strongly conditioned by what is known in Italian public law as the 'moral' status of the civil servant. In choosing to 'serve' the state, he accepts a position of subordination to it, different from that of employer-employee relationships elsewhere. The focus of the relationship, even from the employee's point of view, is upon the service he renders rather than the financial reward he obtains. The latter is not seen as a salary for work done but as a means of freeing him from material pre-occupations. Moreover, the distinction is not merely semantic, even though employment in the public service has recently come to take on an increasingly contractual nature in practice. It has served to perpetuate the hierarchical and authoritarian character of the administration, in which conditions of service are determined by law and through which rights to pay, career and pensions vary considerably across the service because of the complexity of laws and regulations governing employment.

The civil servant also has a number of duties. He is expected to show obedience to his superiors but may question the legality (although not the expediency) of orders given and, if he does so, can only be required to execute them on receipt of written instructions. The 1957 law also makes generous use of the concept of honour. The civil servant must maintain 'good conduct', his behaviour at work must serve as a 'guide and example' for his colleagues, and 'even outside work. . . he must maintain conduct conforming to the dignity of his office'. More generally, he is expected to maintain absolute confidentiality in his work (an obligation which is often used by civil servants in different parts of the administration against each other) and is expected to take an oath of loyalty to the Republic and to defend its Constitution and laws.

This raises the complex issue of political rights. Perhaps surprisingly for a political system as ideologically fragmented as that of Italy, the practice is in many ways more liberal than in Britain, Germany or France. The Constitution declares that the law may place restrictions upon the right to membership of political parties on the part of judges, officers of the armed forces and the police, and members of the diplomatic service. The only other constitutional limitation, however, is that civil servants cannot obtain promotion, except by seniority, while serving as members of parliament. The requirement of an oath of loyalty to the Republic, which potentially could serve the same purpose as the German *Berufsverbot,* has not in practice been used in this way. There may in the forties and fifties have been some discrimination against Communists but since then the party has become increasingly respectable. Nor has the rise of terrorism or student radicalism in recent years led, as yet, to much pressure for a system of discrimination against those whose loyalty to liberal democracy may be questionable.

Part of the reason for this may be that there is a quite clear distinction in Italy between the personnel of the civil service and the political class itself. Unlike Germany or France, the two form almost mutually exclusive career groups and very few senior officials ever leave the service to enter parliament. Moreover, although the nineteenth-century distinction between the role of policy formulation, to be performed by ministers, and the administrative role reserved to the civil servants is no longer tenable in modern Italy, this fact has not given rise to the same debate about the decision-making power of the latter as in some countries, notably Britain. In some ways the problem is seen as lying in quite the opposite direction and recent reforms — in particular the creation of the new managerial group — have actually been designed, without great success, to increase the autonomy of senior officials in administration while improving their capacity to participate in the policy-making process.

Except in matters dealing with the organisation of the service itself, senior officials have probably not been as prone to develop a conventional departmental wisdom on policy matters as their counterparts elsewhere. To the extent that a minister has difficulty in securing the execution of his policies, the problem has so far been seen to lie in two rather different directions: first in the overall efficiency of civil service (i.e. in its ability rather than its willingness to implement a given policy) and second in the capacity of a minister to persuade his colleagues in other departments to pursue policies compatible with his own. This, of course, takes us back to the previously discussed problem of coordination in Italian government.

There is another reason, however, why the question of politics has not been as salient in Italy as in some other countries. Italy has experienced no real change of government since 1945. The major party in all coalitions has been the Christian Democrats. Italy has not had a 'politicised' administration so far for this reason but in practice the administration has tended to collaborate very closely with the Christian Democrats and civil servants have found it to be in their interest not to upset this relationship. It is by no means clear, however, that if a left-wing government came to power there would not be a series of major conflicts between Communist and Socialist ministers and senior officials.

Moreover, senior posts in bodies outside the civil service proper — in the state holdings, banks, insurance and pensions institutes, the broadcasting services and other special agencies most definitely are political appointments. These considerations lie behind the Communist Party's strong support for regional devolution. The more functions it can remove from central government and place in the hands of Communist-controlled regional authorities, the more it believes it will have a chance of improving the quality of Italian administration, and especially of implementing its policies once in power at the centre, since fewer key areas of the administration will then be dominated by those whose contacts, loyalty and policy views were shaped under thirty years of Christian Democrat dominance.

THE CONTROL OF ADMINISTRATION

Like other continental societies, Italy places relatively greater stress than Britain on law, as opposed to parliament, as a guarantee against an overpowerful or arbitrary executive and as a mechanism for the protection of civil and political liberties. Even though Italian governments have traditionally lacked cohesive parliamentary majorities, the legislature itself has not been able to exploit this position to assert any substantial power of scrutiny over the executive, largely because of its own ideological fragmentation.

The Constitution itself, which unlike its predecessor, the *Statuto Albertino*, is a rigid one, provides the fundamental source of legal constraints upon the executive. It is protected, moreover, by a

Constitutional Court which has the power to annul laws which violate the civil, political and economic liberties guaranteed by the Constitution. In this role, the Court has supressed a great deal of legislation that survived the Fascist era. It also performs other functions: it rules, for example, in disputes between various branches of the state and in conflict between state and regions or one region and another.

The second set of legal constraints on the executive is the body of administrative law which defines and limits the behaviour of the public services, and the special courts established to uphold this law. The protection of the citizen against the administration is entrusted, in part, to special courts, not only because of the particular, complex and at times discretionary nature of administrative action, but also in order to uphold the principal of the separation of powers which would be violated if the ordinary judicial authorities were empowered to revoke or change administrative acts. Under certain circumstances, such as action over alleged breach of contract entered into by the administration, an individual does have recourse to the ordinary courts, but in such cases the court has power only to award compensation and not, as in the case of the administrative courts, to annul or modify the action or substitute it, in certain cases, with another.

Administrative justice is not, of course, the only mechanism by which control is exercised over the administration. Parliamentary scrutiny, while less well developed than in Britain or America, does play a role, as do pressure groups and to some extent the press, while intervention by members of parliament on behalf of constituents is often a particularly effective informal channel. Moreover, is we expand the notion of control somewhat from the strict idea of supervising what the administration has already done (audit, redress of grievance) and include within it prior participation in the policy-making process, then it is important to consider procedures by which the administration consults outside advisors and interested parties about its proposed activities.

The Administration Courts

The main special court dispensing administrative justice to individuals is the Council of State. However, this is not the Council's only function; it also performs a consultative role for the government,Moreover, the Court of Accounts, rather than the Council, hears cases dealing with certain financial matters. The Council of State, like the Court of Accounts, dates back to the period of unification, when it played an essentially consultative role, advising the executive on legal and administrative matters submitted to it. In 1889 a new section, the decentralised Provincial Administrative Junta, was added to act as an administrative court for cases brought by private citizens against the various branches of administration. The Republican Constitution envisaged that the latter function would be taken over by regional administrative tribunals but these were only established in 1971 and until then the Council itself, through the administrative juntas, acted as court of first instance.

Since 1971 there has been a two-tier system of administrative justice with regional tribunals (TAR) serving as courts of first instance and the Council of State acting as court of appeal. The regional tribunal is competent to judge the legality of any action by the administrative authorities of the state, the three tiers of local government and some of the special agencies. It also deals with electoral disputes in local government. An action can be judged illegal on the grounds that the administration had no legal competence in the matter, that it used its legal powers for purposes other than those established by the law itself or that it violated the law. Normally, the authority of the tribunal is limited to the simple annulment of the action in question. In a range of cases specified by law, however, it may judge on the merit as well as the legality of the action and in such cases it has authority to modify the action and thus to take over the administrative function itself.

The introduction of regional tribunals has not totally allayed criticism of the slow, rather cumbersome and allegedly conservative nature of administrative justice in Italy. Moreover, they are facing an increasing backlog of work. Their members are still centrally appointed and it is argued that this is an additional element of central control over administrative bodies which have been devolved to the regions, particularly since the magistrates who man the regional tribunals can obtain promotion to the Council of State itself.

In addition to recourse to the regional tribunal, the individual may resort to direct appeal to the administration itself, to the responsible minister or ultimately to the President, who will then refer the issue to the Council of State.

The Council of State, besides acting as an appeal court from the tribunals, also acts as court of first instance for individuals seeking to obtain the compliance of public authorities with judgements made against them in the ordinary courts. In addition, it continues to perform its original consultative role. Its opinion is obtained by the administration on a wide range of matters including the legality and the merit of decrees and administrative regulations, government contracts and conventions to be approved by law, and the codification of laws and regulations. In certain cases the administration has the option of seeking the Council's advice but in others (Cabinet regulations, presidential decrees, codification) it is obligatory. In a very few matters, such as grants of citizenship, that advice is also binding on the administration.

Reference should also be made to the State Advocacy, attached to the Prime Minister's Office. Besides representing the state in legal actions, this body provides the administration with legal counsel on contracts, legislative proposals, decrees and other activities.

Financial Controls

In Italian usage the special administrative courts include not only the Council of State but also the Court of Accounts. The latter in fact, however, performs two types of function. First, like the Council of State, it dispenses administrative justice to individuals. It hears cases concerning the mishandling of state funds by public servants, the civil liability of officials in actions against the state or its agencies, and civil or military pension rights. Regional branches deal with matters concerning financial liability at local government level.

The second and more extensive role performed by the Court of Accounts is that of supervising the financial probity of the administration. This role dates back to the unification of Italy, and similar bodies existed in parts of the peninsula even before that date. The Court performs the functions of inspecting and approving the legality of the financial transactions of central government departments. In this task it is directly responsible to the legislature and may be considered as its 'long arm' for the sort of detailed control which a legislature itself cannot perform. The role of the Court has expanded enormously over the years, as public expenditure has increased, but its procedures have not by and large been adapted to meet the needs of its expanding functions, and various proposals have been made, so far unsuccessfully, for its modernisation. In particular, there is an urgent need to coordinate controls exercised by the Treasury, through the *Ragionerie Centrali,* with those exercised by the Court itself, both to economise on personnel and to speed up the administrative process.

The Court operates *a priori* and *post facto* checks. The former are known as 'preventive' controls. All government decrees, ministerial decrees approving state contracts above a certain sum, all state disbursements and all matters of personnel administration in the civil service which concern appointment, salary, promotion and dismissal, must be registered by the Court (i.e. require its authorisation). There is an elaborate procedure for resolving disputes, at the end of which the Cabinet itself may require registration of the act in question. The Court is then constrained to comply but may communicate its reservations to parliament. Second, there is audit, and in addition to a general audit of the national accounts the Court also audits the accounts of those special agencies outside the central administration, the financial affairs of which are not part of the state budget nor subject to the Court's preventive controls.

In principle, the powers of the Court of Accounts are limited to controlling the legality of the financial affairs of the administration. However, over the years the Court has interpreted this in a wide sense which in effect extends to the expediency of many of the actions under its supervision. This has tended to occur especially where the Court regards the practices or accounting procedures of particular agencies as a barrier to any effective audit or where it considers that one piece of legislation neutralises the effect of another. Thus its general audit of the national accounts, which it presents annually to parliament, contains much critical analysis of policy. One of the great problems in the relationship between the Court and parliament, however, is that the latter is often unwilling to act on the basis of the former's reports. The case of the 'comprehensive' nature of the pay of higher civil servants is symptomatic in this respect. The 1975 and 1976 reports set out in great detail the ways in which the 'comprehensive' principle was being systematically undermined through special exemptions.

However, since these exemptions were often the work of parliament itself and enshrined in law, the Court's remonstration tended to be little more than a cry in the wilderness.

Consultation

The Council of State has both a judicial and a consultative role, in that it is not only a special court but a body established to provide an independent and at times binding opinion on aspects of administration. The Council is, however, only one of a series of advisory bodies established either by the Constitution or by law which play an important role in shaping the activities of government.

Another such body is the National Council of the Economy and Labour. It consists of a chairman, fifty-nine members to represent the various interests of the economy (private industry, finance, the public sector, the unions, the self-employed) and twenty 'experts' from advisory committees attached to government, the National Research Council, the Chambers of Commerce and so on. It advises the administration, the legislature and the regions on economic and social matters and can also present legislative proposals to parliament. Like any purely consultative body, it is difficult to estimate the impact of the Council upon the administration. It has enjoyed considerable prestige over the years as a forum for debate on a wide range of affairs but in the seventies it has probably had far less influence than bilateral negotiations between the government and the union confederations or employers' organisations.

There are also a number of special advisory committees attached to particular ministries which enjoy legal status. These are generally composed of both civil servants and outside experts, including representatives of the major interest groups operating in the field concerned. Among the most important are those attached to the Ministries of Finance, Defence, Education, Agriculture and Public Works. Without doubt they play an extremely important role in providing the administration with information and in advising it on technical questions, particularly during the drafting of laws and regulations. On occasions, however, it seems that certain interest groups have succeeded in establishing a powerful preferential relationship with the ministry in question through these agencies and in this way have exercised an undue influence over civil service thinking.

Parliamentary Controls

The Italian parliament enjoys, in principle, a wide range of investigatory powers which should give it control over the administration but in practice these powers have not been developed to the full. This may in part reflect the relatively lower prestige which it enjoys compared with, say, its British counterpart. Parliamentary proceedings in Italy tend to arouse little public interest and, as a result, debates and questions, let alone the operations of select committees of inquiry, do not have much impact. Certainly, they neither define the relationship between ministers and senior civil servants, nor constrain the actions of the civil servants themselves, in the way that they do in Britain.

Collective cabinet responsibility and individual ministerial responsibility before parliament have little meaning. Conflict within parliament has been taken for granted because of ideological fragmentation and hence criticism of the government has been rather devalued. The absence of a credible opposition in the first twenty-five years of the Republic further weakened parliamentary control. The ultimate sanction of withdrawal of parliamentary confidence — never a very credible weapon for detailed control of the executive in any political system — has meant little in Italy because a government has generally been secure in the knowledge that there was no alternative to it. The high degree of Cabinet instability in Italy conceals a marked stability in both the parties and the personnel who form the government.

In the seventies the ideological tension has declined and in certain quarters the concept of a left-wing alternative has gained ground, particularly in view of the electoral progress made by the parties of the Left. But the Communist Party itself has chosen to reject such a possibility, preferring instead — for largely defensive reasons — its own proposal of an 'historic compromise' with the Christian Democrats and Socialists; and in disguised form, such a coalition already operates. Critics of the ineffectiveness of parliament find it particularly ironic that in a period when ideological confrontation has begun to give way to genuine policy discussion of a more pragmatic sort and when, as a result, the chances of focusing attention upon the ills of Italian administration are better than they have ever been, the party which could best lead this criticism and form the basis of an alternative government is leaning over backwards to mute its attacks. They are also understandably alarmed at the further damaging effect a massive coalition of more than 80 per cent of the parliamentary seats would have on parliamentary control.

The Italian parliament does, in fact, equip itself with a number of specialised committees — normally joint committees of both houses — to supervise administrative activity. Several, such as the joint committees on the supervision of public broadcasting, are permanent. Others are established to investigate a particular issue, for example the committee of enquiry into the security services, the government agricultural agency, the problem of the Mafia (and its relationship to the administration in the south) and unemployment. In general, however, none of these has had any real impact.

Probably the most serious weakness of parliament arises in relation to public expenditure. Here real control is virtually nonexistent. The annual approval of the budget tends to be a formality. It is enormously complex and few parliamentarians have either the time or inclination to get to grips with it. In any case, it gives no real indication of what public expenditure will actually be or how it will be financed. This is because many of the most important items, such as the budgets of the special agencies, totalling half or more of public expenditure, are not included in the budget.

However, individual members of parliament are able to exercise substantial influence over the activities of the administration in particular cases. Parliamentarians are continually occupied with intervention on behalf of their constituents but often the purpose is to secure a privilege — the grant of a pension is the most ubiquitous example — rather than to remedy some administrative injustice.

CONCLUSION

The Italian administrative system grew up in a world dominated by two assumptions: that politicians and administrators would naturally tend towards corruption, patronage and arbitrary rule unless very firmly held in check by tight legal constraints and that a society constantly prey to fissiparous tendencies needed strong centralised control to hold it together. The expansion of the scope of government and the experience of Fascism modified the resultingly rigid and hierarchical pattern of administration, breaking down the boundary between politics and administration and creating a dual system in which the formal ministry-based hierarchy was paralleled by a plethora of special agencies.

As a result, post-war Italy has in many ways experienced the worst of several worlds. She has an administrative system which until the introduction of regional government was territorially very centralised. However, in order to free certain types of administrative activity from inappropriately strict legal controls, many semi-autonomous public bodies have been established. In this way the advantages of centralisation — in terms of policy coordination — are lost.

Furthermore, although in theory the Italian administration is not 'politicised', in practice it has tended to be so — but in a special way. Because one party has held the reigns of government for so long, there is very little circulation of senior administrators on a party basis; in any case a clear division exists in personnel terms between politicians and administrators. The vast majority of administrators, both in the central departments and the special agencies, nevertheless have close informal links with the Christian Democrat Party. This could have led to a useful working relationship and have facilitated policy formation and execution. However, since the focus of politics in Italy has not, until recently, been upon issues of broad public policy, the crux of the relationship between politicians and administrators has tended to hinge on the occupation of spheres of influence in the administration for the power of patronage which this offers rather than the control of overall policy. Given the firmly established but internally divided regime which the Christian Democrat Party has established, the politicisation of the administration which has taken place has been between different types of Christian Democrat patronage appointees as the party's internal factions have vied for influence. The allocation of influence has not been to different parties but to different Christian Democrat groups. In this way the tendency of the administrative system under Fascism to divide up into a series of fiefdoms, each acting on its own account, has repeated itself in Republican Italy.

Yet the need for modernisation has become increasingly apparent. The extraordinarily high levels of self-generated economic growth in the fifties and sixties turned Italy into an advanced industrial society in a shorter space of time than almost any other European society. Economic development has inevitably made society more complex and has led the public to far greater expectations of government than previously. But the capacity of the administrative machine to satisfy the needs thus generated, especially in social terms — education, health and welfare, housing, transport and urban planning — has signally failed to keep up with this development. In the late sixties and seventies economic growth itself faltered. The need for an administrative system capable of managing the economy has thus become ever more urgent. Unfortunately the attitudes, experience and capacities of the senior civil servants simply do not lend themselves to the creation of a dynamic and managerial role of this type. Some first tentative steps were recently taken towards reform but the public service in Italy remains in greater need of drastic re-organisation and modernisation than in almost any other country of the European Community.

CHAPTER SIX

Belgium

THE BACKGROUND

Belgium is, in European terms, a fairly new state, unusual in that it has possessed a single liberal constitution during the whole period of its independent existence. Its territory essentially consists of those southern provinces of the Spanish-governed Netherlands retained by Spain after the predominantly Protestant north became the Dutch republic in the sixteenth century. For the next 250 years, as part first of the Spanish and then the Austrian Empire, these southern provinces were under pressure from the Dutch to the north and France in the south. They were annexed by France from 1795 to 1815, then united with the Netherlands until 1830. The new arrangements did not last. An independent Belgium was proclaimed in 1830 and the national integrity of the new state was guaranteed by the great powers.

In 1831 the Belgian Constitution was the most liberal in Europe. Its authors were strongly influenced by the democratic but anti-authoritarian side of the legacy of the French Revolution. It proclaimed that 'All powers stem from the Nation'; guaranteed individual rights and equality before the law; and established a parliamentary system with a constitutional monarchy. For nearly 140 years the only major constitutional amendments related to extension of the franchise and reform of the electoral system. However, in 1970 fundamental changes were made with the primary objective of achieving a solution to the 'language question'.

The broad outlines of the present multi-party system have clear historical roots in the development of politically salient divisions in Belgian society — religion, class and language. In common with many predominantly Catholic countries in nineteenth century Europe, a political cleavage developed between the advocates of the lay state and the defenders of a distinctlively Catholic type of society. Towards the end of the century the lay group split with the emergence of a working-class party seeking fundamental economic and social reforms. These tendencies still underpin the three major political groupings and their electoral support. The Christian Social Party is now a broadly based Catholic party which has abandoned its formal links with the Church and attracts support across class barriers. In this it was aided by a notably progressive Catholic hierarchy which took the lead in establishing Catholic institutions for the working class, especially the important trade union confederation and many social and cooperative organisations. The Liberal parties represent a lay, but no longer militantly anti-clerical, political trend suspicious of the role of government and favouring free enterprise. This appeals particularly strongly to business men, the self-employed and small employers, and among the professional classes. The Socialist Party is a reformist or social-democratic organisation, drawing its support disproportionately from the non-Catholic working class and closely associated with the lay trade unions.

There is some geographical bias in party strength. Industrialisation started in the south, which was also the most secularised part of the country, and consequently liberalism and socialism were strongest in this area. The Liberals have always been particularly well established in Brussels. The north, which is more Catholic, and was until recently comparatively backward economically, has provided the most support for the Christian Socials. This bias in the distribution of electoral support on the basis of religion and class is further complicated by the third factor — language. In establishing an independent state the Belgians were agreed on their desire not to be ruled by their neighbours but this was a fragile basis for national unity. Belgium has two major linguistic communities: Flemish (a form of Dutch) in the north and French-speaking Walloons in the south. (There is also a small German community in the east.) Though the Flemish were in a slight majority, the country was dominated by Walloons. French was the language of all branches of government; the legal and administrative systems were conducted entirely in French except at the very lowest levels. Wallonia was the economically dynamic part of the country, so French dominated industry, commerce and the professions. Members of the Flemish community found themselves regarded almost as second-class citizens, part of a culturally inferior rural peasantry. It took over a century before Flemish achieved equal status with French. Paradoxically, this equality produced not bilingual peace but intensified struggle between the language communities. The explanation lies largely in the Walloon fear of being swamped, of losing more than their previously privileged position as their power base is eroded. The Flemish speakers now outnumber the French by about 55:45. Moreover, the economic positions have been partially reversed since 1945: Wallonia, whose economy was based on the traditional products of the industrial revolution, suffered badly from their decline and is now a suppliant for government grants while Flanders benefitted from the rise of more prosperous industries.

Simple bilingualism has not been seen as a satisfactory solution for a number of reasons. With the important exception of Brussels, most parts of the country are linguistically homogenous, either French or Flemish. In addition, the two groups are not equally willing to reciprocate in learning the other language. Nearly all Flemish speakers (except the most extreme nationalists) are willing to learn French and can see the practical advantages of doing so; but many Walloons are not keen to learn Flemish, which they consider a minor language in the international context, and would much prefer their children to be taught English or German as a second language. The political saliency of the language issue has two consequences for the party system. In addition to the rise of language-issue parties — the Volksunie, Rassemblement Wallon and Front Démocratique des Francophones in Brussels — the language wings of the old major parties have become increasingly independent. Since 1968 the Christian Socials have two parties which have shown quite serious disagreements, the French wing of the Liberals has identified very closely with the French language parties, and in 1978 the Socialists decided on separation.

Since the early 1960s there has been a general movement towards cultural autonomy for the linguistic groups and devolution of some central government functions to the regions but the precise measures have been the subject of great controversy between the political parties. In 1962-63 legislation was passed fixing a language boundary across the country, on each side of which one language is used exclusively by the public services and in education. Brussels, however, is bilingual. This was followed by a number of constitutional amendments in 1970 carrying the process of linguistic

Election to Chamber of Representatives, 1977

	Votes (%)	Seats (212)
Christian Socials		
Flemish wing CVP	26.2	56
French wing PSC	9.7	24
Socialists		
Flemish wing BSP	11.3	27
French wing PSB	15.1	35
Liberals		
Flemish party PVV	8.6	17
French party PRLW	5.9	14
Fr. Brussels PL	1.1	2
Language Parties		
Flemish VU	4.2	10
French RW	2.8	5
Communists	2.7	2

apartheid further and entrenching the rights of the two communities. However, much of the subsequent legislation required to implement these policies has proved very difficult to pass because it needs a two-thirds majority. The chief stumbling block has been over the status and boundaries of Brussels. Special provision had to be made for the capital city because it is a predominantly French island on the Flemish side of the boundary. Moreover, its suburbs are expanding into Flemish territory: thus the French-speaking majority in Brussels, the Flemish minority in the city and the French and Flemish communities on the periphery are not easily reconciled on any set of proposals.

The language question in the last twenty years has become one of the principle obstacles to forming coalitions and has shortened the life of many governments. Coalitions in the twenty-two governments since the war have included all possible permutations of the three major parties but it is only since 1974 that any of the language parties have participated. It is the Christian Socials who enjoy the pivotal position in coalition formation since on social and economic questions they can lean to the right with the Liberals or to the left with the Socialists. Along with the distribution of posts between the coalition parties, the maintenance of balance between the languages had become a tradition and it is a sign of the strength of the language issue that the 1970 constitutional amendments provide that with the exception of the Prime Minister there must be an equal number of French- and Flemish-speaking ministers.

The Institutional Framework

The basic structures of Belgian public administration are now in a process of wide-ranging reform which makes the system rather difficult to comprehend. Traditionally Belgium has been a unitary state with a single legislative authority (Chamber of Representatives and Senate): a single executive under the political leadership of the Prime Minister and Cabinet; and geographical decentralisation provided by a two-tier local government system whose executives were under a loose central supervision. This simple scheme started to be modified with the enormous increase in the range of activities of the state, leading to a proliferation of new agencies on an *ad hoc* basis at both national and local level.

In the last two decades, under the political stimulus of the language issue, more fundamental reforms have been introduced. The legislature has been divided for certain purposes, with exclusive jurisdiction on specified cultural matters being given to single-language groups of deputies and senators – the Cultural Councils. Special ministers have been appointed to the Cabinet, some with responsibility for the cultural affairs of the language communities, others with territorially defined functions. Advisory councils with executives have been established for the three regions of Wallonia, Flanders and Brussels. A partial restructuring of the lower tier of local government has been instituted.

In May 1977 the parties forming the new coalition signed a *Pacte Communautaire* committing them to more drastic reforms which would involve the devolving of a very wide range of central government functions to three directly elected regional councils (possessing legislative powers and financial autonomy) and their executives, and to two language community councils. These proposals, while avoiding the actual word, seem to imply an unusually complex federal system. At present many of the reforms which have been instituted are either incomplete or so recent that it is not yet clear how they will operate in practice. Some of them may be viewed as merely transitional stages towards the implementation of the *Pacte Communautaire* or other similar proposals.

The Cabinet

At the apex of the central executive stands the Cabinet. While executive acts are carried out in the name of the monarch, they must be countersigned by the relevant minister(s) who are individually responsible to the legislature and bound by collective responsibility. The composition and overall programme of the Cabinet depend on the interparty discussion which take place under the direction of the 'formateur' (Prime Minister designate). This means that the authority of the Prime Minister and the autonomy of the Cabinet are restricted by the preliminary conditions laid down by the parties. The distribution of ministerial posts is the result of bargaining between the coalition partners, with each party filling its share from its own nominees. Much of the policy of the government may be defined in advance and is often embodied in a written agreement. Participation is normally ratified by the executives and/or special congresses of the parties concerned.

The Cabinet includes all ministers but not Secretaries of State who usually attend only for those matters relevant to their responsibilities. The number and nature of the posts is not fixed and since the second world war there has been a marked tendancy for the Cabinet to expand, which has been accentuated by the establishment of offices with particular responsibility for the regions and linguistic groups. Ministers usually have a parliamentary background although this is not required under the Constitution and parties do sometimes put in office technocrats, academics or leaders of special interest groups from among their external supporters.

Tindemans Government, June 1977

	Flemish	*French*
Christian Social	Prime Minister Minister of Finance Justice Transport Public Health and Environment Secretary of State for Flemish Culture/Flemish Affairs Reform of Institutions Flemish Economy	Minister of Defence (and Deputy Prime Minister) Social Security Agriculture/Middle Classes French Education Secretary of State for Social Affairs
Socialists	Minister of. Interior Economic Affairs Pensions Flemish Education Secretary of State for Economic Affairs	Minister of. Public Service (& Deputy Prime Minister) Foreign Affairs Employment Public Works/ Walloon Affairs French Culture Secretary of State for Reform of Institutions Walloon Economy
Language Parties	Minister of. External Trade Scientific Policy Secretary of State for Flemish Culture	Minister of Development Cooperation Posts/Brussels Affairs Secretary of State for French Culture

The party balance gives 9 ministers + 3 Secretaries of State each to the Christian Socials and the Socialists, 2 + 1 each to the language parties. The linguistic balance gives 11 + 4 for each language.

Meetings of the Cabinet normally take place weekly. After the formation of the government the Prime Minister circularises his colleagues with a memorandum laying down the procedures and functions of the Cabinet which are fairly complex since it combines two rather different roles. It provides political leadership, linking the executive with the democratic institutions of the country. Thus the Cabinet asssumes responsibility for government policy, decides priorities, discusses draft legislation, etc. In addition, because of the divisions in Belgian society and the coalition system, questions involving government patronage often come to the Cabinet. It has also acquired a large number of detailed administrative tasks. While constitutional theory gives the power of executing policies (by decree and specific decision) to individual ministers acting in the monarch's name, the practice has grown up of requiring the minister to act with the approval of the Cabinet. Indeed, particularly since the second world war, many laws have expressly required Cabinet discussions before the responsible minister can take the necessary executive measures to implement them. This has overloaded the Cabinet with largely trivial matters and since 1961 various attempts have been made to deal with these in committees but without complete success.

The delegation and coordination of business within the Cabinet are largely secured by the role of the Prime Minister and the use of committees. As in most systems, the Ministry of Finance also exercises a coordinating role in policies involving expenditure. Since 1918 the Prime Minister has had his own office with staff which can advise him on all aspects of government policies, including a high proportion of able junior and senior officials as well as some personal advisers. A number of other administrative groups are placed under the Prime Minister. These include the Chancellery, which provides the Cabinet Secretariat; the Economic Research and Coordination Department to investigate and advise on all aspects of economic and social policy; and the Main Supervisory Committee — which has the job of 'policing' the conduct of the public services — especially in relation to such matters as government contracts. The three organisations responsible for the management of the civil service sometimes come within the Prime Ministerial sector (recently under a special Secretary of State). Sometimes, however, they were placed under the Ministers of Finance or the Interior and in the 1977 government responsibility for the public service was allocated to one of the two Deputy Prime Ministers.

Since 1938 a system of functional Cabinet committees has developed to spread the burden of work. The number and titles of these committees has changed frequently but they typically include Economic and Social Coordination, Budget, Institutional Reform, Environment, and Scientific Policy. The structure is laid down by decree after the formation of the government so that (unlike the

British system) the titles, membership and functions of the committees are a matter of public record. All committees have the Prime Minister as chairman and perform two main functions: preparatory work on policy before full Cabinet discussions and settling many of the technical details theoretically must be discussed in Cabinet. A peculiarity of the Belgian system is that the same formal procedure has often been used to establish an inner circle of senior ministers, most recently under the title of the Inner Cabinet on General Policy.

The Ministries

In the nineteenth century the pattern was simple, with five traditional ministries — Foreign Affairs, Finance, Interior, Justice, Defence — each headed by a single minister. However, the rise of the newer social and economic ministries and the regular reshuffling of administrative responsibilities make it impossible to give such a definitive list today. But the growth in the number of ministers has been even greater than the number of departments, so the principle of a single minister identified with a single ministry has almost completely disappeared. One of the causes is political: a comparison of the ministerial titles in the government above with the ministries in the following table suggests the difficulties imposed by the need to satisfy coalition partners. One may now find a minister at the head of a ministry, possibly with another minister or Secretary of State subordinate to him; several ministers of equal status controlling different divisions of a ministry; a minister without a ministry but with responsibilities defined regionally and/or functionally. The role of the three ministers with responsibilities for the regions is unclear. In their regional capacity they do not stand at the head of ministries, nor do they have authority over other ministers or executive authority in any ministries. The regional minister has a coordinating role and acts as chairman of the ministerial committee for his region. There has been some parliamentary criticism of the consequent blurring of responsibilities and the alleged inefficiencies arising from this situation.

Ministers are aided in their political and administrative work by their own personal staff, the ministerial *cabinet*, paid far out of public funds. In theory each minister is limited to a *cabinet* of seven

Ministries and Associated Bodies, 1976

	Depart-mental Staff	Special Corps	Public Organisat-ions
Prime Minister	700		
Foreign Affairs and External Trade	3,400		500
Finance	32,400		6,600
Interior	2,800	15,900[1]	
Justice	5,800	7,900[2]	
Defence	5,600	56,400[3]	200
Economic Affairs	3,500		900
Agriculture	2,500		1,900
Public Health and Family Affairs	3,200		5,500
Employment	1,200		3,000
Social Security	600		6,400
Public Works	9,300		5,200
Communications	2,100		148,600[5]
Middle Classes	400		1,500
National Education and Culture	3,900	88,600[4]	6,400
	77,400	168,800	186,700

1 Includes 15,700 Gendarmerie, responsibility for whom is shared with Justice and Defence, and the staff of the Conseil d'Etat
2 Judiciary and court staff
3 Military personnel
4 Staff in nationally administered education. Not included are the 57,100 employed by local government and the 134,600 in the subsidised private (Catholic) sector
5 Railways, postal services, telecommunications, civil aviation, shipping

advisers but this rule is widely disregarded and the average is probably twice this number. The majority are normally drawn from within the civil service but will be politically sympathetic to the minister and others may be outsiders from his political party, trade unions and the universities.

The division between ministries is based on the specialised performance of the functions of government. The general approach has been to retain the same administrative units in spite of changes in ministerial titles. But the principle of a unified administration is under great strain with the move to language-based and regional reforms. Already, with the establishment of the cultural councils, the Ministry of Education and Culture is divided from top to bottom on linguistic lines. If the widespread devolution of powers to directly elected regional councils and their executives should take place, then the internal division of most of the domestic ministries will necessarily follow. In practice the laws relating to the use of languages in public administration have already caused some internal divisions. While Brussels is bilingual, ministry field services in Wallonia and Flanders must use exclusively the language of their region, both internally and in their dealings with the public. The central offices of ministries, while largely bilingual internally, must use the appropriate language when communicating with field services in a particular region.

In addition, the type of work undertaken by different departments varies considerably and this is reflected in the staffing figures above. Finance deals with other ministries and also directly with the public; other ministries such as Defence, Foreign Affairs, and Public Works are directly responsible for the implementation of government policies. Economic Affairs has a largely advisory and consultative role. Social Security is mainly concerned with supervising and coordinating work which is actually carried out by public organisations, local government, Public Assistance Commissions and private institutions. This partial dispersal of the administration is both functional and geographical.

Functional Decentralisation

About 38 per cent of the ministry's ordinary staff work in Brussels, with most of the rest dispersed in field services throughout the country. Some ministries also have groups of staff known as 'special corps' which in effect constitute their principle field services. These include the gendarmerie, armed forces, judiciary, teachers and research staff in state institutions. They are all directly under a ministry and carry out its policies but are largely self-contained with a specialised function and professionally competent personnel.

A greater degree of decentralisation is provided by the public corporations (*organismes d'intérêt public*). In 1976 there were eighty-seven concerns, varying greatly in size and type of activity. They include the Belgian Railways (SNCB) with 55,700 employees; the State-School Building Fund with 1,400; the Fund for Occupational Disease with 500; the Belgian National Orchestra with 100; and the

Leather Trades' Council with 2. These bodies are established by separate laws which determine the precise status, functions and structure of each, although a law of 1954 did set up a general framework for some of them. Every public organisation has a 'tutelary' ministry which oversees its activities but the actual degree of supervision and control varies considerably. The ministry with the largest empire is Communications which has the major utilities: railways, postal services, telecommunications, civil aviation and marine transport. In general the public organisations work in the fields of savings, credit, insurance, health and welfare, economic planning, industrial organisation, specialist construction, culture and education, as well as the publicly owned utilities and industries.

Geographical Decentralisation

There is a strong local government tradition in Belgium and its existence is guaranteed by the Constitution. Local authorities have a general competence, subject to financial and administrative supervision by central government and the administrative courts, and also many statutory functions.

There are nine Provinces which constitute the upper but less important level of local government, their main functions being vocational further education, drainage and some roads. The elected council meets infrequently but nominates an executive committee of six which is presided over by the provincial Governor who is appointed by central government, in effect until retirement, and acts for the Ministry of the Interior. His basic responsibility is the preservation of public order, dealing with emergencies and generally acting as an ambassador for the national government in his area. In practice he often works as an ambassador in the opposite direction. Unlike the French Prefect, he does not coordinate local field services of central ministries, nor does he have such wide powers of interference in the running of local government.

The basic unit of local government is the commune. It also has an executive, made up of aldermen and headed by the burgomaster. This paid official, who is neither anonymous nor politically neutral, is nominally appointed by central government but in practice this is merely a ratification of the local choice. Among the services provided by communes are local police and fire service, many local utilities including water, sewerage and gas, education and local roads. They are also responsible for local Public Assistance Commissions which administer local health care and social security.

For many years the problem with the communes was that there were too many (about 2,600), they were too small (about 60 per cent under 2,000 population) and their boundaries no longer corresponded to the real structure of the country. The first solution was to authorise the piecemeal creation of intercommunal associations to provide particular services. This was followed by legislation encouraging mergers between communes, culminating in the law of 1975. A law of 1971 also set up two types of multi-purpose agglomerations of communes — Urban Areas and, in less densely populated areas, Federations — both of which involve the compulsory association of groups of communes into a new intermediate level of local government. As well as encouraging coordination of services among the constituent communes, the new Urban Areas and Federations have had certain functions transferred to them by law — public transport, planning, sewerage and the fire service. In addition the members concerned may agree to transfer other functions. This makes for a rather complex system, particularly in Brussels where wholesale reform and the merging of communes has not been possible because of language-based political objections. Thus the Brussels connurbation is administered by nineteen communes, which also comprise the Urban Area, plus a further six 'peripheral communes' in the suburbs and five neighbouring Federations of communes.

Local Government Staff, 1976

Communes	122,700[1]
Intercommunal Associations	13,600
Urban Areas and Federations	2,700
Public Assistance Commissions	40,700
Provinces	29,900[2]
	209,600

1   Includes 45,700 teachers
2   Includes 11,400 teachers

Another level of government is in the process of creation. The 1974 law set up advisory Regional Councils and Ministerial Committees for Regional Affairs as a temporary first step towards the implementation of the 1970 constitutional amendments. The Walloon and Flemish councils consist of the senators who speak the appropriate language and whose legal residence is in the region concerned. The Brussels Regional Council consists of the senators resident in the area plus forty-two members of the Urban Area Council. The regional councils and the ministerial committees have only a consultative status with an advisory role on the regional aspect of such policies as land development, economic and employment policies, housing, public health, tourism and forestry. If the 1977 Pacte Communautaire proposals are carried out a great many central government functions will be devolved entirely, leaving only foreign affairs, defence, justice, national finance and economic management, and the fundamental principles of social security at the national level. The Provinces would be abolished but sub-regions would be introduced. The levels of government and administration would then be very complex and probably represents at least one level too many for a country the size of Belgium.

THE CIVIL SERVICE

The present formal structures of the civil service in Belgium have only been developed in the last forty years. The system which grew up in the nineteenth century was based on individual ministries with no uniform criteria of appointment or service. Patronage was the norm as ministers and their political parties colonised the ministries in succession. In the 1930s there was increasing criticism of this state of affairs and a new system was gradually inaugurated on the recommendations of Louis Camu who had been appointed a Royal Commissioner for Administrative Reform. Working in the British Northcote-Trevelyan tradition, he advocated a politically neutral unified career service, recruitment on the basis of educational qualifications into a four-class structure, promotion on recognised merit and uniform conditions of service. Legislation to implement the Camu reforms came into effect in 1937-39 but was delayed by the war and post-war upheavals so that many of the provisions were not really applied until the 1950s. During this transitional period the service was swollen by the admission of many new staff under the pressure of events, generally without correct procedures, although most had their position regularised afterwards.

The framework of the civil service is now established by legal rules, backed up by internal tribunals and the administrative courts. Its management is shared by three bodies. The Permanent Recruiting Secretariat, dating from 1939, controls the admission procedure which for the two higher classes is by written competitive examination and interview. The successful candidate will be admitted to a particular ministry and is likely to remain within it. After a probationary period of two or three years, the recruit has to pass an examination in subjects relevant to his duties. Supervision of the probationer is undertaken by the General Selection and Training Directorate, set up in 1963, which is responsible for career management and training. The general practice is to recruit professionally qualified specialists for those posts which require a high degree of expertise. For other entrants a rather limited amount of in-service training is provided which, in fact, largely takes the form of acquiring practical experience — learning on the job — with some short courses, although there is a fairly generous attitude to staff who wish to study privately for professional qualifications. Overall supervision of the service is the duty of the General Administration Department, also set up in 1939. This body is responsible for regulations on conditions of service, pay and grading.

The service is divided into four horizontal classes each of which is subdivided into grades. Excluding the special corps, personnel were distributed (in 1976) as follows: class 1 — 9,300; class 2 — 24,700; class 3 — 21,300; class 4 — 14,600. Class 1 is often referred to as the administrative class, being concerned with the highest levels of management and policy formulation. Those members who are recruited directly into this class from outside the service are normally university graduates. In practice promotion from class 2 to class 1 is quite frequent. Class 2 is responsible for much of the detailed execution of policy, in which no great element of individual discretion is required, and for the supervision of members of classes 3 and 4. Its members must normally have at least satisfactorily completed their secondary education. Class 3 is largely made up of clerical staff employed in routine tasks and some skilled tradesmen.

Class 4 includes porters, messengers and a large group of unskilled maintenance staff. In practice all established civil servants, about 90 per cent of total staff, enjoy complete security of tenure, are entitled to a pension and have the right to join a trade union and to strike.

Management within each ministry is in the hands of the *Conseil de Direction,* made up of the heads of the divisions within the ministry. This small committee puts forward names to the minister for appointment and promotion. To deal with internal conflicts and disciplinary proceedings each ministry has an appeals' tribunal, half the members being nominated by the minister and half by the civil service unions. An interesting feature is the entrenched official status given to the four main public service unions. Their representatives sit on a central consultative commission for the whole service and on the committees covering individual ministries and all other administrative units which must be consulted on all proposals affecting public officials. The duty to consult these bodies is statutory and if a minister should fail to do so the Conseil d'Etat could annul his decision. The use of languages adds a further complicating factor to staffing within the service. Since all field services (and local government and the courts) in Wallonia and Flanders must use the language appropriate to their region, this means that staff will in practice be drawn from that linguistic group. Staff in the field services and central offices in Brussels must be prepared to work in either language but whole classes of central administrative work such as communications with regional field services must be carried out in a specified language. Thus while the staff are bilingual, there is a tendency for duplication of posts and work to be allocated along linguistic lines. Jobs such as filing are made more difficult and significant time is spent on translation.

The Higher Civil Servants

The members of class 1 — the administrative class — are responsible for general management, policy formulation and specialised advice to ministers. The class show some surprising features in terms of size and age structure. It makes up to 13.2 per cent of the civil service, a much larger proportion than was to be found in the equivalent British group, for example. Camu had envisaged that

'Secretary' would, as the entry point for young university graduates, serve to introduce these potential 'high-fliers' to high-level administrative functions. Of this large group of staff only just under 30 per cent are university graduates. These facts are interconnected. An

Administrative Class, 1976

Grade	Title	Numbers
17	Secretary General[1]	24
16	Director General	140
15	Inspector General	320
14	First Adviser	240
13	Director	1,100
12	First Engineer	800
11	Adjunct Director	2,900
10	Secretary	3,700

Includes Governors of Provinces
The titles of grade designate rank rather than strict job descriptions relating to the organisation of work in administrative units. While the class is not divided by specialisms, grade 12 is in fact largely filled by professionally qualified specialists including accountants in the Finance Ministry. An Inspector General may be employed either within the administrative hierarchy or as an inspector

examination of the age distribution for this grade (in 1976) shows that there is a 'double peak' for ages 27-33 and 48-55, as well as substantial representation for every year up to 65. The younger peak indicates the graduate entrants, the older group corresponds to the irregular direct entrants into this class in the post-war period who were established permanently in the service through trade union pressure. In addition, the presence of significant numbers of staff in this grade throughout the age range up to retirement testifies to the success of the trade union policy of keeping a very wide door open for entry into the class by promotion for non-graduates from the executive class 2. This has swollen the administrative class as a whole, especially the lower grades with a very large group of personnel who have no practical possibility of being considered for the very highest posts; it is dominated numerically by middle-aged men with very limited promotion prospects.

The career structure is now a very stable closed system. New graduate entrants aged about 24 have no other employment experience; more than 80 per cent of the two highest grades are graduates who on average have served 27 years to reach Director General. The typical civil servant who has reached these grades may expect to serve another 7-10 years before retirement. This makes for a high degree of continuity among the permanent heads of ministries, particularly when compared with the political leadership. There were nineteen Secretary Generals but seventy Ministers of Finance between 1831 and 1970.

There is a strong tendency for staff to remain within the ministry, or related group of ministries, to which they were appointed. The service is unified so that professionally qualified 'specialists' enjoy realistic prospects of an administrative career although traditionally this is related to the nature of individual ministries. In 'technical ministries', such as Public Works, Agriculture and Public Health, it is very common to find the most senior general administrative posts occupied by qualified specialists — engineers, doctors and agronomists. The highest offices in other ministries used to be dominated by law graduates but there has been a swing towards economics and the social sciences. In 1970 the academic background of the top two grades was: law 30 per cent, engineering 22 per cent, economics and social science 20 per cent, agriculture 10 per cent, medicine 8 per cent. The nature of Belgian public administration is less legalistic than, for example, the German, and while some knowledge of law is useful to the high official, it is by no means necessary.

Politics and Bureaucracy

The Camu reforms were designed to ensure a politically neutral civil service but this objective has not been achieved. It is widely acknowledged that the service is highly politicised, that appointments and promotions are partly determined by political affiliation and that the behaviour of public servants is influenced by their partisan preferences. One study asked high officials to rank the factors which actually influenced promotion to their levels. The top five criteria were membership of a ministerial cabinet, connections with a political party, university degree, attracting the attention of politicians by showing knowledge of certain problems and connections with a trade union.

This situation has often been attributed to the practice of importing outsiders into the higher levels of the administration for political reasons but after the immediate post-war period this has become increasingly unusual. It depends, rather, on the fact that the 'objective' procedures for assessing appointments and promotions culminate in the presentation of a short-list of approved candidates to the minister who makes the final choice. For the most senior posts Cabinet approval is necessary. In a society which is highly segmented on religious, political, linguistic and regional lines there are strong pressures on ministers and their advisers to favour their own. Thus many ambitious civil servants will seek to gain the support of a political party, or a faction or interest group within it. Political groups strive quite naturally to influence their ministers in such matters. There is a general perception that a degree of proportionality between the major parties and groups in society should be maintained in the public service but this is roughly attained by the expectation that as ministers change each group can expect to take its turn. It is often observed that the need for proportionality can increase the career chances of individuals with a less than usual combination of personal characteristics, e.g. a Flemish, non-Catholic, socialist graduate in agriculture.

The system has functional disadvantages. With a number of groups pressing on behalf of their nominees, the temptation is to enlarge the administration in order to satisfy them. This is intensified by the fact that the public service unions, closely linked with the Christian Social and Socialist parties, are themselves among the lobbyists. Beside the pressure to overmanning, there is a tendency to under-utilise the existing manpower because ministers find it easier to work with their political sympathisers while by-passing the uncommitted and especially the politically hostile. In the most extreme case, a new minister coming into a ministry which has been 'colonised' by another political party over a long period may feel that he has to rely on (and consequently expand) his personal cabinet while almost ignoring much of the departmental hierarchy. Conversely, it is often alleged that partisan civil servants tend to sabotage or delay the policies of a minister from another party.

These divisions are bad for morale in the service, having a particularly bad effect on those who choose not to be politicised. They also reduce the collective influence of senior civil servants which is much lower than in France, Britain or West Germany. It is probably only in Foreign Affairs and Finance that the higher civil service is sufficiently united to have a strong and coherent effect on policy. Paradoxically, a senior civil servant is likely to exert maximum influence not through his official position but through his work in political and associated bodies.

THE CONTROL OF ADMINISTRATION

Control and accountability of the public services is here considered primarily in its formal aspects, in terms of parliamentary and judicial control. However, it should be stressed that, particularly in Belgium, some of the most effective courses of action available to the aggrieved citizen may lie elsewhere. The citizen who secures the support of a political party or organised group, or through them has contacts in the administration, or whose cause is taken up by the mass media, may well secure satisfaction without recourse to the official channels.

Parliamentary Control

The familiar concept of the political responsibility of ministers to the legislature for the actions of their branch of the administration is recognised by the Constitution. As in most liberal democracies, the increased size and complexity of ministries and the rise of disciplined parties supporting the government in parliament have reduced the practical scope of this doctrine. The weapons available to the deputies and senators include regular sessions of oral questions to ministers as well as written questions. In addition there is the 'interpellation' — a question followed by a short debate in which the minister has to defend himself against criticisms. If the questioner is not satisfied he may table an order of the day, a vote of no confidence which, if passed, would force the minister to resign but this procedure is rarely taken to a vote today.

Both houses may set up commissions of enquiry under the Constitution. These can require the attendance of witnesses and the production of documents. There have only been six cases since

1880 but several of these exposed serious administrative short-comings — most recently the 1972 investigation into the introduction of advertising material into television broadcasts.

Ministers do also have to stand up to examination during the legislative process and the passage of the budget. Each house has specialised legislative committees corresponding to the structure of ministries and all legislation is referred to the appropriate committee which is attended by the relevant minister and his senior civil servants. The committee meets in private and the proposed legislation has to be explained and defended by the minister; sometimes additional witnesses may be called and the conduct of the department concerned may be criticised. The committee issues a report with a summary of the arguments and the conclusions reached which is printed and distributed. The with-holding of financial legislation is no longer likely but the passage of the budget is the occasion for a large number of questions on government policy in general and its administration in particular.

Parliament has attached to it the Court of Accounts provided for in the Constitution and set up in 1846. In order to guarantee its independence, this audit office was placed under the Chamber of Representatives which appoints its members. It is divided into two chambers, each comprising a President, four Counsellors and a Registrar, and has a total staff of about 520. It is responsible for checking the accounts of all government departments, ensuring that the budget figures are not exceeded and that the money has been spent on the items authorised. It has access to all accounts relating to revenue and expenditure and may call for further information and explanations. Any infringements are reported immediately to the legislature and an annual general report is published.

But in addition to these powers its position is enhanced by the system of 'prior endorsement' of payments. The Treasury section of the Ministry of Finance cannot pay any accounts which have not been approved by the Court of Accounts. If its approval is withheld the Court refers the matter to the Cabinet which may overrule its reservations and authorise payment: the Cabinet must then accept political responsibility before the two houses which will receive a full report from their watchdog. There are complaints that the prior endorsement system causes unnecessary delays and special arrangements have been made for regular payments such as salaries.

The audit office is concerned with legality and compliance with procedures rather than the merits of government policy, although in its reports it does refer to a very limited extent to general questions of efficiency and value for money. However, within its terms of reference it is a very effective instrument and one which enjoys considerable public standing.

Legal Controls

The authors of the Belgian Constitution deliberately excluded the idea of specialised administrative courts on the French model because they associated these (not unreasonably at the time) with the authoritarian tradition of government. Citizens who had complaints against the actions of the administration would seek redress in the ordinary courts but in practice these took a very narrow view of their jurisdiction. They had no power of judicial review of legislation, took a restricted view of their right to investigate the legal basis of ministerial decrees, and were extremely reluctant to intervene in administrative decisions where any question of the discretion of the minister or his agents was involved.

It was growing dissatisfaction with this timid approach by the ordinary courts to the rights of the individual against the state which led to the creation of an administrative court, the Conseil d'Etat, in 1946. (Ironically in 1956 the highest ordinary court, the Court of Cassation, in a judgement on the right to unemployment benefits, extended its own jurisdiction over the administration.)

The Conseil d'Etat, which has a staff of 172, was partially based on the prestigious French institution. It has three basic duties. It vets all government legislation and decrees, giving an advisory opinion which is published. Since 1973 it has the task of adjudicating in the event of disputes arising over the activities of the French and Flemish Cultural Councils. It is the highest administrative tribunal in the land with jurisdiction over central and local administration and the specialist administrative tribunals dealing with matters such as social security. It investigates complaints against the administration and can find for the complainant if an act is *ultra vires*, if correct procedures have not been observed or if legal powers have been improperly used. In this last case it may decide that an administrative decision was within the law and that correct procedures were followed but that legal powers were being exercised for a purpose other than for which the authority was originally conferred. Thus the Conseil d'Etat may look to the 'purpose' and 'intention' of the law and assess the exercise of administrative discretion in the light of such criteria. It can award damages and may annul certain improper administrative decisions. Its relationship with the ordinary courts is uncertain and causes disquiet to academic lawyers but an attempt to clarify the situation by giving it constitutional status in the revision of 1967-71 was not successful. However, in its practical activities during a comparatively short period it appears to have built up a strong record of cases and has a public reputation for independence.

CHAPTER SEVEN

Netherlands

THE BACKGROUND

Although the Netherlands has a national history of at least four hundred years, the characteristic forms of the nation state were absent until the last century. The seven — Protestant — United Provinces of the Netherlands which came together in 1579 formed a loose republican confederation governed by mandated delegates drawn from the aristocracy and urban merchants. This system was destroyed by the French invasion in 1795, completely remodelled on Napoleonic lines, and subsequently amended during the period of rule by the monarch from 1814. William I retained the French-inspired unitary state and, although the Belgian provinces seceded in 1830 and the monarchy was not able to sustain its activist role, the principle of a strong central government survived. After a struggle between liberal political leaders and the monarch a parliamentary system with ministerial responsibility was grafted on around 1848.

The principal political movements in the modern Netherlands may be viewed in terms of religion and class. The Netherlands, although predominantly a Protestant country, has always had a large minority group of Catholics who constitute the largest single denomination. The Protestant community is divided between several Calvinist churches and there has always been a substantial liberal secular bloc. Disputes over education in the nineteenth century led to the political mobilisation of the religious blocs, in which Catholics and Protestants were in uneasy alliance against the liberal proponents of secular public education. A little later the emergence of class issues split the secular bloc between liberals and socialists. Thus by the beginning of the twentieth century Dutch politics were dominated by five tendencies — Catholic, two Protestant, liberal and socialist. Some of the most divisive issues were settled in 1917 by an all-party agreement. This guaranteed equal state aid to all forms of education for which there was a demand, secular or religious, and also introduced universal franchise and an electoral system ensuring strict proportionality between votes cast and the seats won by the parties.

However, Dutch society was still marked by its vertical divisions or 'pillars'. Education, from primary to university, is available on triparite segregated lines. The major interest groups such as trade unions, employers' organisations and farmers associations were separately constituted for Catholic, Protestant and lay members. Broadcasting and the press show the same divisions. But in spite of these tendencies to separate development and their representation in distinct political parties there has been a remarkable degree of consensus and stability. None of the groups were in a position to dominate the others, and recognition of the need to accommodate diverse interests engendered a spirit of 'live and let live'. The major parties have, after hard bargaining, generally been willing to enter into stable coalitions. Government has been viewed as a serious business, based on pragmatism, the consultation of all community leaders and respect of informal rules on proportionality.

In the last fifteen years the party system has been undergoing some changes. Both fragmentation and concentration have occurred. The electoral system allows very small parties to secure representation, which facilitates splits from the major parties and the formation of new ones such as Democrats-66 on the centre-left which bases its appeal to the electorate on the irrelevance of the old party divisions and the necessity of making government more directly accountable to the people. The country has gradually become more secular and the main religious parties have seen their share of the vote decline from over one-half to under one-third. This finally led them to present a joint list in the 1977 election as the Christian Democratic Appeal. In addition, the Labour Party has undergone a radicalisation since the late 1960s, moving significantly to the left and becoming less prepared to make compromises in order to enter coalitions. With an increase in industrial militancy as well as the rise of protest movements demanding greater public participation in policy making on environmental issues, some observers have suggested that the tradition of accommodation and compromise is breaking down.

THE INSTITUTIONAL FRAMEWORK

The Netherlands is a unitary state, a constitutional monarchy with a strong central executive but also a very well established system of local government. The States-General (parliament) is bicameral with the directly elected lower house dominant, although the indirectly elected upper house possesses important powers. At the head of central government stand the Prime Minister and Cabinet who are both collectively and individually responsible to the States-General.

The Cabinet is relatively small, consisting of about fifteen members in recent years. Ministers may not sit in parliament and it is very common for ministers not to have any parliamentary experience. Between 1848 and 1958 only one-third of the ministers were appointed to office for the first time from a parliamentary background, although the proportion has increased since the Second World War. The Cabinet will have been formed after intensive negotiations, often lasting months, between potential coalition partners. One result is that many decisions on the principles of policy will have been agreed before the government takes office.

Leadership and coordination of the Cabinet lie in the hands of the Prime Minister, the Deputy Prime Minister and the Minister of Finance, although sometimes none of these is the dominant political figure in the government. The Prime Minister heads a small coordinating Ministry of General Affairs which is responsible for concerting the activities of the various ministries. He also controls the Cabinet Secretariat. However, his political position is not strong. Not only does he preside over a carefully balanced coalition, partly owing his position to his acceptability to the coalition partners, but he may not even be the most powerful leader within his own party and may also have difficulties in controlling the activities of his parliamentarians. A Deputy Prime Minister, usually also holding a departmental post, is normally appointed to represent the other major party within the coalition. These two men are bound to work closely together. Thus the role of the Prime Minister depends greatly on his personality and individual skill; he cannot generally be more than 'the first among equals' in the Cabinet and must lead largely by consultation and persuasion of the different groups concerned.

The role of the Minister of Finance consists largely of bilateral contacts with individual ministers over the financial aspects of their policies, with the Cabinet acting as a final court of appeal in the case of unresolved disputes. He is often a 'technician' rather than a political heavyweight. His position is strengthened by the requirement that even after parliament has approved ministry budgets the Minister of Finance must authorise actual expenditure.

Each of the ministers who constitute the Cabinet will normally preside over a single ministry, usually with the aid of one or two junior ministers. These State Secretaries, inaugurated in 1948, are political posts, strictly subordinate to their minister and not members of the Cabinet. Often they will be appointed with special responsibility for a particular activity. In the 1977 Van Agt government one of the State Secretaries in the Ministry of Education and Science was given special responsibility for nursery, primary and special education, while a woman in the Ministry of Culture, Recreation and Social Work was made responsible for promoting women's emancipation. In addition, ministers without portfolio are sometimes appointed to coordinate work in particular fields, often in areas where there is some public feeling involved.

Along with their lack of parliamentary background, there is a strong tradition that ministers should be specialists in the work of their ministry. This often means that they are actually civil servants from within the ministry — thus the Minister of Foreign Affairs has frequently been a career diplomat, and the Minister of Justice a lawyer from the ministry. Another major source is the university professor in the relevant subject — professors of economics having a particularly strong hold over the Ministry of Finance. So ministers tend to have the considerable advantage of possessing specialist knowledge and/or administrative experience when taking office. Because of this emphasis on specialised pofessional competence, ministers tend to confine their career to a single ministry rather than to progress up a hierarchy of ministries as is the case in Britain. Both individually and collectively ministers in office seem to cultivate an air of executive expertise, holding themselves aloof from party strife.

In some areas of policy the Cabinet is under considerable pressure from the very influential Social and Economic Council created in 1950. This body, with fifteen members each from employers, trade unions and independents nominated by the Cabinet (mainly

Ministers, Ministries and Personnel. Van Agt Government, 1977

Prime Minister/General Affairs/Cabinet Secretariat	520
Home Affairs/Deputy Prime Minister (1)	2,400
Foreign Affairs (1)	3,500
Justice (1)	22,700
Finance (1)	29,500
Education and Science (2)	3,500[1]
Defence (2)	28,300[2]
Housing and Planning (1)	6,900
Public Works, Water Control and Transport (1)	17,000
Economic Affairs (2)	5,000
Agriculture and Fisheries/Antilles Affairs	12,300
Social Affairs (1)	5,000
Culture, Recreation and Social Work (2)	3,900
Public Health & Hygiene (1)	3,200

Ministers without Departments:	
Development Aid	—
Science Policy	—

Non-Ministerial Organisations:	
Council of State and Court of Accounts	500
General Pension Fund	1,900
Posts & Telecommunications	77,400
Other Government Services	1,300[3]
	224,800

The number of State Secretaries is given in brackets
1 Teachers (25,300) employed by central government not included
2 Armed forces (103,000) not included
3 Includes the Mint

university professors), has the right to be consulted on all social and economic legislation and policies, and may offer its advice unsolicited at any time. In practice its recommendations carry great weight, particularly when they are unanimous in which case the Cabinet and States-General are inclined to accept them in full.

The ministries are based on functions but as can be seen from their titles a single ministry may include some varied activities. Although the number has expanded with the growth in government, the pattern has recently remained fairly stable and there has not been the constant reshuffling of administrative units found in some other countries. Certain government activities have been hived off to largely autonomous bodies such as the General Pension Fund, Posts and Telecommunications, and the Mint. Some ministries employ much of their staff centrally, such as the Ministry of Economic Affairs, while others, such as the Ministry of Agriculture and Fisheries, have large field services. In addition, there is decentralisation to local government and also a special form of decentralisation which is part territorial and functional to deal with water control.

Geographical Decentralisation

Dutch local government has two tiers and shows some similarities to the Belgian system. The eleven Provinces and 842 municipalities have elected councils which nominate executive committees headed by a centrally appointed official. The Queen's Commissioner presides over the provincial executive. He is a permanent official responsible to the Minister of Home Affairs, with the duty of preserving public order and supervising public bodies within his Province and making regular inspections of the municipalities.

Local Government Staff, 1977

Provinces	15,700[1]
Municipalities	207,400
Education Staff	214,600[1]
Water Control Boards	5,600
	443,300

1   Includes staff employed by local government and in state-subsidised schools, both secular and religious

The Province does not have many functions; the most important is physical planning, bridges and ferries, psychiatric institutions and water control. About 40 per cent of their staff are employed in trading activities, particularly electricity and water supply.

The main features of the municipality remain as they were laid down in a law of 1851 which constituted them as the basic all-purpose units of local government. The most striking aspect to the outsider is the role of the burgomaster, a permanent official appointed for six-year terms but in practice with security of tenure. He presides at meetings of the elected council, without a vote but taking a leading part in its deliberations. He is chairman of the executive committee of two to six aldermen, with a vote and a casting vote. By statute he is chief of the local police, fire brigade and civil defence. He also has a suspensory veto over decisions of the council and committee which may be confirmed by central government within thirty days.

The process of appointment throws some general light on the Dutch approach to official appointments. All vacancies must be advertised nationally. Each of the major parties has a parliamentary member who watches over such appointments and applicants will consult their own party representative who may well make represen-tations to the Queen's Commissioner for the Province and also to the Minister for Home Affairs. The local council will normally make representations on the qualifications, religious and political affiliations and any other qualities they would prefer. After extensive consultations the Queen's Commissioner submits a list of three names in order of preference to the minister who almost invariably appoints the first choice. In the case of municipalities with a population over 50,000 the appointment must be made by the Cabinet. There is always a surplus of well-qualified applicants, including serving administrators and burgomasters from smaller municipalities, as well as local and sometimes national politicians. In 70 per cent of cases the appointment corresponds with the dominant religious-political group in the local community, while the other 30 per cent are made to maintain overall national proportionality. The minister does not favour applicants from his own group.

Municipalities are concerned with housing and planning, public health, education, social work, culture and recreation, police and fire services. About 30 per cent of staff are employed in commercial trading operations. Size and obsolete boundaries represent the familiar local government problem but, although the number of authorities has been reduced by one-fifth over the last century, resistance to major structural change is very strong. A law of 1950 provides for voluntary cooperation between municipalities. When special legislation was required, however, to deal with the enormous problems of the Rhine estuary area which is dominated by

Rotterdam, it was only possible to set up a new additional tier for the area with limited power over the constituent authorities because of the opposition of the smaller municipalities involved. Similarly, frequent proposals to divide up the country into new administrative areas have yet to be carried out. It should nevertheless be stressed that Dutch local government is highly professional in outlook and staff morale is high; the provision of many specialised services (e.g. research, staff training and joint purchasing) as well as the presentation of a collective voice to national government are facilitated by the highly effective Union of Netherlands Municipalities.

Because so much of the country is at or below sea level, water control is a vital service. Constitutionally the Crown, i.e. central government, is responsible for supervising the whole sector and may take direct control in an emergency. There is a large section of a ministry staffed by a very prestigious group of specialist engineers while the Provinces carry out some duties and also supervise the local Water Control Boards. These are constituted from local landowners and must maintain water defences, control the water level and drainage and, more recently, monitor water pollution.

The Civil Service

The Dutch civil service has a long history as a career service and a tradition of efficient administration, with many of the features of a 'classical' bureaucracy. But it has several comparatively unusual aspects. It has never developed a uniform central system of recruitment and management within the service, nor has it the common horizontal class structure based on educational levels commonly found elsewhere. However, uniformity does extend to conditions of service. In so far as general responsibility for the service may be located anywhere, it lies in the Ministry of Home Affairs but its control is strictly limited.

This ministry has attached to it the Central Personnel Service, created in 1946, which has a number of advisory functions, dealing with recruitment and conditions of service, administrative reform, training schemes and negotiations with trade unions. In recruitment it acts as a 'labour exchange', steering registered applicants, internal and external, towards the vacant posts of which it has been informed.

conflict-resolving manner. The degree to which the higher civil service excercises a collective political influence is difficult to assess. In general, it is higher than in Belgium. The engineers in charge of water control, whose work enjoys popular support, constitute a most prestigious expert group largely immune from political control and the supervision of the Ministry of Finance. But as a rule, while playing an important part in policy formulation and enjoying the possibility of landing in a political ministerial post, officials have to work within limits defined by competent ministers, a multi-party system and very well established interest groups.

The view on training varies and has altered recently. In the technical ministries professionally qualified entrants develop their expertise through the experience of working within a specialised group of staff. For other ministries there was very little tradition of post-entry training apart from learning through experience. However, in the last twenty years there have been marked developments encouraged by the Central Personnel Service, the independent Institute for Administrative Sciences and the growing (non-legalistic) study of public administration in the universities — particularly Amsterdam. Ministries now send staff on course in management and methods of organisation, and there are a variety of short full-time courses and part-time specialist courses and conferences in which many civil servants participate.

THE CONTROL OF ADMINISTRATION

Traditionally, the style of administration has not been open. Public interest was low and decisions were left to political and administrative elites unless immediate rights and interests were threatened. The administration, stressing professional competence and efficiency, worked in an atmosphere of confidentiality, consulting the relevant well established interest groups in advisory committees behind closed doors. In the past decade public concern about a range of issues concerned with the environment, such as pollution and nuclear energy, has led to agitation for greater public participation in policy planning. There has been some response from governments in the 1970s, with a commitment to release and publicise information on planning and development in sufficient time for views to be formed and representation made to the authorities.

The general mechanisms of parliamentary control of the administration in the Netherlands are those which are found in parliamentary systems with ministerial responsibility. They include questions to ministers, the interpellation and the scrutiny of legislation and the budget. Most observers agree that the Dutch separation of ministers from parliament increases the effectiveness of parliamentary control. Members do have a collective sense of identity distinguishing them from the executive, so that even representatives from the coalition parties feel free to criticise ministers and even vote against them on particular issues. The budget, which is debated ministry by ministry, affords an opportunity for the scrutiny of policies and their execution. It is the departmental minister rather than the Minister of Finance who has to defend each section of the budget. Although there is a power to set up investigative Commissions of Enquiry, it is hardly used. In the recent Lockheed bribery scandal it was the government which set up a 'three wise men' commission made up of a senior judge serving with the European Court of Justice, an ex-President of the Netherlands Central Bank and the President of the Court of Accounts.

As in many other countries, the ordinary courts slowly developed only rather limited jurisdiction in the field of control of the administration. However, in recent years the Dutch courts have been willing to scrutinise the use of administrative discretion but the remedy they provide is compensatory damages rather than annulment of the decision. The legal body which can bring about annulment and reversal of decisions is the Council of State. This old-established advisory body was partly remodelled on Napoleonic lines at the beginning of the nineteenth century but has never developed the power or prestige of the French Conseil d'Etat. It is consulted on all legislation and international agreements, and for these purposes it is organised into sections with overlapping membership which cover ministries. Most of its members are not lawyers but distinguished public servants. There is also the Administrative Disputes Section whose position was redefined in 1964 to act as a court of appeal against the decisions of central government and provincial and municipal authorities. It also applies the principles of fair administration. It shares with its Belgian counterpart an unsatisfactory ambiguous relationship to the ordinary courts but its chief weakness lies in its staffing. It really lacks a sufficient number of high calibre administrative lawyers to pursue its investigations.

The Court of Accounts has a long ancestry but its present composition and powers are defined by a law of 1927. Its presiding members are appointed by a procedure in which the Court sends a list of nominees to parliament which may alter the list and then sends it in a stated order of preference to the government, the latter always respecting this choice. The Court appoints its own staff, now over 200. It has a general responsibility for scrutinising state revenues and expenditure, on a post-audit basis. Its main function is to check the legality of transactions, ensuring that the accounts correspond to the financial legislation and that proper accountancy procedures have been followed. If the Court does not approve of expenditure, the departmental minister concerned will have to move legislation to regularise the position — giving parliament the last word. The Court also checks on the efficiency of administration and the execution of policies, publishing critical reports which are the subject of parliamentary debates. For both its functions it has specialised sections which work within the ministries. Because of staffing constraints they cannot check everything and in practice use the internal audits of the ministries as the basis for detailed spot checks.

Selective Bibliography

GENERAL

J. ARMSTRONG *The European Administrative Elite* Princeton University Press, 1973.

B. CHAPMAN *The Profession of Government* Allen and Unwin, 1959.

J. CORNFORD (ed.) *The Failure of the State: The Distribution of Political and Economic Power in Europe* Croom Helm, 1975.

C.J. HAMSON *Executive Discretion and Judicial Control* Stevens, 1954.

J. HAYWARD and M. WATSON (eds.) *Planning, Politics and Public Policy: The British, French and Italian Experience* Cambridge University Press, 1975.

F. HEADY *Public Administration: A Comparative Perspective* Prentice-Hall, 1966.

S. HOLLAND (ed.) *The State as Entrepeneur* Weidenfeld and Nicholson, 1972.

S. HOLT *Six European States* Hamish Hamilton, 1970.

B.G. PETERS *The Politics of Bureaucracy: A Comparative Perspective* Longman, 1978.

F.F. RIDLEY (ed.) *Specialists and Generalists: A Comparative Study of Professional Civil Servants* Allen and Unwin, 1968.

P. SELF *Administrative Theories and Politics* Allen and Unwin, 1972.

A. SHONFIELD *Modern Capitalism: The Changing Balance of Public and Private Power* Oxford University Press, 1965.

B.C. SMITH *Field Administration: An Aspect of Decentralisation* Routledge and Kegan Paul, 1967.

G. SMITH *Politics in Western Europe* (2nd edn) Heinemann, 1977.

F.A. STACEY *Ombudsmen Compared* Oxford University Press, 1978.

BRITAIN

A.H. BIRCH *The British System of Government* (2nd edn) Allen and Unwin, 1973.

A.H. BIRCH *Representative and Responsible Government* Allen and Unwin, 1964.

R.G.S. BROWN and D.R. STEEL *The Administrative Process in Britain* (2nd edn) Methuen, 1979.

Sir R. CLARKE *New Trends in Government* HMSO, 1971.

H.J. ELCOCK *Administrative Justice* Longman, 1969.

A.H. HANSON and M. WALLES *Governing Britain* (2nd edn) Fontana, 1975.

H. HECLO and A. WILDAVSKY *The Private Government of Public Money* Macmillan, 1974.

M.J. HILL *The Sociology of Public Administration* Weidenfeld and Nicolson, 1972.

J.P. MACKINTOSH *The Government and Politics of Britain* (4th edn) Hutchinson, 1977.

B.C. SMITH *Policy-Making in British Government* Martin Robertson, 1976.

F.A.STACEY *British Government 1966-75: Years of Reform* Oxford University Press, 1978.

J. STANYER *Understanding Local Government* Martin Robertson/Fontana, 1976.

H.W.R. WADE *Administrative Law* (4th edn) Clarendon Press, 1977.

FRANCE

M. ANDERSON *Government in France: An Introduction to the Executive Power* Pergamon, 1970.

J. BLONDEL *The Government of France* (2nd edn) Methuen, 1974.

L.N. BROWN and J.F. GARNER *French Administrative Law* Butterworths, 1967.

S. COHEN *Modern Capitalist Planning: The French Model* Weidenfeld and Nicolson, 1969.

M. CROZIER *The Bureaucratic Phenomenon* Tavistock Publications, 1964.

J. HAYWARD *The One and Indivisible French Republic* Weidenfeld and Nicolson, 1973.

H. MACHIN *The Prefect in French Public Administration* Croom Helm, 1977.

F.F. RIDLEY and J. BLONDEL *Public Administration in France* (2nd edn) Routledge and Kegan Paul, 1969.

F.F. RIDLEY *The French Prefectoral System* (Commission on the Constitution, Research Paper) HMSO, 1973.

E. SULEIMAN *Politics, Power and Bureaucracy in France* Princeton University Press, 1974.

V. WRIGHT *The Government and Politics of France* Hutchinson, 1978.

GERMANY

G. BRAUNTHAL *The West German Legislative Process* Cornell University Press, 1973.

R.A. CHAPUT DE SAINTONGE *Public Administration in Germany: A Study of Regional and Local Administration in Rheinland-Pfalz* Weidenfeld and Nicolson, 1961.

D.P. CONRADT *The German Polity* Longman, 1978.

K.H.F. DYSON *Party, State and Bureaucracy in West Germany* Sage Publications, 1977.

A.J. HEIDENHEIMER and D.P. KOMMERS *The Government of Germany* (4th edn) Crowell, 1975.

H. JACOB *German Administration Since Bismarck: Central Authority versus Local Authority* Yale University Press, 1963.

N. JOHNSON *Government in the Federal Republic of Germany: The Executive at Work* Pergamon, 1973.

N. JOHNSON *Federalism and Decentralisation in the Federal Republic of Germany* (Commission on the Constitution, Research Paper) HMSO, 1973.

R. MAYNTZ and F.W. SHARPF *Policy Making in the German Federal Bureaucracy* Elsevier, 1975.

E.L. PINNEY *Federalism, Bureaucracy and Party Politics in West Germany: The Bundesrat* University of North Carolina Press, 1963.

K. SONTHEIMER *The Government and Politics of West Germany* Hutchinson, 1972.

ITALY

J.C. ADAMS and P. BARILE *The Government of Republican Italy* (3rd edn) Houghton Mifflin, 1972.

P.A. ALLUM *Italy: Republic Without Government?* Weidenfeld and Nicolson, 1973.

R.C. FRIED *The Italian Prefects* Yale University Press, 1963.

D. GERMINO and S. PASSIGLI *The Government of Contemporary Italy* Harper and Row, 1968.

M. POSNER and S.J. WOOLF *Italian Public Enterprise* Duckworth, 1967.

R. ZARISKI *Italy: The Politics of Uneven Development* Dryden Press, 1972.

BELGIUM & NETHERLANDS

F.E. HUGGETT *Modern Belgium* Pall Mall, 1969.

F.E. HUGGETT *The Modern Netherlands* Praeger, 1971.

A. MOLITOR *L'Administration de la Belgique* Institut Belge de Science Politique, 1974.

G.L. WEIL *The Benelux Nations: The Politics of Small-Country Democracies* Holt, Rinehart and Winston, 1971.